A Passion for the Particular

Dorothy Wordsworth: A Portrait

**This book is to be returned on or before
the last date stamped below.**

09. SEP 81

CAR -2. SEP. 1981

30. SEP 81

28. OCT 81

'24. NOV 81'

CH -2. DEC. 1981
CAR
16|2|82

12. MAR 82

23. JUL 82

25. FEB 84

07. MAR 84
28. MAR 84

19. APR 84
21. AUG 84
27. MAR 85

24. MAY 85

14 JUNE 85

15. APR 86

20. SEP 86

02. 11. 93

A Passion for the Particular

Dorothy Wordsworth: A Portrait

by

ELIZABETH GUNN

LONDON
VICTOR GOLLANCZ LTD
1981

ISBN 0 575 02700 2

To P.N.G.

Nel mezzo del cammin di nostra vita
Mi ritrovai per una selva oscura,
Che la diritta via era smarrita.

Dante, *Inferno*

Photoset by Rowland Phototypesetting Ltd,
Bury St Edmunds, Suffolk
Printed in Great Britain by
St Edmundsbury Press, Bury St Edmunds, Suffolk

Acknowledgments

I have written this book off the back of the scholarship of others. It includes no original research and has no pretensions to being more than my personal interpretation of the spadework done by specialists in the field. As such my debt is great. And where I have parted company with the scholars, I have done so with humility and with a full recognition of all I owe.

Having said this I would like, without causing embarrassment, to express my supreme debt to Dr Mary Moorman. Not only have I relied heavily on her work. For her singular personal kindness to me, and patience in replying to my pestering letters, I cannot thank her too much.

Further I must thank Mrs Narasimhan, Director of Studies in English at Newnham College, Cambridge; Dr Robert Woof and the Trustees of Dove Cottage; Commander Dane, curator of Rydal Mount; the Rector of Forncett St Mary's; the Librarian of the Keswick Public Library; the National Trust (Ambleside); the Librarian and staff of the Cambridge University Library and of the London Library.

I have also to thank the Oxford University Press for permission to quote extensively from the *Journals* of Dorothy Wordsworth edited by Mary Moorman (1971); from *The Letters of William and Dorothy Wordsworth* edited by Ernest de Selincourt, Vol. I revised by Chester L. Shaver (2nd ed. 1967), Vol. II revised by Mary Moorman (2nd ed. 1969), and Vol. III revised by Mary Moorman and Alan G. Hill (2nd ed. 1970); and from the following works: the *Letters* of Mary Wordsworth edited by Mary E. Burton (1958); the *Letters* and *Unpublished Letters* of S. T. Coleridge edited by E. L. Griggs (1956–9 and 1932); *The Prelude* (1805 text) edited by Ernest de Selincourt, corrected by Stephen Gill (1970). I am warmly indebted to Messrs Macmillan for permission to quote from the *Journals* of Dorothy Wordsworth Vols I and II edited by Ernest de Selincourt (1941); to the Nonesuch Press for their permission to quote from *Minnow among Tritons* edited by S. Potter (1934); to Messrs Routledge & Kegan Paul for permission to quote from the *Notebooks* of S. T. Coleridge edited by K. Coburn (1957–73); and for that of the Toronto University Press to quote from *Letters of Sara Hutchinson* edited by K. Coburn (1954).

A Passion for the Particular

I have written a portrait or sketch of Dorothy Wordsworth and her circle. Those who seek a full biography cannot do better than turn to E. de Selincourt's *Dorothy Wordsworth* (1933).

SWALEDALE
YORKSHIRE
OCTOBER 1980

ELIZABETH GUNN

Contents

Illustrations

FOLLOWING PAGE 118

Dorothy, *c.* 1800. Silhouette by artist unknown. (Courtesy Dove Cottage Trustees)

Alfoxden House (Courtesy the Alfoxton Park Hotel)

Racedown, Dorset (Courtesy Mrs H. Marsden-Smedley)

William Wordsworth by H. Edridge, 1805. (Courtesy Dove Cottage Trustees)

Sara Hutchinson (Asra) *c.* 1815. Silhouette by artist unknown. (Courtesy Dove Cottage Trustees)

Greta Hall, Keswick (Radio Times Hulton Picture Library)

Samuel Taylor Coleridge in 1795, by P. Vandyke (National Portrait Gallery, London)

Mary Wordsworth, watercolour on ivory by Margaret Gillies (Courtesy Dove Cottage Trustees)

Rydal Mount (Radio Times Hulton Picture Library)

A page from Dorothy's Journal showing the entry for 16th November 1801 (Courtesy Dove Cottage Trustees)

Dove Cottage, Grasmere, today (Radio Times Hulton Picture Library)

. . . Where'er my footsteps turned,
Her Voice was like a hidden Bird that sang,
The thought of her was like a flash of light,
Or an *unseen* companionship, a breath
Of fragrance independent of the wind.

William Wordsworth, *The Recluse*

I

She is a Woman indeed!

Coleridge, Letters

July 1797—June 1798

'FEBRUARY 3RD. A mild morning, the windows open at breakfast, the redbreasts singing in the garden. Walked with Coleridge over the hills ...' (Alfoxden Journal)

The year is 1798, the diarist Dorothy Wordsworth, the words themselves as unobtrusive as sparrows. They nevertheless contrive to bring us the scale, the scope, the very breath of a morning on the hills. The name Coleridge may open for us like Keats's magic casements on perilous seas in faery lands forlorn. But here we meet it on different ground—ground where each word counts, and its power consists in cropping up so simply.

In the minds of the Somerset locals, however, in 1798, it was far from figuring so simply—or doing so in the context of Miss Wordsworth, who, brown as a berry, thought nothing of being out upon the hills day-long with the husband of Mrs Coleridge. The couple it is true were commonly a trio, Miss Wordsworth being accompanied by her brother. But the fraternal relationship, too, the locals thought suspect, loverlike as the pair were seen to be. All this (and that Mrs Coleridge was conspicuous by her absence) was no more than Dorothy's relatives had foreseen. It was now four years since her horrified aunt had written sharply denouncing her habit of 'rambling about the country on foot', and worse—travelling not by coach, *hiking* across England with no fitter protector than her brother.

But Dorothy went her way; and wrote as one who did so. Her contemporaries, with the Picturesque in vogue, could not have heard her redbreasts singing in the garden as we may do close on two hundred years later, singing with a sweetness and distinctness the more singular since conveyed in a bare statement of fact. Yet today it remains possible that we too will not hear, that the words will be too simple for us; that we will pass them over for the very reason that they are part of our modern vernacular.

They were not so passed over by two young English poets, William Wordsworth and Samuel Taylor Coleridge, although she had begun to keep a journal only some ten days before the extract quoted above. Wordsworth, not content with reading the first entry, copied it; and whether or not her description recapitulated their talk or was Dorothy's own, found netted there exactly what he needed for his poem. He was not alone in this; into Coleridge's *Christabel*, into *The Ancient Mariner* itself, went things Coleridge had not seen, echoes, images, phrases lifted from her Alfoxden Journal.

'Three persons and one soul', 'the Concern' Coleridge called it, meaning himself, Wordsworth—and Dorothy. And with Wordsworth, the man he most reveres, for the first time under his roof, it is not of the latter that he writes but of 'his exquisite sister . . . She is a woman indeed! in mind I mean, and heart; for her person is such, that if you expected to see a pretty woman, you would think her rather ordinary; if you expected . . . an ordinary woman . . . pretty!'

It is not just that in person she is not exquisite. Coleridge's own last exclamation mark betrays him as at a loss to define what it is about her. Slight and small, a mere five foot beside Wordsworth's five foot ten, she has light brown hair and, as Wordsworth has, grey eyes. You would pass her in the street without a second glance. Wordsworth might have helped Coleridge out: You cannot see the face itself for the play of thought and feeling. Like cloud shadows chasing over the hills, these are constantly changing; and as constantly transparently reflected. It is this that bewilders, enchants and impresses Coleridge—a woman who is not only prepared to discard dissimulation but is incapable of it. And as he writes there suddenly comes to mind a line of his own: 'Guilt was a thing impossible in her'.

But then she lacks the ordinary woman's need to dissimulate, 'various', wrote Coleridge, as was her information, her 'eye watchful in minutest observation of nature—and her taste a perfect electrometer. It bends, protrudes, and draws in, at subtlest beauties, and most recondite faults.'

Coleridge found her remarkable. Sara, his wife, did so only in ways that bring Dorothy nearer to us. Miss Wordsworth, the chatelaine of a mansion, Alfoxden, behaved like a vagabond and looked like one—in what Mr Wordsworth poetically pleased to call her woodland dress. She was as often out at night, even out alone, thought nothing of being seen so—and soaked to the skin. The locals did not like it and the gentry did not call. Miss Wordsworth was throwing away her advantages. One might be poor but this did not mean that one could not be genteel. And had she, Sara, been Mrs St Albyn's tenant, the gentry would have called, as they never would on one in all things as outlandish as Miss Wordsworth.

In 1807 a timid twenty-four-year-old De Quincey, while in no way thinking along the lines that Sara Coleridge did, was clearly taken aback by the sister of the bard he had come to see. Avant-garde as he was in regarding Wordsworth as one, and himself as a boy of fourteen odd enough to devour the first of the latter's poems, when he read of 'the shooting lights' of Dorothy's 'wild eyes' he had clearly ascribed these to poetic licence. In 1838 recalling their 1807 meeting, his initial shock still reverberates in the first thing he singled out to say about her: '"Her face was of Egyptian brown"; rarely, in a woman of English birth, had I seen a more determinate gypsy tan.' In other words he had seen it, but only in beggars and pedlars, never in a woman of Dorothy's class. 'Her eyes were not soft . . . nor were they fierce and bold', but 'wild and startling and hurried in their motion . . . some subtle fire of impassioned intellect apparently burned within her'. This 'being alternately pushed forward . . . then immediately checked . . . gave to her whole demeanour and conversation an air . . . of self-conflict . . . almost distressing to witness. Even her very utterance . . . often suffered, in point of clearness and steadiness', from her agitation. While 'at times the . . . self-baffling of her feelings' actually made her stammer, and so badly that her case might have seemed as chronic as Charles Lamb's. He was further rattled by 'the glancing quickness of her motions'. Miss Wordsworth 'did not cultivate the graces which preside over the person and its carriage', despite having lived as a girl with her uncle, a Canon of Windsor and personal favourite of the royal family. Her sister-in-law, unlike her, 'had seen nothing of high life, for she had seen little of any'. Nevertheless 'Mrs Wordsworth would have been pronounced very much the more lady-like person.'

But if Dorothy neglected to cultivate the graces this was not the neglect of a blue-stocking. And it did, De Quincey admits, astonish him to find that in what she had read or failed to read 'she had obeyed the single impulse of her own heart. Where that led her, *there* she followed, where that was mute . . . not a thought had she to bestow upon a writer's high reputation. And thus', he thought, 'the strange anomaly arose, of a woman deeply acquainted with some great authors . . . out of the fashionable bent' and content to be quite unacquainted with others; 'careless of literary history', yet 'with the stamp of originality upon all she uttered'. For she was (and not just as a woman) 'a person of very remarkable endowments intellectually'. But perhaps the gift most peculiarly her own was one at the disposal of all-comers 'viz. the exceeding sympathy always ready and always profound by which she made all that one could tell her, all that one could describe, all that one could quote from a foreign author, reverberate, as it were . . . to one's own feelings by the manifest impression it made upon *hers*. The pulses of light are not more quick . . . than were the answering and echoing movements of her sympathizing attention'.

The 'creature of an impulse', 'too ardent and too fiery for the reserve essential to dignity', it must not 'be supposed that there was any silliness or weakness of enthusiasm about her'. She was simply 'liberated from that false shame which, in so many persons, accompanies all expressions of natural emotion'. And remained 'the very wildest (in the sense of the most natural) person' that De Quincey has 'ever known'.

De Quincey's and Coleridge's portraits differ and overlap. Neither mentions Dorothy's dress, despite the fact that Coleridge—as his brilliant and beautiful daughter recalled—'had particular . . . fancies about' the subject, 'as had Mr Wordsworth'. Her father liked women in white,

3

expressive of 'delicacy and purity'. 'Mr Wordsworth . . . wished that white dresses were banished', 'loved all that was rich and picturesque, light and free in clothing'. Purple or Prussian blue were his favourite colours.

The chief interest of this may lie in its power to expose our preconceptions: the two men's tastes must surely have been reversed; but also it throws light on the radical difference existing even at this level between the two. It also conjures up Dorothy's appearance. Not only did she look and behave like a gypsy. Her clothes were free and flowing, were purple or Prussian blue—and were so in accordance with Wordsworth's taste.

The picture may seem complete with her chaotic scrawl. Her letters invariably end 'Hope you can read this'. It does, however, come as a shock to find that in her journals, too, her writing sprawls across the page.

For how reconcile this, or Dorothy herself—'her very utterance . . . often suffering in point of clearness and steadiness' from her agitation—with utterance so objective, clear, distilled? With an eye that headed clear as a bird, as untrammelled by self-conflict, for what she called things 'all for themselves', for it might be 'Young lambs in a green pasture in the Coombe, thick legs, large heads, black staring eyes'. This from one of Dorothy's stamp, as colourful and dynamic, may strike us as an oddly limited statement. Limited in its scope and prosaic in its language. Lambs are all very well. But from a woman whose feelings leapt to life with such disastrous violence, surely we might have expected something more. Where in this is 'the subtle fire of impassioned intellect'? How understand Coleridge's estimate of her?

It may help here to see what she meant by things 'all for themselves': 'the Coniston Fells in their own shape and colour, not Man's hills but all for themselves . . .' This might seem merely to echo her passionate cry after inspecting a formal 'picturesque' garden: 'Happily we cannot shape the huge hills, or carve out the valleys according to our fancy'. It is not only, however, a rejection of the man-made. A purple crag 'stood upright by itself. Its own self and its own shadow . . .' It is this that fulfils her need, the otherness of things 'all for themselves'.

But things are re-made man-made, manhandled by language. Language comes between things 'all for themselves'; as do one's feelings. And so she will minimize both the words and the feelings, and leave us to make what we can of the lambs in the Coombe.

But surely when Coleridge is present almost as often as William, when she can record 'At 11 o'clock Coleridge came as I was walking in the still clear moonshine in the garden. He came over Helvellyn', she might have done better. Might have exclaimed at the recklessness of this nocturnal route, instead of continuing, 'Wm was gone to bed, John also . . . We sate and chatted till ½ past three; W. in his dressing-gown. Coleridge read us a part of Christabel. Talked much about the mountains etc. etc. . . . Losh's opinion of Southey—the first of poets.'

This in fact for Dorothy is positively lavish. At least we know what is talked about, perhaps because she *had* flared up—Southey the first of

4

poets! But the talk itself she does not give, since if this takes place *à deux* between herself and William it is pointless. A letter comes from 'the Frenchman' and William must go to Mary: 'The fine day pushed him on to resolve' and off he sets in his blue spenser and pantaloons fresh from London. Just why he goes may be obscure but was not obscure to them, and no reader but themselves was ever envisaged. Still less does she aspire to record the eloquence 'that rose like a steam of rich distilled perfume', to give us Coleridge as Hazlitt does, 'launching upon his subject like an eagle dallying with the wind'. For how possibly give the gist of talk so labyrinthine, how—even if one had the time to do so—recapitulate with any accuracy long arguments about the poet's function? And accuracy in observing and recording is her business. If this seems a far cry from the poetic, it is intended to be so; William's mission is to throw this out, to write of the poetry in common things without a plum in one's mouth, and look without a platitude in one's eye.

In this, the new movement in poetry, it might almost be said that it was Dorothy who led the way. For her power was her own and not derived. Her power to *see* a leaf, not to ask its meaning, not to ask why is the world as it is, but simply to look at a leaf or at life and find this sufficient— extraordinary, ordinary, meaningful in itself. Herein—though not for the reason that may leap to mind—lay her value for Wordsworth and for Coleridge. Both men wanted what she saw because they could not so see it, or write of it with her unencumbered pen. Coleridge's eye, it is true, was a marvellous and delicate organ. And his visual notes might often be taken for hers. But even when he sets out and describes the hues of autumn as Dorothy might, these in the end are lost in the 'infinite shades of brown and green', submerged by his life-long obsession: 'the diversity that blends the whole'.

In Wordsworth's case the impediment might appear to have consisted less in having lost the innocent eye, than in his conviction that he had done so; the conviction that he had not only left the garden of Eden but forfeited the right to inhabit it.

As to why Dorothy wrote how and of what she did, it may seem that De Quincey unwittingly put his finger on the spot in his word 'self-baffling'. She looked and wrote to find release and exercise control, 'because I will not quarrel with myself'. Because as she sets this down she can see no other way to bear the anguish of separation from William who will be gone from her for three whole weeks. Her agony is intolerable and for once she does admit this, admit that, on finding herself alone, she sat on a stone by the lake and wept; and was powerless to be objective: 'The lake looked . . . I knew not why dull and melancholy, and the weltering on the shores seemed a heavy sound.' This state of affairs is one she can neither allow nor afford. And so she takes the only measure she knows and resolves to keep a journal. This will not only ensure that her days are filled, nor will she keep it merely for discipline's sake; but—already she is more cheerful —'because I shall give Wm pleasure by it when he comes home again'.

5

But it is time to picture the man Dorothy did as she wrote this. For the figure still engraved on her mind's eye, striding away on a morning in May 1800, is markedly different from the authorized version. For one thing he is more 'Quixote-like', quaintly and casually dressed—or so Hazlitt had seen him two springs before—in 'a brown fustian jacket and striped pantaloons'. There was 'something of a roll, a lounge in his gait'. This, with his sombre complexion, suggested nothing so much as a man recently shipped from foreign parts, even perhaps a Spanish monk in disguise. But 'the intense . . . high forehead' Hazlitt might have foreseen; likewise in a poet the 'fire in his eye (as if he saw something in objects more than the outward appearance)'. Despite this the impression was somehow less that of a mystic than one of arresting vitality. But then if one was awestruck and merely William Hazlitt, one did not expect to meet a famished mystic; one who, after walking twenty miles from Bristol, instantly laid in to his host's cheese—triumphantly remarking 'that "his marriage with experience had not been so productive as Mr Southey's in teaching him a knowledge of the good things of this life"'—while disposing no less effectively of the play he had seen with the phrase that '"it fitted the taste of the audience like a glove"'.

A caustic mystic. 'Cheeks furrowed by strong purpose and feeling'—this had the proper rigour, a fanatic. But 'a convulsive inclination to laughter about the mouth'? And then 'the depth, the manliness of the voice', 'with its guttural intonation, and a strong tincture of the northern *burr*, like the crust on wine'? Strong meat this and strange. Even without De Quincey to comment on the Roman nose being large, 'always . . . accounted an unequivocal expression of animal appetites organically strong'.

Presented with Hazlitt's portrait few people today would perhaps identify the sitter. Anne Wordsworth, his mother, might have done so despite the fact that William in 1778, at the time of her death, was not yet eight years old. Her prediction that he would be remarkable either for good or evil is startling, and the more so in a mother who was neither an ambitious nor anxious one. Tranquil and comfortably off in the red-brick Cockermouth mansion that fell to Sir James Lowther's agent, she indulged in no fears of the stream that ran through the garden for the small girl born sixteen months after William, on Christmas Day 1771. Nor for her five fledglings was the countryside beyond this out of bounds, perilous as were its quarries and castle ruins. She was not a woman to exaggerate. But always waiting in the wings, loving and serene, supplied the axis of her children's world.

'My Aunt, you know', Dorothy was to write, 'has been my mother'. There could be in her eyes no higher praise. And—with four brothers, no tomboy—the gentleness she exhibited early may well have been Anne Wordsworth's, lifting her up to see but not disturb the sparrow sitting on its nest in the 'privot hedge'.

6

That this gentleness, however, did not in these early days prevent her being William's boon companion, can only make their mother's prediction the odder. For if her second son was more difficult than his brothers— was moody, headstrong, passionately loving, dreamy—she could not, on 7 April 1770, have seen the faintest connection between his birth and that of one Napoleon nine months earlier; still less have linked this son, aged four, with events in distant France, the crowning of Queen Marie- Antoinette.

She none the less saw what Dorothy saw, what William Hazlitt saw, still saw in 1825—that Wordsworth's manner betrayed him as 'either mad or inspired', saw too 'the peculiar sweetness in his smile'. But Hazlitt, by now no slavish admirer, writing a literary essay, in fact wrote a biography of Wordsworth that for penetrating insight has never been surpassed. Mr Wordsworth, he remembered, wrote a tragedy when young in which occurred some 'energetic' lines:

> '. . . . . . Action is momentary.
> The motion of a muscle this way or that,
> Suffering is long, obscure and infinite.'

lines he recalls hearing quoted 'as put into the mouth of a person smit with some rash crime'.

Hazlitt was only just in time. Twelve years later the figure, in 1825 still 'Quixote-like', would vanish with table-legs and mantlepieces. The poetry is still being restored to us freed from its later accretions, but the rebel Dorothy loved is not loved today. Yet her love was not mere idolatry; she was as passionately loved by a man we have never troubled to understand, a man of great charm and hugely attractive to women. I shall therefore, taking a leaf from her book, deal first with the being who dominated Dorothy's horizon.

II

What spell so strong as guilty fear

Wordsworth, *Peter Bell*

1770–1787

HE WAS VERY MUCH Anne Wordsworth's son; but perhaps still more his father's. 'It is indeed mortifying to . . . find that amongst all those who visited at my father's house he had not one real friend', Dorothy wrote. Words so extreme could never have been applied to William's case. Dorothy's cottage in the Grasmere days was constantly 'edge-full' with friends old and new. But gregarious by nature though he was, there were times when he had good reason to feel his plight as not unlike John Wordsworth's. Dorothy was six when she was parted from a father she had rarely seen and could hardly know. The relationship with his sons was more prolonged. Despite this he evokes in *The Prelude* no affectionate tribute, for reasons which are perhaps not far to seek. The hated Sir James Lowther, later Earl of Lonsdale, did not spare his agent-cum-attorney. Rich, ruthless, ambitious, constantly adding to his estates and as constantly involved in litigation (he would always go to law rather than settle the smallest debt) perhaps his agent's least enviable function was that of political vigilante on his employer's behalf; of ensuring, if only by means of liquid refreshment, that votes were forthcoming without as within the Lowther pocket borough.

As such John Wordsworth could neither afford nor readily gain friends. But if any resemblance to William's own later position was accidental and entails no likeness, a likeness does I think strongly suggest itself. Both men chose, and possessed the strength, to swim against the tide. John Wordsworth's motive may well have been ambition. But if he suffered inordinate demands to be made on him, his duties were not confined to Sir James's service. He rode himself no less hard, with an almost fanatical zeal— or need to match the stress of his temperament. The little we know of him must suggest a man with powerful drives. For we know, too, that he passionately loved his wife. Centering on her alone feelings almost too strong, her death was a blow from which he never recovered. For five years he lived on stricken, plunging himself in work, seldom at home and when home doubtless morose. And since then has had, if not a bad, what may seem an inadequate press as the poet's father. Anne Wordsworth had reared her children on fairy stories and not on the improving moral tales

8

already taking over from these. The neglectful unhappy father did something more. It was he who introduced William to poetry and taught him to get by heart 'large portions of Shakespeare, Milton and Spenser'. Youth, however, has a need for callousness. Nor was De Quincey alone in remarking in William 'animal appetites organically strong'. William, to describe himself, recalling his youth as 'thoughtless', 'the coarser pleasures of my boyhood days', employs both words—'animal', 'appetite'.

Meanwhile despite their mother's death, despite the unfettered pleasures (surely unique) permitted at Hawkshead school, despite the second home Dorothy's brothers found lodging together with lenient Anne Tyson—the time spent at their father's house was eagerly awaited, as Wordsworth vividly conveys. The passage is the well-known one in which he describes how one Christmas, 'on the glad eve of its dear holidays', feverish with impatience, he restlessly went to see if he could not sight the ponies coming for them. Unsure by which of two roads these might travel, he stationed himself on a crag at the junction of both, to sit peering through the mists with as his sole companions a single sheep and a blasted hawthorn tree.

That this was no mere romanticizing of boyhood is proved by the sequel; at Cockermouth he found his father dying and ten days later stood by the grave in bitter wind and snow. 'The event, / With all the sorrow that it brought / Appeared a chastisement.' Such chastisement might well seem to refer solely to the dire fate which now overtook the children. Wordsworth expanding on this, however, is explicit: he was punished for his impatience awaiting the ponies, 'that day so lately past when from the crag / I looked in such anxiety of hope'. Then 'in the deepest passion I bowed low / To God who thus corrected my desires'. Perhaps he did. But this is a very much later Wordsworth speaking, the voice of a deist, one for whom bowing low was an attitude that for most of his life he would signally fail to adopt. How is one to understand what follows? That afterwards that day,

> . . . the wind and sleety rain
> And all the business of the elements,
> The single sheep and the one blasted tree
> And the bleak music from the old stone wall,
> The noise of wood and water, and the mist . . .

were images to which he 'oft repaired; and thence would drink, / As at a fountain'.

Of what did he drink? Of boyish hope or of hope chastised? Here for the first time he is not explicit. And perhaps he did not know himself; poets are not required to know their meaning. But up to this point he expressly deals with one emotion—guilt, for an act unwittingly committed. A propensity to guilt—without which we might never have had the poet, nor an Ancient Mariner an albatross; and without which we must certainly have lost the Grasmere Journals. Such was John Wordsworth's legacy to the world.

To his children at the time it appeared a calamitous one: penury, dependence, humiliation; debts to the tune of £4,700 incurred by their father on his employer's behalf. Lord Lonsdale predictably refused to pay, and a lawsuit was set in train in which the Earl—an adept in such matters —contrived at the end of twenty years to die still in pocket when the debt was honoured by his heir.

Meanwhile the Wordsworth boys were left worse than homeless. They inherited their Penrith grandparents. Though class distinctions were less distinct than they subsequently became, William Cookson, draper, had done well in carrying off a Crackanthorpe, heiress of Newbiggin Hall, and could not or was not allowed to forget it. Philistine, petit-bourgeois, puritanic, this insensitive couple left their mark perhaps on all the children. In Richard, the eldest, reticence became extreme caution; shy, silent John, eclipsed by William whose daring he could not emulate, learnt to ask little of life; Kit, the youngest, motherless at three and bred up to the rigours of Penrith, put his nose in his school-books and kept it there. As for William, his mother's prediction may well have been in great part prompted by his life-style when at Penrith.

The shop on the site, still a pleasantly old-fashioned draper's, still keeps its eye on the little market square of what Dorothy called 'that petty place'. In it we may still seem to glimpse the drawing room upstairs, hung with portraits (doubtless of Crackanthorpes) with the carpet kept rolled up, laid only on rare occasions. A shrine of that death-in-life ordained below, it invited desecration, incited one to violence with its bare floor made for whipping tops—if whipping nothing else: 'Dare you strike your whip through that old lady's petticoats?' was William's challenge, his own lash at the ready. Richard declined. 'Then here goes', and the lady was left in a highly unsuitable state. This perhaps in the term he almost certainly spent attending the dame school in Penrith before his mother's death. To the miseries of the year that followed—before, at nine, he could be transferred to Hawkshead—belongs perhaps an episode potentially still more desperate: 'Upon some indignity', he says, 'having been put upon me', he went up into the attics at Penrith 'with the intention of destroying myself with one of the foils . . . kept there. I took the foil in hand, but my heart failed.'

It is true that Wordsworth accuses himself of having been at this time 'of a stiff, moody and violent temper'. He qualifies this, however. 'But possibly, from some want of judgement in punishments inflicted, I had become perverse and obstinate in defying punishment and rather proud of it than otherwise.'

The child is father of the man, and if Wordsworth did not see it here he none the less tracked matters to their source. For the concrete in him, surely, was pure Penrith Brighton rock. No such traits can apply to the small boy, always adventurous, whose chosen companion was a younger sister, one who refused to rifle a bird's nest and who when he took her off with him butterflying stayed his hand—and ruined the sport? No, 'who . . . God love her! feared to brush the dust from off its wings'.

Dorothy, admittedly, was to describe what she later found in him as 'a sort of violence of Affection, if I may so Term it'. And the phrase—she is conscious that it is odd; but nothing less strong will convey the force of the impression, his delicate unremitting attentiveness to her, 'a sort of restless watchfulness, I know not how to describe it'. It is 'a tenderness that never sleeps'.

The commodity was not one dealt in by genteel Penrith drapers, there was no label marked Vitality; there was one writ large, Wickedness, and others—Intransigence, Uncouthness—that less happily stuck. But yoked as it was with this regime, the paradise of Hawkshead was to prove perhaps a hardly less dangerous terrain. Not for nothing is Wordsworth's life-work known to us as *The Prelude*. If this had been conceived as an ante-chapel, the great cathedral nave he had planned refused to follow, the altar remained stubbornly in the past. No poet has so persistently dwelt on his youth and its passing away, none so prematurely and strangely held that his powers were lost to him before their realization— and embodied the loss in an *Immortality Ode*.

So mighty were the hymns that one forgets, if not the altar, the extreme oddity of its position. For if in age we may come to lament youth, there can exist few people however fortunate who do not shake off its bondage with relief. And if 'Full soon thy Soul shall have her earthy freight, / And custom lie upon thee with a weight, / Heavy as frost, and deep almost as life', Wordsworth when he wrote this was not contemplating a lifetime spent commuting to the City. He was looking back—to his schooldays, to days when he exchanged penal Penrith and its docile countryside for mountains that tumbled sheer to lakes, for cliffs and cataracts, a land itself rugged, tumultuous, brooding. There after school 'when cottage windows blazed through twilight gloom', he, William Wordsworth, need not heed their summons. 'Clear and loud the . . . clock tolled six'; but he, 'all shod with steel', 'proud and exulting as an untired horse', might 'wheel about' to join the hue and cry across the ice; or, Penrith children long pent in their narrow cribs, a boy of nine spend half the night out upon the fells inspecting the snares he had set—and not only his own. At times the temptation to plunder would be too strong; and then the solitary hills would quicken with noiseless footsteps, with 'low breathings coming after me'.

Terror was half the game, one itself fearful enough for a child alone at night upon the fells. And for Wordsworth such escapades brought in their train more than the moon and stars, the strangeness and scale of the world in which these took place. He was 'fostered', he wrote, 'alike by beauty and by fear'; and was not in this expressing a debt to Penrith. He did court fear—and once at least in a form not fully foreseen. This too was 'an act of stealth and troubled pleasure', the theft one summer's night of a boat in which he had pushed off 'not without the voice of mountain echoes'. He was soon, however, lustily plying the oars of an 'elfin pinnace', keeping his eye on the ridge that framed the lake, when suddenly from behind this a huge black peak, 'as if with Voluntary power instinct / Upreared its head'. He 'struck and struck' but 'growing still' the shape with 'measured motion like a living thing / Strode after' him. For days no known or pleasant things remained; but 'mighty forms that do not live / Like living men' moved in 'By day, and were a trouble to my dreams'.

Given his hair-raising taste for hanging pinned to crags by nothing more it seemed than the biting blast, and the policy of an 'outward-bound' school (if one that expected its scholars to proceed to Cambridge) Hawkshead was for boys a very heaven. Exertion itself may generate a fusion with time and place, a bond in the heat of the moment with that moment. At puberty this bond became for Wordsworth something more—a sense of vital relationship lacking elsewhere. Henceforth Hawkshead exploits were to be less heightened than displaced by what before had been their context, a context vaster than what in Penrith man had made of man, a world which now claimed him for its own.

In bed now at Anne Tyson's he lay listening as 'the frost raged bitterly with keen and silent tooth'. Now as he set himself to raise the owls and hung there in the silence awaiting their reply, hearing his own hallooing die away, that silence would overtake him as the roar of mountain torrents. Now as the orange evening died and still the noisy gang flew on over the ice in the dark and cold, the crags 'tinkled like iron', while the surrounding hills gave back an alien melancholy sound. Now as

> . . . on the perilous ridge I hung . . .
> With what strange utterance did the loud dry wind
> Blow through my ear . . .

It was his native tongue.

He listened, he deciphered and struck up with a pedlar who sold not only 'fine knacks for ladies', but dealt in country customs, in strange tales and ballads. This motley race who travelled the roads—tramps, beggars, old soldiers, had always held a fascination for him. And the pedlar with his love of life, mother-wit, mad-cap ways would long be an inspiration and archetype. Another if different bond was that with Hawkshead's young headmaster, in whose study it would seem he was free to browse, to take down from the shelves whatever took his fancy—or find out what took that of William Taylor. There beside the works of Taylor's own poet-friend, George Dyer, were poems by men named Thomson, Collins, Crabbe; but also the poems of a dead boy, Thomas Chatterton, written at little more than his own age. He himself, at fifteen, had been given a leatherbound notebook—and the only possible giver seems William Taylor—in which to enter verses of his own, not merely those set by the school and not always in the Gothic vein in vogue. For as he wrote and walked it struck him more and more that no one for some reason had ever written of what he wished to write—of ordinary things; of the sudden startling clarity with which, for instance, an oak-tree might stand out against the glow of evening. Taylor was the man he most wished to please and impress; and did not Taylor rate poetry exceptionally high?

But a term came round when the headmaster's study stood empty, he was ill; then unthinkably given out as dying. He took his leave of the boys and talked on his death-bed of Gray. He was thirty-two. For his perhaps potentially most intractable pupil the loss, at the crucial age of sixteen, of this liberal spirit—the only being to whom he had ever looked up— meant the removal not only of a guide who might have rendered the stormy years ahead less convulsive, but of a civilizing influence. Had Taylor lived we should hardly have lost the poet-*enfant terrible*, but we might have been spared the puritan.

Meanwhile there were few, if any, with whom he could talk of poetry, none to whom he could turn for understanding. Nor could he guess that this loss would be made up to him, a year away, in his sister Dorothy.

III

Nuns fret not at their Convent's narrow room

Wordsworth, *Sonnet*

1778–1787

IT WAS NINE years since they had met, since their mother's death had left them 'destitute, and, as we might, / Trooping together'. Had Wordsworth chosen here to have his revenge on Penrith he could not have done so more effectively. Destitute they indeed were, if not yet literally so. But if there was still their father to pay the bills rendered as a matter of course for the keep of their daughter's children by these unbelievable grand-parents, the doors of an orphanage could hardly have closed more grimly on the five. Nor an extended statement better convey the misery and bewilderment that now united the children left 'trooping together' as best they might; consigned, no doubt, to some bare back room where there was nothing to damage and where such noise as they made would least be heard. And initially perhaps there was little to hear. But if, as would seem likely—with their father in no condition a mere ten weeks after their mother's death to have the children at Cockermouth for the boys' summer vacation—they were left to endure together for some ten months, at an age when hours are days and weeks years, it is more than probable that the muteness of misery gave way to something a good deal less convenient.

Unloved and unwanted, constantly checked and reproved, living as if they had always done something wrong, the children—lost, tear-stained, defiant—hung together. Accustomed to a climate of tenderness, they now had only each other. With the glow of the Cockermouth days a distant dream, there was now only Dorothy to take up the sobbing Kit, only the brothers to comfort their younger sister. From this plight there derived in the long term perhaps something more than a stronger affection than that normally found between brothers and sisters—a physical demonstrative-ness unusual in this sphere, and rare perhaps in the context of northern reserve.

Their mother had died in March 1778. Deliverance for Dorothy came in the December, in the shape of a new guardian, Miss Elizabeth Threlkeld, the cousin and close friend of her mother. But if the carriage which arrived to fetch her away ought to have seemed like Cinderella's coach, one can hardly doubt her anguished desire to explain that she could not leave Kit, could not endure to be parted from her brothers. If, however, she clung to

14

the sound of the Penrith cobbles under the wheels, to find herself when this ceased in the grip of despair, she had found she must quickly have realized something else. For the first time for months someone addressed her sympathetically, kindly, and—as her mother might have done—took out a handkerchief, wiped away her tears and told her about her cousins in Halifax. And perhaps asked would she not sleep a little; the journey ahead was a long one. And the answer would be she would like to look out of the window. So, at least, she did and continued throughout her life to do. The houses and haystacks were quite different here. She had indeed, in reality, entered another country, and did not need her aunt to explain to her that in leaving Penrith for Halifax she was leaving Jehovah's Kingdom—for the sweetness and light of the Northgate-end Chapel.

Dorothy's Halifax has been buried by Halifax, and I do not propose here to disinter the colourful life of a wool town with its weavers on cloth-market days bringing their bales to display to her merchant uncle. Dorothy never employed her pen in describing this, although whenever she could she returned there. Her silence is marked and revealing; the setting of her youth could hold no possible interest for anyone—in contrast with any scene or site remotely connected with William. And so it remains an invisible backcloth that nevertheless provided what she would always delight in, 'a living prospect'; the bustling lively ambience of a thriving town where everyone was busy and business pleasure, conducted on a basis of mutual trust and respect—but also a shared distrust of the easy notion that a God so benevolent should, by way of return, be conveniently disposed of as a mystery.

Unitarianism may ring no bell today, but it rang one powerfully enough in Dorothy's time not only to attract to its pulpits such preachers as Godwin and Coleridge, but to ensure them packed pews. Coleridge in fact might well have been the founder of the sect, though its tenets assumed for him a more awful cast than they possessed for the simpler conscience of, if not the rich, an essentially prosperous middle class. If He had—and He had—been good to one, then one must try to please Him. But this entailed knowing how to do so, dispensing with mysteries like the Trinity which were the works not of God but man. A mystery did no one any sort of moral good. It was necessary to start with God as One. And go from there, go back it might be to the Neo-Platonists, to philosophers—never to drunken priests, an uneducated crew—and on Sunday to go to the Northgate-end Chapel where bigotry was not and reason reigned.

It is hard today to conceive of an enlightened bourgeoisie, one 'not puffed up by false unnatural hopes / Nor selfish with unnecessary cares'. But in Halifax it existed; and to it Dorothy owed a freedom from tension and a stability without which, with the cargo she carried, she might well have foundered. Wordsworth's words quoted above were used to describe his mother. I have used them designedly in another context. 'The loss of a mother', Dorothy wrote, 'can only be made up by such a friend as my dear Aunt'. Elizabeth Threlkeld, still in her early thirties and already with five

orphans on her hands—the children of her sister, Anne Ferguson—
succeeded where many parents fail. Perhaps in part because she possessed
the attribute which made Colette's Sido so fascinating—a life of her own
which did not hinge on theirs. If she was always busy she was doing what
she enjoyed, whether darning or teaching Dorothy to darn; was alert, was
gardening or reading; was a woman of wide culture and, clearly,
considerable charm and distinction. Shrewd, firm, tolerant, interested,
amused, she was besides Dorothy bringing up Sam, Martha, Edward,
Elizabeth and Anne—'all without effort, from a blessed nature'.

On Dorothy, with her susceptible temperament and with Penrith ways
still fresh in mind, her aunt's blessed nature made a profound impression.
But young as she was she was quick to see more than this—that though
the trick might be done 'all without effort', always gladly never grudgingly,
there none the less lay behind this, if no stern and loveless precept, great
unselfishness, rigour, a keen sense of duty. 'My Aunt', she wrote, was the
person 'the most thoroughly intent upon doing right of any I ever knew'.

This is saying a great deal and perhaps a little too much, by which I do
not mean to imply that Aunt Threlkeld was not all that Dorothy said;
merely that her example seeded itself on ground perhaps almost too ready
to receive it. In Halifax Dorothy found an ideally happy home. Impulsive,
warm, with her eager response to all things, stuttering in her excitement
and haste to share some discovery, she was quickly the pet of her older
Ferguson cousins; and later the leading spirit in a circle where, if many
were called, not all were chosen. Despite this, despite the fact that now
and for many years as the inmate of another happy household (that of her
uncle William Cookson) she continued in the fullest sense to contribute,
she was never free, she said, from 'the painful idea that one's existence is
of very little use, which I really have always been obliged to feel'. Penrith
apart, no one obliged her to feel this but herself. And if in her desire to be of
use she resembled her aunt, she needed, one may feel, no exemplar and
might have been better off without one.

For much as she owed Aunt Threlkeld, Dorothy's qualities—her self-
lessness, frugality, keen sense of duty, the happiness she found in devoting
herself to others—were traits that if reinforced by her aunt's example,
derived from a deeper, more painful source, less wise and as such
potentially more dangerous in character. By the time she reached her
aunt's hands it was already too late; Halifax could not undo what Penrith
had done. No amount of love or security could by this time efface the
imprint, the traumatic shock so early on of, at a stroke, losing her mother,
her home, her brothers—all that was familiar, loved, *her own*.

Aunt Threlkeld, however, was practical, and Dorothy's education
uncannily fitted to meet her future needs. With this the rational light that
fell through the plain glass windows of the Northgate-end Chapel had
something to do. Polite accomplishments were not on the schedule, any
more than the notion that it was by such trumpery tricks (combined with
as little learning as possible) that young women achieved their end—

finis indeed—a husband. Things might be ordered differently in Bath. But if William Pollard took his pew in the Northgate-end Chapel with the sense that his pockets were comfortably lined, he, like Miss Threlkeld for Dorothy, paid the five shillings entrance fee and sent his daughters to day-school in Halifax. Plain sewing and high thinking—though never too high for sense, nor to allow of Dorothy, at fourteen, devouring *Clarissa Harlowe*—were to serve her a great deal better than sketching and warbling to the pianoforte.

Dorothy's fingers were perhaps to account for as much plain sewing as her brother's legs, it was reckoned, accomplished in miles. But she learnt something still more vital to her: a feeling for literature—for Homer, Shakespeare and Milton, for poetry but also the best in prose—which, joined with her urgent temperament, was to give her what Coleridge remarked as perfect pitch. Quite as intent as her aunt upon doing right, when it came to keeping a journal this form of osmosis would make her no less intent upon saying it right, on being exact.

Posterity has its own special debt to the Northgate-end Chapel in the shape of William Pollard's eldest daughter. Plain Jane Pollard was Dorothy's dearest friend, and in youth was perhaps not plain—or endearingly so. Her likeness at Dove Cottage is certainly endearing. One feels it must be unequivocally Jane; because she would not equivocate, would not connive with her nose being depicted as smaller than it was. And if in middle life as Mrs Marshall she recklessly scraped her hair high on her poll, not in a plain bun but in tier upon tier of, it must be said, astonishing sausage rolls, perhaps she enjoyed them or Mr Marshall did. Or perhaps when Dorothy—at fifteen normal enough to be interested in such things—wrote to her 'I wear my hair curled about my face in light curls friz'd at the bottom and turned in at the ends. How have you yours?', Jane's hair had been her one beauty, and later she left her maid to go to town on it with the curling tongs.

But if in a friend of Dorothy's the sausage rolls come as a shock, more remarkable is the fact that they cease to do so; that we entirely forget these as we look at the face below, a sensible, no-nonsense sort of face. The face of Halifax, for this is what it is, of one who growing up amidst its gaieties was to prove no faithless flibbertigibbet. In Dorothy's hour of need extending to years, Jane never forgot her childhood friend, not merely providing her with a vital outlet but preserving Dorothy's letters if only in a drawer in the hope of finding time to decipher them. To this, to the excellent Jane, we owe Dorothy's story told for the first time by herself.

We owe it, of course, also to her departure from Halifax and initially to the miseries of Penrith. Possibly when the summons came—the stern if implied injunction that she was old enough to return and make herself useful—her feelings were mixed. To part from her beloved aunt, to be reft from all her friends just as she and they were growing up, to leave them to dances and routs for a place where there were no such things must have been a hard pill to swallow. But then the thought that at Penrith there would be her own brothers could hardly fail to outweigh all the rest.

The depths of misery to which she was reduced in a matter of weeks, at most a month, before these brothers arrived, and which she was not too proud to reveal to Jane Pollard, come vividly through her first extant letter. It is dated simply 'Sunday eveng', and, as she agitatedly explains, is a whole week later than intended: 'On Monday my Grandmr was in a very bad humour and I could not get out of the room for a mo[men]t', on Tuesday Aunt Threlkeld had first claim; 'on Wednesday night I begun one . . . but the shop was shut up, and I could get no inkstand but one . . . quite dry. I desired my Br John to put a little water in it, and he filled it so . . . it blotted all my paper.' On Thursday night she tried again 'but my Br Wm was sitting by me and I could not help talking with him'. She might perhaps have snatched an hour to write, 'but I have so few, so very few to pass with my Brothers . . . You know not how happy I am in their company . . . I do not now pass half my time alone. I can bear the ill nature of all my relations, for the affection of my brothers consoles me in all my Griefs'. But how soon she will be deprived of this, and how soon she will become 'even more melancholy than before. They are just the boys I could wish them, they are so affectionate and so kind to me as makes me love them more and more every day. Wm and Christopher are very clever boys'; John 'has a most excellent heart, he is not so bright as either Wm or Christopher but he has very good common sense' which will serve him well as a sailor. 'Richard . . . is equally affectionate and good, but is far from being as clever as William' and stayed one night only. (At nineteen he is training to be what he is, a born solicitor.) Meanwhile 'Many a time' have the three at Penrith 'shed', wrote Dorothy, 'tears of the bitterest sorrow, we . . . each day, feel more sensibly the loss we sustained' in 'our parents, and each day do we receive fresh insults'. Of what kind Jane will wonder: 'the most mortifying kind; the insults of servants'. But could she write half what she wished, Jane must be 'as much in the dark as ever. I was for a whole week kept in expectation of my Brothers, who staid at school all that time after the vacation begun owing to the ill-nature of my Uncle who would not send horses for them. . . . This was the beginning of my mortifications'. Indeed nobody but herself 'expressed one wish to see them, at last however they were sent for, but not till my Brother Wm had hired a horse . . . and ccme over because he thought some one must be ill; the servants are every one of them so insolent to us as makes the kitchen as well as the parlour quite insupportable . . . We are found fault with every hour of the day both by the servants and my Grandfr and Grandmr, the former of whom never speaks to us but when he scolds which is not seldom'. And their fortune, she fears, will indeed 'be very small as Lord Lonsdale will most likely only pay a very small part of his debt. . . . We shall have I believe about six hundred pound apiece if Lord L. does not pay. It is but very little, but it will be quite enough for my Brothers' education and after they are once put forward in the world there is little doubt of their succeeding, and for me, while they live I shall never want a friend'.

IV

A gift then first bestowed

1787

DOROTHY, AS WILL later be seen, was no moaner. And if from now on her whole emotional life revolved around brothers seldom seen, she never in other circumstances complained, or allowed herself to repine when for years she did not see them or when William's rare visits ended. .

It is none the less probable that the tyranny of Penrith did more to bridge the gap of nine years than could another happier ambience. Dorothy's closest affinity had early lain with William. That he should now be the one singled out for particular obloquy—and his attitude must have laid him open to this—could only in Dorothy's case have one effect. 'I absolutely dislike my Uncle Kit', she wrote, 'who never speaks a pleasant word to one, and behaves to my Br Wm in a particularly ungenerous manner.'

It may be as well to dispose here briefly of Uncle Kit. There is in fact not much to be said for him. As Christopher Crackanthorpe Cookson and a chip of the old block he, however, and not the grandparents, was one of the children's two official guardians. As such it might have been thought in Uncle Kit's own interest not to rub in the children's indigence, but to do what he could to ensure its termination. Instead he not only washed his hands of this, leaving it to the son of their Wordsworth guardian—with whom the boys spent the brief Christmas vacations—to shoulder the burdensome suit against Lord Lonsdale, but did not scruple to damage its favourable outcome. 'My Uncle Kit', as Dorothy wrote to Jane Pollard, 'having said many disrespectful things of him [the Earl] and always espoused the cause of the Duke of Norfolk [Lord Lonsdale's particular enemy] has incensed him so much that I fear we shall through life feel the effects of his [Uncle Kit's] imprudence.'

In thrall to such guardianship a contemptuous truculence must have seemed the only line to take commensurate with self-respect, with being left at school, imposing on old Anne Tyson, a whole week. And not only seemed so to William; Dorothy herself came to indulge in more than mortification—in a spirit of rebellion that must have astonished her aunt in one so willing, grateful, eager to please. 'We have been told thousands of times that we were liars', she wrote, and 'treat such behaviour with the contempt it deserves'.

Had she and William not met after so long as accomplices, Dorothy to pour out her 'mortification'; had she instead felt obliged to curb her impetuous feelings, their instant *rapport* might not have flared as it did. Nor might it have done so had she stayed a year more in Halifax, had she not at fifteen and a half been 'so very little', had she met and been attracted to other young men; had William, in short, not entered her life as and when he did, forever to take possession of her heart.

As it was, for two days she had him to herself. This may have been due to Uncle Kit's intransigence or to William's reluctance to go for his luckless brothers without first establishing that his sister (labelled by her grandparents 'wild and intractable' and treated like himself as a limb of Satan) was really as extraordinary as she seemed. Extraordinary in her quickness, her candour, her freedom from affectation, her ardent interest in all that related to him, her knowledge and love of literature—her desire to know if he could without too much trouble procure her some new poems by a Scottish poet named Burns about which her friend, Jane Pollard, had written to her.

The poems were procured and read and the draper's shop forgotten as for six weeks they strolled in the sun on the banks of the Eamont; or, with Dorothy not too old to enjoy the recklessness of it, scrambled into the ruins of Brougham Castle and—hidden from all the world, secure on the top of its turret—lay 'listening to the wild flowers and the grass'. The presence of John and Kit is ignored in *The Prelude*, though this may be due to nothing more than the fact that Wordsworth in this confuses or blends two summers, wrongly bringing Dorothy back in 1788 by which time John had gone to sea. But Kit aged twelve may well have preferred his rod and line to Burns, as assuredly did the intensely private John, whose qualities emerged only later, when removed from William's sphere he at last, as a seafaring man, gained the self-confidence he had lacked. Now at fourteen he could only hesitate to intrude on all that William found in Dorothy.

William had not, in fact, been unhappy since Taylor's death. On the contrary he had seldom been happier, never lived more intensely than now that his own days at Hawkshead were drawing to a close. '. . . left alone, / Seeking the visible world, nor knowing why', this, 'sought for' its 'own sake', now 'Appeared like something in myself, a dream / A prospect in the mind'. The fusion of inner and outer was so complete that at times he would grasp at a tree or a wall to confirm its reality. In other words he was adolescent, his faculties expanding, but also free as only youth is free. Whether his own happiness transfigured the world around him, or whether his exalted state derived from communion 'with things that really are', he could not himself in retrospect decide. At sixteen he knew only that

> In all things now
> I saw one life and felt that it was joy.

Had he returned to Penrith in a less buoyant mood, had he been lonely and bereft, the overwhelming effect on him of reunion with Dorothy must have been more explicable. As it was her recovery was 'a joy above all joys', 'another morn risen on' mere 'mid-noon', the years between reduced to 'separation desolate', and she herself 'a gift then first bestowed'. That she could be so, beset by the miseries of Penrith, seems an achievement in itself. Nor was she merely bathed in the glow of his mood. The words quoted above were written in 1804. But neither were they conditioned by retrospect. There exists both a moving glimpse of Dorothy herself and an insight into William's feelings in a passage written at the time, recalling her as she stood, perhaps, in a niche of Cockermouth Castle, unaware of the eye that marked her every mood:

> Sister, for whom I feel a love
> That warms a Brother far above,
> On you, as sad she marks the scene,
> Why does my heart so fondly lean?
> Why but because in you is given
> All, all my soul would wish from Heaven?
> Why but because I fondly view
> All, all that Heav'n has claimed, in you?

In Dorothy he had not only found all that he could have wished for, not merely the love he had lost with his mother's death. He was far from friendless at Hawkshead, was nothing if not manly and had found a loving pillar in Anne Tyson. It was nevertheless as if in meeting Dorothy he had stumbled on an unknown side of himself, on the sudden recognition of how deep was his need for love—and on the violence of his own affections.

No such violence had coloured his feelings for Mary Hutchinson, once his playmate at Miss Birkett's dame school and with whom, before Dorothy's reappearance on the scene, he had consoled himself when at Penrith. Mary's feelings would early seem to have been of a stronger order; she can certainly hardly have failed to feel put in the shade by a girl so flame-like and voluble, so unlike herself. If so, this was merely a foretaste of what, after marriage even, was for many years to be her lot. When in 1804 as William's wife she took her place in *The Prelude* this was below and second to Dorothy, and in no such eulogistic terms. She was merely 'another maid . . . who cast a gladness on that season by her . . . exultant outside look of youth'—if only by this it could only make matters worse. When she is then given a 'placid under-countenance' this is almost as bad as a double chin.

There are happier words in which to evoke a serenity which in Mary did give an illusion of beauty. But in 1787 no such words had been written; and Dorothy was a sister, not a rival. No one, moreover, was better fitted than Mary to understand William's and Dorothy's pleasure in being together.

For the Hutchinsons were yet another family of orphans, and had likewise, in Dorothy's phrase, been 'squandered abroad', likewise, in consequence, later to form a tight-knit clan. 'Stockton is just the same as ever, bright and clean and dull! But we, the Hutchinsons, are all so agreeable ourselves, and to ourselves . . . that we are quite independent of other society.' So wrote Mary's sister Sara in 1821. Their plight had, however, been far less grim than the Wordsworths'. Mary was not an only girl. She was thirteen, the third of ten children, when in 1783 her mother died. On the death two years later of her father, an unsuccessful importer of tobacco, the children were dispersed but to loving relations. Mary (with Peggy, George and Joanna) remained in Penrith with Aunt Monkhouse, her 'Good', as opposed to 'Bad Aunt', Great-Aunt Gamage, the three oldest boys going to their great-uncle, Thomas Hutchinson, a gentleman-farmer at Sockburn in County Durham. Sockburn, as Dorothy would find, was 'not at all like a farmhouse'. Bounded by a magnificent reach of the Tees, the demure red-brick doll's house still stands keeping its secrets— the talk, the scenes played out under its roof, its pivotal role in the lives of Dorothy, William, Coleridge, Sara Coleridge and Sara Hutchinson.

Sara, Mary's sister, had also been farmed out and from the age of ten brought up in Kendal. There, at the hands of James Patrick (the Wanderer in Wordsworth's *Excursion*, and widely known as 'the intellectual Pedlar') she received an education then rare for a woman, one that would do much to create her extraordinary destiny—and, yoked with this, of necessity Dorothy's own.

Mentally the Hutchinsons were a tougher breed than the Wordsworths. From where exactly, one wonders, has been derived the watered-down figure of Mary? Certainly not from her letters. Her reserve it would appear deceived many. Perhaps 'Slave-trade Clarkson'—as Southey was to christen the abolitionist—was the chief culprit. Wit was not, however, Clarkson's forte; and his famous remark of Mary, that she could only say 'God bless you', clearly was meant as high and serious praise—to live on as his one *bon mot* and never intended as such. Coleridge, admittedly, said she 'was of a more solemn cast than her sister', meaning than the irrepressible Sara. But this indicates only a matter of degree in a family which was nothing if not lively. The best explanation of Mary seems to be that she kept herself to herself not because she had nothing to say, but because, not easily impressed and often tart in her reactions, she could thus quietly enjoy her own amusement.

Meanwhile that first summer William bequeathed to Dorothy what she would most need when he came to leave her—a friend, an escape route. This parting came cruelly unexpectedly early. One might, it seemed, treat Uncle Kit with the scorn he fully deserved but Uncle Kit retained the upper hand, could still decree that William—with close on three months to fill in before going up to Cambridge in October—should not remain at Penrith to take Dorothy from her duties, but return to Hawkshead with his brothers. But if Uncle Kit possessed the power to part him from Dorothy, Uncle Kit was as powerless to make him unhappy as to demolish Hawkshead in his favourite season, autumn; to stop him putting the time to excellent use in polishing and copying his poem, *The Vale of Esthwaite*, and adding to this his lines to Dorothy.

For Dorothy, alas, there were no such compensations; and no new-made friend could replace an old one. The day after their departure she is writing to Jane, had in fact rushed to her ink-pot the day before and finished 'one side before Church time'. But 'I cannot paint to you my Distress . . . I can only tell you that for a few hours I was absolutely miserable, a thousand tormenting fears rushed upon me . . . Could I write to you . . . in this situation?' Dorothy's self-discipline tells her, no. This morning she rose early and should certainly have written,

. . . if I had not had some work to finish before my Grandmother's coming down stairs, it was what I had neglected doing while my Brothers were here, as when they were with me I could always employ my time much more agreeably than in mending an old shirt. . . . My Grandmother is now gone to bed and I am quite alone. Imagine me sitting in my bed-gown, my hair out of curl and hanging about my face, with a small candle beside me, and my whole person the picture of poverty (as it always is in a bed-gown) and you will then see your friend Dorothy. . . .

Tuesday evening. I have stolen a moment again to take up my pen. . . . You know not how forlorn and dull I find myself now that my Brs are gone neither can you imagine how I enjoyed their company when I could contrive to be alone with them. . . . Ah! Jane if the partial affection of a Sister does not greatly magnify all their merits, they are charming boys, particularly the three youngest. . . . I often say to myself. . . . 'I have the most affectionate Brothers in the world, while I possess them, while I have you my Dear Dear Jane . . . can I ever be entirely miserable?' . . . I thank you . . . for your inquiries after my health, I have been perfectly well since I came to Penrith excepting for a pain in my head now and then, but I think crying was the cause of it. . . . I am determined to read a great deal now both in French and English. My Grandmr sits in the shop in the afternoons and by working particularly hard for one hour I think I may read the next, without being dis-covered, and I rise pretty early in a morning. . . . I am at present reading the Iliad and like it very much. My Br Wm read a part of it.

The life which now fell to Dorothy's lot proves that the tormenting fears which had rushed upon her in her first anguish were no mere morbid figment of the moment. Only now, for the first time, do the horrors of Penrith become fully comprehensible, in a letter she wrote to Jane some three months later. One would imagine, she says, that a grandmother would feel tenderness for a grandchild, particularly one with no other parent. But there was 'so little of tenderness' in her grandmother's manner to her,

> or of anything affectionate, that while I am in her house . . . I feel like a stranger. You cannot think how gravely and silently I sit with her and my Gfr, you would scarcely know me, you are well acquainted that I was never famous for taciturnity, but now I sit for whole hours without saying anything excepting that I have an old shirt to mend . . . our only conversation is about *work*, *work*, or what sort of a servant such a one's is . . . what places she lived in, why she left them, &c.&c. What my dear Jane can be more uninteresting . . . ? Yet I am obliged to set upon the occasion as *notable* a face as if I was delighted . . . notability is preached up to me every day. . . . My Gmr's taste and mine so ill agree that there is not one person who is a favorite with her that I do not dislike. You are well acquainted with the characters of those two amiable Ladies, the Miss Custs, they are a mixture of Ignorance, Pride, affectation, self-conceit, and affected notability.

She now sees 'so many of those *useful* people' that she has 'quite an aversion' to 'notables'. But 'I have filled above half my paper with talking about those . . . whose meanness only deserves my contempt, I will therefore, no longer vex myself with thinking of them nor you with reading about them.'

That this letter was written in new, much ameliorated conditions, in the study of her uncle, William Cookson—'where we have a fire'!—only makes the indictment more forcible. The life she depicts was in fact one improved out of recognition by 'that Uncle whom I so much love', who daily gave her fresh proofs of his affection, and who was quickly to become the 'friend to whom (next to my Aunt) I owe the greatest obligations'.

The draper's second son, an enlightened man of the world, was as different from his brother as cheese from chalk. A Fellow of the College (St John's) for which William was destined, where he had been a close friend of Wilberforce; since then acting as tutor to the royal children, he now arrived and took Dorothy under his wing. Possibly, as a bird of a patently different feather from the rest of the Cookson clan, he had had some special fondness for his sister. Or possibly, unlike his relatives, he simply found it natural to take an interest in his sister's children. At all events he was quick to appreciate in Dorothy all that the rest of his family deprecated, to perceive her intelligence and her misery; and, cultivated and scholarly, to combat her grandmother's view that a girl's sole proper business was sewing shirts.

From now on, each morning, Dorothy could count on two blessed hours of release from the Miss Custs, and the gloom of being cooped up with her grandmother; could instead spend the time pleasantly with her uncle studying geography, French and arithmetic. Nor was this all. Divining her loneliness and perceiving that once back in her grandmother's clutches she would undoubtedly have to make up for these 'wasted' hours, he allowed her to write letters in lesson time.

Almost certainly it was his desire to meet his nephew that now procured William's return to Penrith and Dorothy three weeks of unlooked-for happiness. If so, this alone would have won her heart. But that her uncle was as impressed as she could have wished by William, had not the least doubt of his brilliant nephew gaining a fellowship—after which he would be ordained, and from then on his whole future assured—enrolled William Cookson among the saints. William, it was true, had had thoughts of being a lawyer. But it did not much matter what he became. Dorothy busily packing his trunk for Cambridge could examine with something more than wonder and pride the velvet coat lined with silk made for him at Hawkshead (cost of tailoring 1*s*.10*d*.). Could, when her kindly uncle drove off with her brother to install and recommend him at his old college, feel something nearer to hope, to confidence in the future, to security, than she had long known.

V

The Glimmering Prizes

1787–1791

THE PRIDE WITH which Dorothy wields the prefix 'my Br' in her letters, before mentioning William, John or Kit is pathetic and indicative of her feelings. Of Richard, who had left school before she came to Penrith, she saw little and was less fond. An articled clerk, Richard in fact was well on the way to becoming not only a thorough bore and old woman—selfish and complacent; but also an arch muddler, as Dorothy and William would learn to their cost. But all three of her other brothers were to prove men of distinction. She long had a special maternal feeling for Kit, but was not blinded by this when she classed him at thirteen with William as both 'very clever boys'. At forty-six Kit would be Master of Trinity College, Cambridge, and Vice-Chancellor of the University.

More important, meanwhile, for Dorothy was the fact that William was for once in good odour with his relations. Within a week of his entering St John's, his proficiency at Euclid (doubtless helped out by a timely word from his uncle) had obtained him a Founders' Scholarship. If to avaricious Penrith this meant something, to Dorothy it must have seemed to set the official seal on her new-found confidence in the future.

One could not, however, at least in the dark little rooms behind the draper's shop, live indefinitely on good news or in the future. And perhaps her depression that winter was heightened by hope—the hope of spending Christmas with John and Kit. An invitation to join them at all events arrived from their Whitehaven uncle and guardian, Richard Wordsworth. '. . . but I must not go', she wrote, 'poor Lads I shall not see them'; perhaps because, although William would stay in Cambridge, there would not only be her brothers but her cousins—young folk, dancing, sinful goings-on. Newcastle held no such forbidden fruit, merely her loved Aunt Threlkeld who was staying there. But, despite an emissary who offered to act as escort, this gallivanting too was denied her.

A week before Christmas, however, she did have cause for rejoicing but, with almost incredible charity, indulged in no such feelings even to Jane. Her grandfather's sudden death, she wrote, 'was a great shock to us all', but she is 'thankful that he did not linger longer, for, poor man! he has for these two years been a burthen to himself and his friends'. Her grandfather's 'ill-nature' running in tandem with Uncle Kit's had, in fact, been her own chief burthen. And now—this might, if possible, be worse—she may have to go and live not only with Uncle Kit but with the future Mrs Uncle Kit, and who, perfect as this was in its way, should this be? None other than a notable Miss Cust. Meanwhile if the carpet for once was unrolled in the upstairs drawing-room, the wake three days before her sixteenth birthday must have been one of the grimmest—with the draper's establishment, not excluding Dorothy, decked out (and doubtless herself charged for it) in every bale of black the shop could raise. Dorothy, however, typically mentions none of this (one cannot help wishing that she had—the Penrith obsequies from her pen must have been worth having). Instead she made a brave if unsuccessful effort to poke fun at her own dolefulness: 'I have sent you', she wrote in January to Jane, 'a lock of my hair, it will serve to remind you of poor Dolly . . . You cannot think how I like the idea of being called poor . . . Dolly, . . . I could cry whenever I think of it.' But she will not blow her nose on the handkerchief Jane has made her, embroidered with love for *her*, with *her* initials. 'I have just this moment pull'd it out to admire the letters. 'Oh! Jane! it is a valuable handkerchief!'

And so it was, valuable out of all proportion. But she will not enlarge on what gives it its heightened value; will instead take measures against doing this and make use of the escape route furnished by William. At night, defying her grandmother, will slip out of the house and praying that she will not be identified (in what even the reticent John would explosively call 'the most scandalous place I ever was in—everything one says and does is known to the whole town!') hasten to Mary and Peggy Hutchinson. There, with the servants in bed and the kitchen fire to themselves, she might warm herself—and talk at last.

Taciturnity, as she said, was never her strong point, talk always a vital outlet to her. If at Penrith she had learnt to sit for hours together saying nothing, the solemn hush which now reigned at the draper's shop must have stretched her nerves to breaking point. But with Mary and with Peggy—whose 'laughter light', it would seem, after her death still rang in William's ears—Dorothy could stammer away, grow calmer, talk of her brothers, and be regaled with the latest about Great-Aunt Gamage.

With the fire growing low and Penrith peeping Toms safely abed, the three girls, setting out to see Dorothy home, would pace by moonlight or starlight down one street and up another, prolonging their talk and delaying their separation. A further obligation Dorothy owed to her Uncle William was another meeting place, the Vicarage. The vicar's, Mr Cowper's, second daughter Anne was the Hutchinsons' aunt by marriage, having married their uncle, William Monkhouse. And now Dorothy's Uncle William was courting Dorothy Cowper (was everyone called William and Dorothy?). Not only was the vicar's beautiful fourth daughter good enough for 'that Uncle I so love'; she was better, the opposite in all things of a Miss Cust—she had actually turned down Uncle Kit.

When the summer vacation came round, of the three boys only the youngest, Kit, returned to Penrith. John was away, off on his first voyage to Barbados; and William a little surprisingly returned not to Dorothy, not to Mary, but to Anne Tyson's at Hawkshead. He loved and owed much to Anne Tyson who was ageing and near retirement, and whom he knew it would fill with pride and joy to see him still in his glory, 'in splendid clothes, with hose of silk, and hair / Glittering like rimey trees when frost is keen'. And he endured being duly paraded and mobbed up on the score of his powdered hair by his former school-fellows. But the chief call of Anne Tyson's was the place itself. He had pictured Cambridge romantically, reverently, as a place of learning: the reality had proved disturbingly different. 'The glitter of the show' had both gone to his head and come as a shock to this raw country-bred idealist. He wanted now not to go back but to revisit his former self; to lie in his old bed at Anne Tyson's, to look out at the moon in the ashtree—and digest the difference. He had been away in another world; now he wanted to take its measure, and his own, in the light of the old touchstones. After sophistication he wanted simplicity, after the fens he wanted fells. He wanted to be free for the first time for months to think; he did not want to be bothered with Uncle Kit.

And he arrived at the need to take a far-reaching decision; or rather took himself to a country dance, and with its exhilaration still upon him, walked home as the sunrise broke on Helvellyn. The effect was the same: 'I made no vows, but vows / Were . . . made for me'—vows that, if they had larger implications, were, if only indirectly, to bear closely and painfully on Dorothy's life over the next six years.

Not till early August now did he join her at Penrith, but with in his baggage a far more ambitious poem than anything he had hitherto attempted, *An Evening Walk. Addressed to a Young Lady*. This was not addressed to the belle of the country dance. To it when published he appended a note retained throughout his life: 'The young lady to whom this was addressed was my sister'.

We do not know if Dorothy at this stage saw the poem—still in an uncompleted state—since during this summer her correspondence lapsed. Possibly in August, at least, because she did see the poem; or if she did not could still inspire lines written when he returned for a further month to Hawkshead. In these 'Even now' he sees 'a distant scene, / (For dark and broad the gulf of time between)', a cottage 'gilded' with hope's 'fondest ray, / (Sole bourn, sole wish, sole object of my way . . .)'. Here he intends with Dorothy 'to happy days' to 'rise'—and here remain 'till our small share of . . . sighs / (For sighs will ever trouble human breath) / Creep hushed into the tranquil breast of death'!

The scheme is so extraordinary that one feels bound to dismiss it as a mere piece of youthful Utopianism in a young man with life and love before him. Nor was Mary herself out of the picture; on the contrary, this is held to have been when she entered it to inspire the opening lines of his famous lyric:

> She was a Phantom of delight
> When first she gleamed upon my sight;
> A lovely Apparition, sent
> To be a moment's ornament . . .

This, admittedly, is not the language of passion. It specifically evokes a passing fancy. That she was 'a moment's ornament' may, however, suggest that Mary helped to set up the gilded cottage. For William's Hawkshead vows had not been vows of celibacy, and even were the Lonsdale debt not paid there was nothing in 1789 to lead him to decide that he could never support a wife and children. One can only conjecture that he had not yet plumbed his unknown self, that his feeling for Mary led him, at eighteen, to suppose he would never feel anything stronger for a woman—or find a woman to equal Dorothy.

The letter that eventually reached the faithful Jane in December—'I believe nearly half a year has elapsed since I last wrote'—was postmarked Norwich and rapturous; but on an entirely different score. Rapturous partly, perhaps, in proportion to Dorothy's dread of the event that has wrought this miraculous change—the marriage of Uncle William and his departure out of her life to live in distant Norfolk with his bride. The fact that her 'happiness was very unexpected . . . I knew nothing of it ten days before', suggests that her mounting misery, a more and more silent Dorothy, finally obtruded itself on the notice of the much occupied future rector, or on that of his bride, herself up to the eyes in wedding arrangements. They must have been touched by how much they meant to her, and more than had their reward when Dorothy heard that permission had been extracted from Uncle Kit and that she might go with them if she chose. 'When my Uncle told me I was almost mad with joy; I cried and laughed alternately; it was in a walk with him and Miss D that the secret was communicated . . . you may be sure the short time I had to stay at Penrith was very busily [and blissfully] employed in preparing my cloaths.'

The wedding took place and after a wedding breakfast at the Vicarage Dorothy left on her first honeymoon trip; she was to go on three in all, not—as she was to say in later life—always an enviable fate. But on this one the bride herself could scarcely have been happier or more eager to see her future home. Anywhere would have been perfect in not being Penrith. 'But to live in the country and with such kind friends! have I not every reason to be thankful?' And with Cambridge and William no way off.

They now, in fact, passed through Cambridge and saw him in excellent spirits. Dorothy, however, clearly herself felt something of the bewilderment he had done: 'I could almost imagine myself in a different country when I was walking in the College courts and groves. It looked so odd to see smart powdered heads with black caps like helmets only that they have a square piece of wood at the top, and gowns something like clergymen wear; but I assure you (though a description of the dress may sound strange) it is exceedingly becoming.'

Becoming, doubtless, to William. But for once he is given short measure. She does not mention the rooms where he lived so cheaply, sandwiched between the clatter of the College kitchens below, the boom of the organ in Trinity College Chapel, and 'the loquacious clock' that did not spare the quarters 'twice over with a male and female voice'. And perhaps she did not see them, due to there already existing a coolness between uncle and nephew. If William in the vacation had kept his plans to himself, it would have been natural for his kindly relation to ask him how he was finding life at Cambridge. And equally in character with William to burst out against enforced attendance at Chapel. Or perhaps —on his uncle's expressing disappointment that, when the Master of his old College died, his nephew had refused to join in the time-honoured custom of pinning an epitaph on the coffin pall—William had been a shade too outspoken about dons who took not the faintest interest in one; who were there it seemed not to teach but merely to kill time while they waited on a college living. Certainly, after having lingered a fortnight in Newcastle, one day only was reserved for Cambridge—'since', as Dorothy explained, 'as you may be sure we were anxious to see our destined abode'.

Forncett St Peter's can hardly have changed since the day when Dorothy drove up its gravel walk, bordered by limes, to have her first glimpse, on its right, of the church with a round tower, and at its end her bourn, the Rectory itself—red-brick, William-and-Mary in style with its Dutch-style gables, still today a remote and tranquil spot. If Dorothy yearned for country life she had got it with a vengeance. The few local inhabitants were all farmers. There was only one neighbour, a widow, with little to recommend her according to Dorothy's satiric pen.

But from the outset Dorothy was full of delectable schemes that, identifying with her uncle and aunt, centred on the plot of ground which was their new home, but also they allowed her to feel hers. The gardens were to be charming. 'I intend to be a great gardener', and she was to be given charge of the poultry, a rustic role from which 'I . . . promise myself much pleasure'. 'We [not her uncle, nor he and her aunt between them, but Dorothy too] have sketched out a plan' of the way they will spend the time: 'We are to have prayers at nine oclock (you will observe it is *winter*), after breakfast is over we are to read, write, and I am to improve myself in French till twelve oclock', when they are to walk or visit the poor till three, 'which is our dining hour; and after tea my Uncle will sit with us and either read to us or not as he and we find ourselves inclined . . .'. She is thoroughly looking forward to Christmas in the country. 'We have had many consultations in what manner we are to keep my Birth day but we have at last agreed upon roast-beef and plumb pudding as the best Christmas-day dinner . . . you know the manner in which I spent last Christmas. How different is my present situation!' Different indeed. But then how long it is since her wishes have been consulted in anything. And then she has as her own room 'one of the pleasantest in the house'; 'some of the views are beautiful'.

When the summer came round she rose about six and indulged in a pleasure today reserved, it would seem, for the monastic orders—walked 'with a book till half-past eight if the weather permits' or, if not, read in the house. In the evening 'we walk together till about eight, and then I walk alone as long as I can in the garden'. Later a confirmed nocturnal walker, she was already 'particularly fond of a moonlight or twilight walk. It is then I think most of my absent friends'.

She thought of them but she did not pine for them, nor envy Jane her Halifax gaieties. 'Indeed', she wrote, 'I am sure I should make the worst rake in the world. I was at Norwich a few days in the summer and returned quite jaded and pale as ashes.' Returned with relief to the robins ('There are . . . two in the room' as she writes, 'which are gone to rest . . .') who hopped about the room as they would, to the day of her death, hop about any room where Dorothy was. Her nervous, rapid motions would, one might think, have startled birds, but they too are swift, nervous creatures. Was not her nervousness theirs, that of a wild creature, timid and readily startled as themselves? Or perhaps like Coleridge they simply recognized her as guileless, as one utterly trusting whom they could trust; instinctively divined her to be like themselves a 'natural', one whose proper home was the outdoors.

She had robins. She had her charming aunt and her cultivated uncle; their society more than supplied her needs—supplied her with an article wholly new to her: 'leisure to read . . . walk and do what I please'. There might be poultry keeping and set hours for study, but there was no one to chivvy or harass her. There were servants to do the work, no babies for two years, and when one arrived nothing more to do than occasionally rock the cradle which she did: 'Mary', she wrote, 'is quite delighted with my *singing*', adding, 'You will wonder at her taste'. Forncett did not swarm like Aunt Threlkeld's with her cousins. In its peaceful studious atmosphere, with her uncle to guide her reading, her intelligence and taste alike blossomed. His niece may have been no bluestocking but William Cookson played his part in forming the 'perfect electrometer'.

In return she helped her uncle with his parish duties and—her desire to be of use never in abeyance—that summer started a part-time village school. 'I have nine scholars. . . . I only instruct them in reading and spelling and they get off prayers hymns and catechisms.' Not surprisingly the mistress was popular, as was proved when smallpox closed the school:

' "Pray Miss," ' Dorothy, waylaid by one of her pupils, was asked, ' "when shall we come to school again?" '

Unhappily, since all her letters for 1789 have disappeared, little more is known than that she had this summer the two visitors whom, could she have chosen, she must have picked. Aunt Threlkeld came in August and, if she knew it herself, kept secret that she would shortly be Aunt Rawson, the wife of a rich widower with cotton mills and a handsome house in the country outside Halifax on the river. William had come straight to Forncett from Cambridge; though how long his visit lasted is unclear. All that is known is what Dorothy happily could not know, that they would not meet again for eighteen months.

I have spoken of Dorothy's life as being for the next six years painfully if indirectly conditioned by William's. At Forncett her quiet days mirrored his reflection—a reflection that in the end would smash the mirror. William had placed himself in an invidious position. There was no real reason why, the previous summer, he should not with his Cambridge record still good, have told an uncle—liberal and well-disposed towards him—that he wished to change his course of study. His decision not to read for a fellowship must have seemed arbitrary and, with his pecuniary problems, unwise. But he could perfectly well have followed what was termed and accepted as 'an independent course of study'. At the end of this he could still have obtained a degree and a curacy. Nominally reading mathematics and classics, he instead pursued an independent course of study—unsanctioned. In this he was influenced by his dislike of a competitive system which aroused a spirit of envy he had despised as early as when, at Hawkshead, he had tripped up his brother—John?—who threatened to outstrip him in a race.

From 1790 he did not stay away from examinations (possibly this would have meant his being sent down). He completed part of the paper, acquitted himself with distinction and walked out, to be classed as 'unplaced'. Terminal examinations did not affect his degree, but they did affect his guardians and Forncett. If Dorothy suffered, however, from her uncle's disapproval, she did not as yet, it seems, worry overmuch. William had doubtless explained his views on his last visit, and doubtless Dorothy accepted these. He would use the University as it should be used, to study; would continue to read the classics, learn Italian and above all soak himself in a field he now dared to think might one day be his own— English poetry. That he was out of favour could only ensure her allegiance. It none the less made her position an awkward one. And perhaps she was not unduly distressed when William (after spending Christmas with Richard and John, back from his first voyage) failed to turn up at Forncett the following June.

Instead to her astonishment she received a letter from France. He was on a 'pedestrian tour' of the Alps with a friend, Robert Jones, and six pounds apiece to last three months. In those days 'gentlemen' went not on pedestrian tours but the Grand Tour. And Dorothy confessed that, had she known, she would like others 'have looked upon it as mad and impracticable'. From this moment on, however, she was not at Forncett at all—she was in France, in Switzerland, climbing the Simplon; she was gliding down the Rhine in a tiny craft purchased at Basle and re-sold at Cologne. But by now he must be back in France, near Calais, that meant near Forncett. For William was to come direct to her.

But although he reached England at the time appointed, in mid-October, the visit did not take place. With his nephew's degree now barely four months off, his uncle could hardly view William's latest achievements in the same glamorous light that Dorothy did. This, if it disappointed her, was powerless to do so deeply. For William had not only troubled while abroad to write her long letters which entailed Jane Pollard crossing the Alps—there were passages she did not copy for Jane: 'I have thought of you perpetually', he wrote, 'and never have my eyes burst upon a scene of peculiar loveliness but I have almost instantly wished that you could . . . be transported to . . . where I stood'. He had missed her—missed her responsiveness, her power to share his feelings. Jones (throughout life to be for Dorothy 'my brother's companion in his pedestrian tour', in her eyes a glorious appellation) was 'the best-tempered Creature imaginable', and as such ideal, said William, for 'me who am apt to be irritable when travelling'. But Jones with all his virtues could not see what William saw. Dorothy alone would have seen it.

The Rector of Forncett meanwhile, it would seem, charitably deciding to make a final effort to do what he could to ensure that William in his degree, at least, made a 'good end', did now invite him to stay for the Christmas vacation. The previous Christmas yet another William had been a guest, the tiny Mr William Wilberforce, who had been greatly impressed by Dorothy. Sufficiently so to be suspiciously so, thought Jane, who enjoyed rallying Dorothy on her 'suitor'. But Mr Wilberforce was nowhere in the picture, as Dorothy walking now not with a book but—a diminutive figure—on her tall brother's arm, could relive step by step the 'pedestrian tour'.

Now too, if not before, he must have read her *An Evening Walk*, divulged and discussed the dream cottage with her. Whatever he did, he this time 'won my affection to a degree which' Dorothy 'cannot describe. . . . Every Day as soon as we rose from Dinner we used to pace the gravel walk in the Garden till *six o'clock* when we received a Summons (which was always unwelcome) to Tea. Nothing but Rain or Snow prevented our taking this walk. Often have I gone out when the keenest North Wind has been whistling amongst the Trees over our Heads.' Since then she has paced that walk in the garden 'which will always be dear to me from the Remembrance of those long, long conversations I have had upon it supported by my Brother's arm. Ah! Jane! I never thought of the cold when he was with me. . . . I am very sure that Love will never bind me closer to any human Being than . . . Friendship binds me to you . . . and to William, my earliest and my dearest Male Friend.'

Some part of their talk must, however, have touched on William's immediate future. Dorothy was all for parsonage life. William was unconvinced; he had no desire 'to vegetate on a paltry curacy'. He could not, in any case, start to do so till he was twenty-three. What was he to do in the interval? He could take his degree. And this he did, at the end of January 1791, a plain B.A. without Honours; but not surprisingly did not, like his friend the amiable Jones who did no better, get offered a fellow-ship. He now, however, knew what he wanted to do—to go into hiding; and did this in the best place to do it, London. There he wandered the streets. Something might turn up and when it did not he went to see Jones in Wales. Here for four months indecision kept him hamstrung, idle. The rector of Forncett, however, was not hamstrung. By September his nephew was back in Cambridge being tutored in Hebrew and Arabic, essential for a scholarly clergyman.

Dorothy, selfless and staunch as she was, could hardly have failed to be pleased by a degree at least of co-operation which held out the prospect of William's renewed proximity in the future and a warmer welcome for him at Forncett. Her attempts to sell him parsonage life had, it seemed, not been in vain. If she herself had acquired a taste for this—how else was one to procure the pleasure of living in the country, afford a dream cottage and *be of use*?—that she was also, in some degree, her uncle's emissary seems probable from the tone of her letter to Jane, written during William's summer of indecision. Her subject is her favourite one and begins in her usual strain:

> I confess you are right in supposing me partial to William . . . probably when I next see Kitt I shall love him as well . . . his disposition is of the same cast as William's . . . but he is much more likely to make his fortune. . . . William you may have heard lost the chance . . . of a fellow-ship by not combating his inclinations, he gave way to his natural dislike of studies so dry . . . consequently could not succeed at Cambridge . . . he wishes that I was acquainted with the Italian poets . . . [and] has a great attachment to poetry; indeed so has Kitt, but William particularly, which is not the most likely thing to produce his advancement. . . .

This is as near as she comes to criticizing William, and betrays her loyalties as clearly torn. They must have been less so had her uncle been harder on William. Instead he exercised the prerogative of one who, not being a guardian, had no powers of coercion—an inestimable advantage in William's case. William Cookson's role was purely voluntary, his motive merely concern to prevent a nephew—unusually gifted but temporarily lost in the maze of post-adolescence—making mistakes he must later deeply regret.

William, however, saw himself in a different maze—Sanskrit; and applied himself to one thing, getting out. 'What must I do amongst that immense wilderness,' he wrote to a friend, 'who have no resolution, and who have not prepared myself for the enterprise by any sort of discipline. . . . A pretty confession for a young gentleman whose whole life ought to have been devoted to study.'

A pretty piece of ebullience—he was already at Brighton—and one which would hardly have earned his guardians' permission for him to scrap Sanskrit and go instead to France to learn the language. But this could be done in a matter of months at the end of which time he would be equipped to earn a living, in the capacity of tutor to some rich young man being sent abroad to finish his education. The seductive prospect of William keeping himself for once, in place of being kept for a further two years at Cambridge, could hardly fail with Uncles Kit and Richard. By the end of November 1791 he was in Paris, gazing not at the Bastille in ruins but at a picture that hung in a convent near by, the *Magdalene* by Le Brun, in fact a portrait of Louis XIV's voluptuous mistress, Louise de la Vallière.

VI

A Violence of Affection

1791–1794

By Christmas 1791, Dorothy's twentieth birthday, her uncle's exasperation with William's failure once more to 'combat his inclinations' and doubts as to the wisdom of always letting this young man have his head, has been tempered by those Christian precepts—charity and forgiveness—which Forncett's rector strove to hold ever before him. In the matter of his nephew these were inclined to wobble. It was then that Dorothy felt most acutely the extent of her debt to her uncle and aunt. This put her in miserable spirits; and these she could only do her best to work off by being always beforehand with her aunt's wishes, and redoubling her efforts to be of use.

But by Christmas she could be happy with, as a birthday present, news of William settled at Orléans. For once, it seemed, he had done the right thing. Orléans was the best place in all France to study French since it was where the purest French was spoken—due to the fact that, formerly a royal residence, the nobility still kept town houses there. This, as her uncle said, would be of great advantage to William who had decided against taking a tutor, a step that seemed a trifle unwise, but charges were higher, perhaps, than he had foreseen. Doubtless he would with no lack of good society pick up the language, as he said, by ear. The one danger lay in the number of Englishmen there for the same purpose, and that he might hear too much of his native tongue.

If Dorothy had counted on William being here for her birthday this year, her disappointment must have been easily dispelled. William would only be away for some six months; she could look forward to frequent loving letters. And now for four whole months of the six she was to have John, 'grown' she has heard, 'a very tall handsome man'.

John, whom his unloving father had lovingly nicknamed 'Ibex', after 'the shyest of all beasts', had, perhaps, as a mere fifth mate, still not emerged from his shell. To shin up the rigging in perilous seas admittedly was something, something William had not done. But to endure danger —and there had, on this last voyage, been moments that might have made one lose one's nerve—was not enough. The real test of oneself must be command; to see how cool one could stay in 'a violent tufoon', such as that they had met with off Penang when one of the crew had gone overboard, or when (as also happened on this last voyage) the ship, thanks to the pilot, ran aground.

It is unlikely that Dorothy heard anything of these hazards. But she must have been eager to know how his trading had gone. For the advantage of serving with the East India Company was that its officers might, according to rank, each carry a certain weight of cargo for sale. A fifth mate's share was small. But John, in any case, had practically no money to lay out. With a captain's wages, however, and allotment of fifty-six tons, one might in a very few voyages grow rich.

But if John was naturally silent, William was oddly so, and when he did write told one very little. She could neither as on his 'pedestrian tour' imagine herself at his side, nor did his letters contain the same assurance that he thought of her continually, wished for her, missed her. But the explanation, she should have seen it, was obvious: he was working day and night at French, was not going out in the country and had nothing to describe or share with her. He answered none of her questions—because he meant to surprise her by returning to answer these in person. In any case she must steel herself, for then, as soon as he could, he must be off again as a travelling tutor.

But in mid-May came wonderful news. Soon after John's departure her uncle, it transpired, had written to William saying that he could arrange a curacy early. And William had now written back—not quite as soon as he might have done, but still a letter of unconditional surrender. This must mean his immediate return to prepare for ordination, mean that he need not be a travelling tutor, mean the dream cottage, if not yet with 'fair lawns', if not immediately dreamlike—tangible. When by late June he had still not appeared, it is difficult to believe that some displeasure was not evinced by an uncle already, no doubt, justifiably sore that an offer— inspired by affection for his niece—had not been acknowledged with something more of gratitude and less of what looked increasingly like reluctance.

From the mounting stress for Dorothy of this situation relief was to come in an unexpected form. Meanwhile from John at Penrith came other news. She ought not to feel it as joyful, but she did—her grandmother had joined her grandfather. Not only was Uncle Kit not going on with the shop—he now had, of course, no need to do so—he was dropping the name Cookson and moving to Newbiggin Hall as Christopher Crackanthorpe Esquire. The draper's shop was gone, as good as wiped off the face of the earth. Nothing, no fate that might now befall, could ever again require her to cross that hated threshold. But then she remembered her grandmother's gift to her of a hundred pounds. This was a chastening thought; but also timely. John's wages on this next voyage would be forty-five shillings a week; Uncle Christopher Crackanthorpe Esquire would be sure now to advance him something for his trading, but she could herself lend John her hundred pounds.

And then she was perhaps thankful that William had not come, since another William, red and squalling, had. This event was followed by one which further took her mind, and happily her uncle's, quite off William: the former royal tutor was not to be left to rusticate all the year round, but had been appointed a Canon of Windsor. They would have to up-sticks, the whole household. And—only conceive, in the summer— live cooped up for three whole months in a town.

She set off glumly via London, and 'did not like London at all'. But Windsor—to her surprise she was charmed with Windsor. There was 'nothing wanting to make me completely happy'. There had, after all then, been something wanting at Forncett? William? No, for she did not have William now. What had been wanting—increasingly wanting ever since the day when William at Cambridge had first been classed as 'unplaced'—was freedom from care, from anxiety as the examinations came round, from the sense of her uncle's mounting disapproval. Now, at a stroke, this pressure was removed. The relief of it literally went to her head like wine; and does much to explain the inexplicable—the violence of her crush on the royal family, who 'staid near a fortnight' at Windsor, and walked (as did Dorothy Wordsworth) each night upon the castle terrace.

When she first set foot there, she wrote,

> I could scarcely persuade myself of the Reality of the Scene. . . . The King and several of the Princesses were advancing, the Queen's Band was playing most delightfully and all around me I saw only well-dressed, smart People. . . . The King stopped to talk with my Uncle and Aunt, and to play with the children, who though not acquainted with the new-fangled Doctrine of Liberty and Equality, thought a King's Stick as fair Game as any other man's . . .

But when she says, 'I think I never saw so handsome a Family', and proceeds to weigh up the respective charms of the Princess Royal and Princess Mary, Jane is not to imagine that she is 'dazzled with the Splendour of Royalty'. To this one can only say all my eye and Betty Martin. She was as dazzled as she was bound to be, as any middle-class girl bred up in backwater, and with or without a chip, would be.

Aware that her raptures, however, must run Jane's mocking gauntlet, she reluctantly decides to change the subject: 'But what other shall I turn to? I am bewildered in a maze of which I can neither see Beginning nor End.' She wends on blithely, however, through races and routs, to end unwittingly in a revealing pendant, an all but incredible glimpse of Dorothy making her 'Entrée' at one of the Egham Race Balls. She has not, it transpires, danced for five years; and, on taking the floor, 'had the most severe tremblings and palpitations . . . that can be conceived by any trembling Female'.

This interlude in the life of one whose natural tendency was to abhor 'notables', to shun the smart and well-dressed, who cared nothing for grandeur and did care, above all, for simplicity, serves as a timely reminder of her youth. How little fun she has had; convivial, high-spirited, gay, how quietly the days flowed by at Forncett, unrippled, it seems, by events even in France. Yet surely some news must have seeped through, surely in Windsor at least, the Canon must have read the newspapers. Were they—as William wrote of himself—all 'Glassed in a green-house', 'Tranquil almost, and careless as a flower . . . When every bush and tree . . .' was 'shaking to the roots', that, in October 1792, Dorothy could lightly dismiss as 'new-fangled' theories of Liberty and Equality? This within weeks of the September massacres, when to the hundreds murdered in prison in Paris, while being held for trial, had been added fifty-three from Orléans sent to Versailles and hacked down in the street.

The answer in Dorothy's case must be the castle terrace, that in Windsor such happenings seemed even less real than at Forncett. William for some extraordinary reason had still not returned; had, in fact, in August applied for more money, but spoke of being back in October, then in September applied for further funds. What could he want with another twenty pounds inside a month? When supplies were at last cut off, forcing him home, it would seem to have been on the score of his having spent time—and money—enough in France, as much as from any fears on his behalf.

But the point for Dorothy was he was back, that by 22 December she could at last report: 'William . . . writes to me regularly, and is a most affectionate brother'. As to why he did not come in person at once to Forncett, he was anxious, he explained, to push through the press some poems that 'might help to prove he could do something'. Her uncle must have been sceptical and displeased by this further delay. But the poems, it appeared, could be got out in only three weeks. And so they were; true, they arrived in a parcel without the poet, but he would be free to follow any day now. Meanwhile she could not but handle with pride the two small quarto volumes 'by W. Wordsworth, B.A. of St John's Cambridge'. *An Evening Walk. Addressed to a Young Lady* (the poet's sister) was uncomfortably like being in print oneself. At two shillings she was cheaper by a shilling than the Alps, which formed the subject, it seemed, of *Descriptive Sketches*.

Fortunately, since she could hardly share her pride with the Canon of Windsor, she had with her 'one of the dearest of my Brothers'. She had last seen Christopher, then called Kit and aged fourteen, at Penrith, so that Jane may 'judge . . . of my Happiness during the Time we spent together'—time spent tearing strips off William's poems. This is, perhaps, less odd than at first appears. Dorothy was as defensive as a tigress with her cubs, forestalling anything but praise from Jane by employing the surest means of defence, attack. The poems have doubtless 'already suffered the Lash of' Jane's 'Criticisms'. Jane is then less asked for her opinion than told what this is to be: the poems prove William a true poet and 'contain many Passages exquisitely beautiful, but . . . also contain many Faults . . .' She now herself lays on the lash in no uncertain manner, a manner which may, on reflection, undo her purpose, may actually damage William's sales. She cannot retract—but can add the afterthought, 'if you have not yet seen the Poems pray do not make known my opinion of them—let them pass the fiery ordeal.'

Her own scorcher to Jane, however, is in a different sense odd. The chief faults of the poems are 'Obscurity, and a too frequent use of . . . uncommon words' which, if beautiful, lose by repetition. Her attack-cum-defence, in short, is made on poetic grounds and on this score *Descriptive Sketches* merit a beating. But their chief fault is hardly obscurity. How with Windsor fresh in mind, and that January the French King guillotined, had Dorothy swallowed their content? And come—within three weeks of Louis's death—to review with no trace of a qualm the ranting rallying cry of a self-confessed revolutionary:

> But foes are gathering—Liberty must raise
> Red on the hills her beacon's far seen blaze
>
> .   .   .   .   .
>
> Rejoice, brave Land, though pride's perverted power
> Rouse hell's own aid and wrap thy fields in fire . . .

Poetically she is right, this is terrible stuff. But politically! Surely she must by now have regretted the 'by W. Wordsworth, B.A. of St John's Cambridge'.

> Great God! By whom the strifes of men are weighed
> In an impartial balance give Thine aid
> To the just cause; and oh do Thou preside
> Over the mighty stream now spreading wide.

A fine prayer to be given out in English parish churches, and one that never would be if Canon Cookson had any say in the matter.

The mystery of Dorothy's attitude seems insoluble, or soluble only in one way: that in the letters which flew to and fro from Forncett William explained—and she accepted. For Christopher is no more than a peg on which to hang William: 'He is like William; he has the same traits.' There follows a string of Christopher's perfections: 'William has both . . . in an eminent degree'—here occurs the passage I cited earlier, which assumes a pathetic significance in the context—'and a sort of violence of affection . . . I hope you will one day be much better acquainted with him' (Jane has never set eyes on this paragon). 'I look forward with full confidence to . . . receiving you in my little Parsonage. . . . When I think of Winter I hasten to furnish our . . . Parlour, I close the Shutters, set out the Tea-table, brighten the Fire. When our Refreshment is ended I produce our Work, and William brings his book to our Table and contributes at once to our Instruction and amusement'. With 'such romantic dreams as these' does she 'amuse' herself in hours 'which would otherwise pass heavily along'.

Her confidence in 'my Parsonage' is as bright and unreal as her parlour. And she does herself know it. At the conclusion of *An Evening Walk*, Jane, she thinks, would be pleased with the lines, '"Thus hope first pouring from her blessed Horn" &c.&c. You would espy the little gilded Cottage on the Horizon, but perhaps your less gloomy Imagination and your anxiety to see your Friend placed in that happy Habitation might make you overlook the dark and broad Gulph between.'

Within days, perhaps hours, the gulf had yawned beneath her, more dark and broad than her gloomiest imaginings.

To explain this, it will be necessary to return to William gazing at the picture of Louise de la Vallière. Although with Robert Jones he had passed through France a year after the fall of the Bastille, the only signs they then saw of the Revolution were joyous ones. As Englishmen—was not England the land of liberty?—and Englishmen not making the Grand Tour, but proletarian figures of fun with their bundles on their heads, they were welcome to join in the revels and gaily did so. The festive board was free, a strong point in its favour. And the nights were spent dancing in the open. It was all very pleasant—and very un-English.

Had William reached the Orléans pictured by his relations his course might have been wholly different. Instead he reached one orderly indeed—to the point of dullness. Not only had its aristocrats judiciously removed, there were oddly few young men around with whom he might in a café have struck up acquaintance. They had all, it seemed, left or were leaving to join two armies—one royalist, one revolutionary. As he wrote later, 'all things were to me / Loose and disjointed, and the affections left / Without a vital interest'. Developed as these were in him, they could not long be left so. Seeking a room, he found one beyond his purse, but made friends with the family and now had somewhere at last to pass some evenings. He passed them to such good effect that in three months Annette Vallon, a guest in the house, was pregnant by him.

What was she like, this young woman who contrived so rapidly to sweep William Wordsworth into bed? Dark-haired, vivacious, artless, trusting—a little like Dorothy? But also like William apolitical. Certainly she was no ordinary girl, nor her boldness that of a hussy; rather was she remarkable for courage—later as an ardent royalist to lead, under Napoleon, the perilous life of a Scarlet Pimpernel. She was, however, as were her family (a long line of Blois surgeons) a staunch Catholic; and, when her state became known, the Vallons were far from insisting—as William, it seems, hoped—on marriage with a penniless Protestant. Instead back at Blois it became almost impossible to meet. But William, for better or worse, had now learnt French. Lodging at Blois as at Orléans in a house where his fellow boarders were army officers, that is, aristocrats, he listened almost incredulously, then with mounting repugnance to the unreality of their talk. He was not an aristocrat and his only experience of one had not improved his opinion of the breed. The people he most prized were—the people; good, simple Anne Tyson, the pedlars of this world, the country folk among whom he had lived, the courageous poor, the beggars and vagrants to be found on every road in Cumberland.

Unable to see Annette or endure the officers' drivel, he began to frequent revolutionary clubs; and there, it would seem, met Michel Beaupuy. Thirteen years older than Wordsworth, a soldier and man of action, an aristocrat but who loved and pitied the poor as William did, Beaupuy with his integrity was perhaps the chief instrument in forming Wordsworth the revolutionary. For four months they walked and talked, until in July Beaupuy left to rejoin his regiment. His departure left Wordsworth friendless. How should he fill the days? He filled them by writing *Descriptive Sketches*. Then in September he followed Annette, dispatched back to Orléans in order that her child might be born in secret. The town's close connection with the September massacres provided another different disturbing awakening. He could still only with difficulty see Annette; and late in October left to return to England via Paris, in order to see for himself what was going on.

What he saw horrified him. The guillotine still stood where two days before it had lopped eleven heads. The moderate Girondists were hopelessly indecisive and no match for Robespierre, Marat and the mob. But something must, could still be done; he even could do something. How actively he was involved with the Girondists is unknown. What is known is that he remained in Paris for close on six weeks and returned to England, 'compelled by nothing else than absolute want'. Presumably much of the money sent him had gone, as of right, to Annette who, on 15 December, gave birth to a daughter, Caroline. By this time he must have been already *en route*, if—allowing for the journey—Dorothy by the 22nd was getting regular letters from him in London.

'I am bewildered in a maze of which I can neither see Beginning nor End.' Little had Dorothy guessed in the cloisters at Windsor the truth of these words, the extent of the maze on the threshold of which she had stood. Nor, in late February 1793, could she have guessed the extent of its ramifications—that these would not only alter her own life, but profoundly affect the course not merely of one but, I shall argue, two great English poets. In the case of William Annette had given birth to more than a daughter, and in this gave Dorothy her mission. For to the passion of this love affair, to Annette as ardent as herself, Dorothy ironically was to owe the few years of her own most perfect happiness—the temporary eclipse of anything so unsullied and ethereal as a phantom of delight.

At Forncett, meanwhile, it seems likely that she pleaded a very real headache, and kept to her room in her agitation and shock; but also to think out how best to advise William. An illegitimate child in itself presented no problem either to Dorothy, no prude, or in the society of the time; though unhappily her uncle was, with Mr Wilberforce, in the van of those now starting to oppose the lax morals of the day. The child might be got round—but to marry one's mistress! That was altogether another matter. And the mistress a Roman Catholic—and to want the curacy. The combination was unthinkable.

With still no light in the maze, however, Dorothy did not falter. There was one thing she could do for William, and she did it instantly—wrote to Annette. In what strain she wrote, with how ready a sympathy and how instinctive a grasp of Annette's plight, is, even allowing for Annette's style —at once unbuttoned and stilted—shown by a letter she wrote to William. She is enclosing, she says, a letter to his sister:

> The earth has not produced two like her. She does honour to her sex. May my Caroline grow to resemble her. How I wept, my dear Williams! What a heart! What soul! How completely she shares the troubles which afflict me, but how distressed I am that she should suffer so much on our account. . . . Your sister talks to me of our little home together with an enthusiasm which gives me great happiness. . . . I pray thee, my dear little one, to forward this letter immediately to my dear sister whom I love with all my soul, [and] to let her say nothing to your uncle; were she to do so it must be a painful ordeal for her. But you judge it necessary.

Annette in her letters indulges in no self-pity. In disgrace, with her 'Williams' far away, their two countries now at war, with her child, her sole comfort, taken from her—put out to nurse where she may only secretly visit it—she pours out no recriminations. Simple, loving, courageous in the midst of her miseries, she is far from oblivious of Dorothy's problems. And the end of her letter must give one pause. Did William leave to Dorothy the task of pleading his cause with his uncle? Annette says, 'you judge it necessary'. There would be a strong case for Dorothy urging him to do so, that she must be the better advocate. But the best advocate must have been one who himself faced the music. William was neither weak nor unmanly. To my mind, however, everything suggests that he did, regrettably, leave Dorothy to intercede for him. Whatever the truth, her position at Forncett now became untenable, and her unfortunate uncle and aunt turn into 'relations not positively con-genial in pursuits and pleasures and with separate and distinct views'. These views included William being forbidden Forncett. To remain in such an atmosphere as a dependant, if as one now more than working her passage as head nurse-maid, was a mounting impossibility. And by June she had leave to visit Halifax. She would stay till after her aunt's confine-ment, but this was only a month off. By late August or September she would be free. William, meanwhile, too was in luck—about to set out on a tour that would take in the Isle of Wight and the West Country, with all expenses paid by a rich Hawkshead friend, William Calvert. Nor, by mid-July, was this all.

'*None of this is to be read aloud, so be upon your guard*', she began to Jane, seizing the chance, she says, to write while her uncle and aunt are out. Jane must have been agog, romance, even elopement seemed certain— but it is only William once again. Dorothy is secretly planning to meet him in Halifax. As to why meeting one's brother must be kept secret, the explanation is that duplicity comes hard to Dorothy—'after the meeting had taken place, I should by no means wish to conceal it from my Uncle yet I should be very averse to his knowing . . . that the scheme was a *premeditated* one'. In between this and the secret Jane has had to endure a long panegyric—from which it emerges, however, that Dorothy's idol is not the idol of his older relations; that the reason is 'an unpleasant one for a letter, it will employ us more agreeably in conversation, then, though I . . . confess that he has been somewhat to blame . . . I think I shall prove to you that the Excuse' lies 'in his natural disposition'! But her real fear is that Jane may expect too much of this brother, of whom she has heard enough to detest in advance. 'In the first place', says Dorothy anxiously, 'you must be with him more than once before he will be perfectly easy in conversation; in the second place his person is not in his favour.' Though Dorothy does not think this, it is better to warn Jane. 'He is . . . certainly rather plain than otherwise.'

Dorothy's escort to Halifax would be their Newcastle relative, Mr Griffiths, coming to Norfolk on business. By the end of August, with no Mr Griffiths, William's own tour was in difficulties. His friend's conveyance, a whiskey, had broken down on Salisbury Plain. Whereupon, Dorothy could write gaily, 'Mr C. mounted his Horse and rode into the North and William's firm Friends, a pair of stout legs, supported him from Salisbury . . . into North Wales, where he is now quietly sitting down in the Vale of Clwyd.'

This was unfortunate; perhaps even tragic, since that very month a young man down from Cambridge was then in the West Country, had attended a literary evening and heard with overwhelming enthusiasm a reading of *An Evening Walk* and *Descriptive Sketches*. He was twenty. His name was Samuel Taylor Coleridge. And he had never heard of Sara Fricker.

The poet he admired was at this moment writing a new poem begun on and entitled *Salisbury Plain*. Or so his sister had grounds in September for thinking. But in early October was he not perhaps in France? The only evidence is Wordsworth's own, transmitted at second hand by Carlyle, who reported Wordsworth as telling him that he had been in Paris when the Girondist Deputy, Gorsas, was guillotined. Gorsas died on 7 October 1793. By mid-October all the English in Paris were under arrest. Had he, in fact, risked this venture it is generally assumed that his motive was purely political. But if he could bear to set foot in France without seeing Annette the inference must strike one as odd. If he did, on the other hand, snatch a few hurried and anxious hours with her, such conditions seldom favour lovers. With Annette's emotional nature, her French volubility, above all the shock of discovering that events affecting her own family had made her fanatically royalist, the meeting could have been a disastrous one.

Meanwhile Mr Griffiths continued to have no business in Norfolk. And for Dorothy it was, perhaps, as well if the Rectory nursery continued, after her aunt's confinement, to keep her 'a very busy woman'. Her twenty-second birthday, which she had counted on spending with Jane, could hardly have failed to be a dismal one. But the snowdrops were out and almost over before she could at last actually leave for the magnetic North.

VII

Windy Brow

1794–1795

IF DOROTHY HAD unhesitatingly yielded up the dream cottage—shared with William but which would be her *own*, where she would be the mistress—to William's wife, Annette, she was now within sight of her reward. In the interval there was happiness enough in Halifax, in being once more with her beloved aunt. There was Mr Rawson, the new house —a new Jane. She should have known she would not be meeting Jane in a mob cap, rushing around with her hair flying about her. But at first had been unprepared for this elegant stranger, the fiancée of a Mr Marshall of Leeds. This feeling, however, soon passed. Dorothy, in fact, was herself the one most strikingly changed. Wherever she went in Halifax she made a profound impression. And though William, as she had feared, was not at his best—was restless and taciturn—his poems had been read and admired. As to his political opinions, Unitarians made it their business to keep an open mind; they were liberal, rational, middle-class. In short she could savour the joy of seeing him for the first time taken at something like her own estimate. And it was with her aunt's amused blessing that she set off with 'that eccentric young man, your brother' by coach to Kendal, from where the eccentric young man proposed that his sister should foot it the rest of the way.

For Dorothy there can have been no day more glorious in its freedom, was never perhaps to be a prouder one, than that on which they got down from the coach and—'I walked with my brother at my side, from Kendal to Grasmere, eighteen miles, and afterwards from Grasmere to Keswick, fifteen miles, through the most delightful country that ever was seen'. Those who today approach the Lakes from the same direction see, from the four-lane straight dual carriageway, a panorama—but not what Dorothy saw. The road from Kendal was then a track winding between hedgerows, each bend of which afforded something new. All her life she would thrill at the sight of Staveley, 'the first mountain village that I came to with William, when we first began our pilgrimage'.

But Staveley was engraved on her mind not only by its location. Here she was able to drink 'a bason of milk . . . and washed my feet in the brook' —a relief, but one could not wash away blisters, so she 'put on a pair of silk stockings by William's advice'. They were still a considerable distance from where they would pass the night. But it was time to eat—above all to drink. They picnicked under the trees by a stream and Dorothy was in heaven, since William too was happy, loving and gay; happy and loving enough to remember seven years later how,

> Two glad foot-travellers through sun and shower,
> My Love and I came hither while thanks burst
> Out of our hearts to God for that good hour
> Eating a traveller's meal in shady bower
> We from that blessed water slaked our thirst.

From here they went on by what later became her favourite walk—'because it is the way I first came to . . . Grasmere, and because our dear Coleridge did also'. Crossing the bridge, once stepping-stones, one might still meet Dorothy on it hastening to Ambleside for letters. After the final haul over White Moss, it must have been a relief to walk downhill. With Grasmere, their 'sole bourn' for that night at last in view, and the lake ahead, she passed, too tired to notice, an unremarkable cottage on her right: 'it was just at sunset. There was a rich yellow light on the waters, and the Islands were reflected there'.

After spending the night in a primitive inn, overlooking the churchyard, they went by a road along which in future years they were to hasten in all weathers to see their dearest friend, so often ill; and, wet and dirty, receive a cool welcome from Sara Coleridge. Their destination this time was a farmhouse, Windy Brow, which today unpretentiously still stands exactly as Dorothy saw it on a small secluded lane high behind Keswick, built in the unmortared local dark red stone, as yet still a farm, plain not gaudy. The simple life of its inmates—'I think I may safely affirm *happier* than any body I know'—was combined with overwhelming grandeur. Below sash windows the precipice fell sheer to a dashing stream, to the lakes of Keswick and Derwentwater, with 'towering above . . . a woody steep of a very considerable height whose summit is a long range of silver rocks'. Behind, on the hill which shelters Windy Brow, she had a yet better view of the whole vale, past Derwentwater to Bassenthwaite, with Skiddaw only one of the mountains tumbling and tossing all around.

No wonder she was ecstatic and no wonder William rallied, as only Dorothy with her own delight, her own powers of seeing, could rally his. To her now he could talk of all that at Halifax had kept him more than usually withdrawn; and find a relief in the sheer unburdening to one to whom, less than a year before, he had written: 'How much do I wish that each emotion of pleasure or pain that visits your heart should excite a similar pleasure or . . . pain within me . . .' Now that wish was granted in reverse. For remote as was Dorothy's experience from his, no nuance of what he said was lost on her.

'Till my brother gets some employment he will lodge here', she wrote to Jane; but this he would hardly get at Windy Brow. Nor could they indefinitely impose on that same William Calvert who had come to his rescue the summer before. In addition, there was not only William Calvert but Raisley, the younger brother, whom William scarcely knew; which made it worse that both had now turned out of their lodgings in order that he and Dorothy might have these. Six weeks was the most they could hope for; then William must seek work which would bring in something more than *Salisbury Plain*, the long poem she was copying for him. Since William's writing was even more illegible than her own, she was now for the first time engaged in what would be in the future a major task. And her heart must have sunk as it was often to do, when —at the end of May with her labours finished—William talked of going to press; and then said he thought there were parts he might want to alter.

Perhaps he was right. The poem was nothing like *An Evening Walk*; but then in this case the walk had been a grim one, alone and at nightfall on Salisbury Plain, with Stonehenge rearing up in fearful shapes. His head full of the Terror newly begun in France and himself shelterless in such a spot, it was hardly surprising that he should recall the tale of a woman to whom, once happily placed, trouble had come; who, friendless and faint with starvation, wandered the face of the earth, a vagrant with nowhere to lay her head.

Did his mind not also run upon Annette abandoned, in a country where God knows what might happen? Abandoned, if through no fault of his, in trouble through his fault? If Caroline had not been an accident, if without Annette's agreement to this step as the only means to marriage—and everything suggests that she was not consulted—if, 'Without a certain knowledge of my own', William had rashly decided for himself, the responsibility was great indeed. Was not, still worse, his love already on the wane when he might furtively see, but not sleep with Annette? Intellectually they had nothing in common. And it is difficult to believe that William enjoyed being made, as he was, to kiss the baby clothes. Or to believe that after Beaupuy's talk, with his own mounting obsession with politics, he found the charm he had done in poor Annette's ingenuous, emotional, now harassed chatter.

Whatever the truth about Annette there seems little doubt that the poem Dorothy copied at Windy Brow embodied more than the views he had shared with Beaupuy; that already she had on her hands one in desperate need of medicine for that troublesome article—guilt.

On a day near the end of April 1794, William's problems, however, were for once not foremost in her mind. *She* felt no vestige of guilt at being honoured with a letter from an aunt not even a Crackanthorpe, a Cust. And gentle though she was, intended both to make this plain and incur none by the manner in which she wrote. (To taste her steel, it should be explained that the Speddings of Armathwaite Hall were, socially, a trump card.)

My Dear Aunt,

I should have answered your letter immediately after the receipt of it, if I had not been upon the point of setting forward to Mrs Spedding's of Armathwaite where I have been spending three days. I am much obliged to you for the frankness with which you have expressed your sentiments upon my conduct and am . . . extremely sorry that you should think it so severely to be condemned. As you have not sufficiently developed the reasons of your censure, I have endeavoured to discover them . . .

She has succeeded in finding only two: one, expense, and secondly '. . . that you may suppose me to be in an unprotected situation'. As to the first, 'I reply that I drink no tea, that my supper and breakfast are of bread and milk and my dinner chiefly of potatoes from choice'. With regard to being in an unprotected situation, 'I affirm that I consider the character and virtues of my brother as a sufficient protection'. She cannot, however, pass over being rebuked for 'rambling about the country on foot'. So far from considering this as a matter for condemnation, she rather thought it would have pleased 'my friends [!] . . . that I had courage to make use of the strength with which nature has endowed me, when it not only procured me infinitely more pleasure than . . . sitting in a post-chaise', but meant a saving of thirty shillings at least.

'I am now', she wrote, 'twenty two years of age and such have been the circumstances of my life that I may be said to have enjoyed [my brother's] company only for a *very few* months.' She now has a chance 'of obtaining this satisfaction . . . which I could not see pass . . . without unspeakable pain'. Besides, she derives much improvement from his society; has regained all the knowledge she had of French and 'added considerably to it'. She has also begun Italian, from which she expects soon to gain 'much entertainment and advantage'. She is 'much obliged to you and my Uncle for your kind [?] invitation which I shall accept with great pleasure'. But Mrs Spedding of Armathwaite, from whom she has 'received the kindest civilities' has pressed her to make a further stay. And nothing 'would make me more happy than to cultivate the acquaintance of the Miss Speddings who are most amiable women'.

Nothing, Dorothy shrewdly guessed, would have made her 'notable' aunt more happy than any civilities from the Speddings, whose son, John, had been with William at Hawkshead. But perhaps her favourite new acquaintance was young Raisley Calvert, who, though William said he scarcely knew him, it would seem now dropped in frequently and hung on, William's words. Later she was to take it as a matter of course that everyone did and should hang on these; there were indeed to be times when they had no option. This was, however, her first experience of seeing anyone else hang upon them as she did herself. But if she had felt no guilt on receiving her aunt's letter, nor in replying to it as it deserved, Raisley Calvert may well have made her feel guilty. Not by anything he did or said, nor exactly on the score of charity. For the Calverts (whose father had held her own father's position, in the opposite camp, as steward to the Duke of Norfolk) had been left very differently placed. Raisley's money was still in trust until he came of age, but the Duke was his trustee, not his enemy. There was money enough, however; their lodging at Windy Brow, which William Calvert owned, was a temporary thing. But Raisley looked frail, as if he should be in his own comfortable quarters, well cared for and fed as he was at Windy Brow.

She was, none the less, doubtless glad when he came since it interrupted William, labouring to improve *An Evening Walk*. Composition seldom tired him, only rewriting, he said; but this was surely because he composed walking, out in the air and not at a table tinkering with his glue pot. And when she got him even up the hill he did compose; and added some quite new things to the *Evening Walk*, among them some lines she could carry away when they must separate, and which made the poem still more her own:

> Yes, thou art blest, my friend, with mind awake
> To Nature's impulse like this living lake
> Whose mirror makes the landscape's charms its own
> With touches soft as those to memory known;
> While exquisite of sense the mighty mass
> All vibrates to the lightest gales that pass.

They must leave—leave Windy Brow where she had been so happy and William made cheerful, cheerful enough to feel a new confidence that he could as a poet do something, a belief she shared and tended, and Raisley shared. Though this, in its way, was for William an added complication, making it more difficult than ever to declare for Grub Street and London where he would have to write reams, but never a line of what he felt he could. Raisley, to whom he had in these past weeks opened up, was dead against his taking such a course. There was, perhaps, a special attraction for this frail young man in one at once so dynamically physical and delicate in his attentiveness to others. It was more than this about Wordsworth, however; and more than his being a poet. Something about the man himself—his talk, his whole manner—gave one the feeling of being in the presence of greatness. Raisley Calvert, if young, was no mere dazzled youth. He had, as will be seen, a sound practical streak. Learning of Wordsworth's dilemma, his proposition now was that they divide his own income between them, until he was twenty-one a hundred pounds a year. This incredible offer was refused, though doubtless pressed again as he took what seemed a final sad leave of his guests.

For Dorothy separation from William was not yet. They must first as a duty go to Whitehaven; and pass through Cockermouth. They stood there and looked at the house—and at more than their memories: 'all was in ruin,' Dorothy wrote, 'the terrace-walk buried and choked up with the old privot hedge which had formerly been most beautiful', mingled with roses, and 'where the sparrows were used to build their nests'. Such wilful neglect clearly brought home their own plight with painful freshness; and Dorothy, on reaching Whitehaven, wrote off to Richard: 'Do not you think that by going to Lord Lonsdale himself you might *gain something?*'

Meanwhile at Whitehaven they had found their uncle seriously ill. His death could afford them little grief. Though it might have done had they known that his children would within weeks come down on them for £460, still owing they claimed for part of William's expenses up at Cambridge.

But their time together had now run out. William must go to London, where he had hopes of starting a journal with friends; but first go back to Keswick and see if Raisley would back him. Dorothy, meanwhile, would stay with his favourite Whitehaven cousin at Ramphill on the lonely Furness coast, in July go to the Speddings and from there take up—oh yes, she had no intention of letting her aunt off lightly—her invitation to stay at Newbiggin Hall.

Duty required it of her. She would not be welcome, but there was a sort of challenge in it. And she was wrong; she was welcome, not admittedly by her aunt, but pathetically so by Uncle Kit: 'I never saw', she wrote to Jane, 'a man so agitated in my life as he was at our meeting.' Uncle Kit had plainly, in marriage, suffered a fiery ordeal and developed a craving for affection, which he found in his gentle, warm-hearted, forgiving niece. She, in fact, forgave so far as to forget, attributing all his faults now to his wife; left to himself she is sure he would always act well. She had her reward not in heaven but at the end of a visit which apparently lasted several months, when her uncle gave her ten guineas, 'which . . . was very kind. . . . and the manner of giving it . . . doubly so'.

The length of her stay at Newbiggin Hall may have been induced by her desire at least to be near William, who had not gone on to London, but remained at Windy Brow where Raisley was as ill as he had looked. Almost deliberately, it might seem, Raisley now interposed himself bodily between William and Grub Street, was as if bent on bowing out with what proved to be consumption. With William Calvert away in the army, William could do no less than stay at first to cheer and then to nurse one who, ill and lonely, had shown himself so generous. And perhaps at the Speddings' he did see Dorothy. But to Newbiggin Hall he would never go; and in fact, relieved at his post, spent August where she had lately been at Ramphill (no doubt to ask the only one of the Whitehaven clan he could ask to intercede in the matter of the debt). And near the beach, where the deck chairs and transistors of Morecambe Bay now jostle for space but in those days desolate, except when at low tide it was used as a thorough-fare, heard a great shout: 'Robespierre is dead!'

The Reign of Terror was over, now Reason instead could reign. The shout was one that echoed throughout Europe. For Dorothy it was bound to carry a special personal message—the weight that this would lift from

William's mind. Now he need not feel his own ideals betrayed, would once again—his faith in men restored—feel hope, and be better able to cheer poor Raisley. But then William was back and found Raisley a great deal worse, ill enough to contemplate going to Lisbon and to draw up a will— in which he left William £600. But not too ill to be practical about this, to insist that measures be taken to prevent the money being seized 'by people that he knows nothing of'. By this he meant Whitehaven. The legacy was intended to free William to follow his poet's calling. And with Raisley now 'so reduced . . . he cannot be long on earth', William wrote frantically to Richard, who was as dilatory in the matter of answering letters as it behoved a solicitor to be. He was also the best off of the family having inherited Sockbridge, one of his father's small estates; but also as he could smugly point out due to his own labours: 'I am happy to inform you that my Bus [iness] . . . increases daily . . . and altho' our affairs have been peculiarly distressing I hope that from the Industry of ourselves at one time we will enjoy more . . . independence than we have yet experienced.' William was bone idle. But Richard for once was prompt and would 'readily enter into the Bond you require', which was that Richard pay Whitehaven and William repay him 'the moment I am worth more than this six hundred pound'. Dorothy must have been as relieved as William; and deeply moved by Raisley's now increasing the legacy to £900 for her benefit.

But the hopes she had had in August would by now have evaporated. She could not but feel more and more anxious as William's task grew daily more harrowing and arduous, when he was far from being as strong as he looked. Not only was Raisley now too ill to be read to, William had barely time to glance at the papers and follow the trial, for high treason, of a group of men who wanted Parliament reformed—not revolution. If the Government wanted revolution this was how to get it. The accused, however, were all—a victory—acquitted, in great part due to Godwin's sane article, even the last man, Thelwall, being got off. That but for a man named Thelwall there might have been no Lake Poets, that she might never have headed her letters 'Grasmere', Dorothy could not know. William's obsession with this trial, as far as she was concerned, could only be one more sign of the strain he was under. And though there might seem light ahead, if Raisley did not live till he came of age the will would be null and void.

The birthday at Windy Brow in November was a grim one, only redeemed for Raisley by the fact that he had lasted out long enough. Death came finally in January. Such had been the ordeal that William by the bedside could actually write: 'cataracts and mountains, are good occasional company, but they will not do for constant companions'. He had not for months had even these. Now he found himself literally thirsting for London, of all places. But he must first consult with Dorothy.

He saw her briefly in Newcastle, where she was staying with the Griffiths. The legacy, she agreed, must be invested. But the proceeds of this could in London, with its now nameless charms, together with literary not hack work, be made to provide an income sufficient for both of them. And Dorothy could help; she could do translating.

William now went on his way to London, and Dorothy went hers, back to Halifax. But her journey would take her almost past the door of Mary and Peggy Hutchinson, housekeeping for Tom on the farm he had inherited at Sockburn. The chance was too good to be missed; she would get down from the coach and pick it up again the following day. Instead she stayed for close on a month, a month of carefree pleasure. Not only was the house 'not at all like a farmhouse . . . , they seem to have none of the trouble which I used to think must make farmers always in a bustle'. Left £1,800, a house on an emerald isle, 'a grazing estate . . . scattered over with sheep', but with very little corn, only two cows; with, above all, no elderly relatives breathing down their necks—Aunt Gamage, the last to depart, had done so this year—the Hutchinsons saw no cause for bustle, and were, besides, not of the bustling kind. Life was meant to be enjoyed and they had a horror of dullness. To Dorothy their existence seemed an idyll. And for once she need not strive to help and please. The sensation was balm and she felt the influence of it, of Mary's unhurried graceful movements as she made the pastry which made her own seem all so agitated. There was plenty of time to make pastry and wander along the river, itself, broad and smoothly-flowing, soothing; time to read, time to play ball as she had not done since childhood, to laugh and be laughed at by Peggy and mocked by Sara.

For not only had the old friendships not fallen away, she now formed a new one with a girl six years younger than herself but not unlike her in externals even: plumper, but just her height, with hair of the same colour, though far longer and more beautiful, which flew about as they played ball, or streamed in the wind behind her as she flashed past at a gallop on her pony. The galloping was impressive to the point of being alarming. She had, in fact, at first seemed slightly alarming, this sharp young woman who rode away and thought foul scorn of those who got upon horseback and never stirred out of a trot. But then one found, when she talked so, that she was only what she called 'granking'; and discovered, as others were to do, that 'Miss Hutchinson, without a spark of malice in her heart had . . . a good deal of intolerance in her head'. As one had oneself. Discovered, in fact, that one had everything in common; that Sara was uncommonly well read and penetrating in her discrimination; that though her hair and skin were beautiful she was plain, knew it, and did not repine about the fact. But ordered a bonnet with zest as she did everything else, and knew just what she wanted: 'a Chip Hat . . . of the very newest fashion . . . cold *pea-green*, else lilac . . . a useful size, that is one to shade the face but not too large, as that . . . would be out of proportion; mind no flowers or kickshaws about it . . . not hemmed with Ribband or anything but simply the Hat itself . . .'

Was not their lack of looks the Hutchinson girls' strong point perhaps, accountable in part for their self-reliance and sturdy independence of mind? Sara certainly thought it an advantage: 'I often congratulate myself on never having been a beauty', she was to write in middle life; 'Mrs Coleridge says she cannot bear to look at herself—"and that it is not a bit a matter what one puts on when one is grown such a sight". Now I shall for ever feel it is my duty to make myself as bonny as I can—one has no [right] to force people to look upon what is disagreeable'.

Sara, in fact, like Mary possessed a sweetness of expression that more than made up for any lack of beauty, and, as Dorothy was not to be alone in discovering, reflected what lay beneath the surface: 'If Sense, Sensibility, Sweetness of Temper, perfect simplicity . . . joined to shrewdness and entertainingness make a valuable Woman, Sara Hutchinson is so.' Such would be the verdict of the husband of Mrs Coleridge, herself a mere four years later still 'in looks'.

Sara's entertainingness was to prove not the least of her assets when later she made her permanent home with the Wordsworths. An asset, but with behind her none of the stress of Dorothy's life—devoted but emotionally detached, with her critical acumen unimpaired also, perhaps, to Dorothy a threat.

Meanwhile, back in Halifax, after the beauty of Sockburn, she began to think that perhaps Aunt Rawson was right—she usually was—that London might be 'a very bad wild scheme'. William himself was finding no work and getting, by the sound of it, none of his own work done and only headaches; but was seeing a lot of Godwin, which seemed to do him good and could do no harm if, as now appeared, revolution would be effected through education. But it might be as well that William was not staying with Richard, who was terrified of William's politics. Though William was a republican, not a revolutionary; he recoiled from the bare idea now of revolution. Richard, however, would hardly see the distinction. Luckily William had met a Mr Montagu with whom he was living in chambers in Lincoln's Inn. Poor Mr Montagu was in a bad way, it seemed. An acknowledged natural son of the Earl of Sandwich by an actress, Martha Ray, later shot dead by her lover, a clergyman (who, it is said, had, if he did not enjoy, the distinction of being escorted to Tyburn by James Boswell), Montagu's background was hardly a steadying one. After being, though unknown to Wordsworth, contemporary with him at Cambridge, he had read for the Bar, led a wildish life, made an unsuitable marriage and, on being cut off by his father, supported himself by taking in pupils. But then his wife had died, and Montagu, wild with grief now, had resumed his former intemperate ways. Such was the condition in which Wordsworth found—and reclaimed him. Not in any heavy-handed manner, but, according to Montagu, 'imperceptibly', with a delicacy he was never to forget.

But perhaps the unhappiest inhabitant of the household was Montagu's son, two-year-old Basil. Wordsworth had not forgotten the misery and bewilderment of Penrith after his mother's death. Basil, lost and neglected, badly needed help. His father could give him no sort of proper home. Two rich pupils of Montagu's, alerted to Basil's plight, however, could and would—with William's help. John and Azariah Pinney possessed, or their father did, a hunting lodge which they hardly used in Dorset. And Wordsworth had—had he not?—a sister. As with the Calverts and Montagu, the Wordsworth charm worked wonders. William could have the house free. Their father in Bristol must first approve the plan and, not being told the financial details, did so.

In Halifax on 2 September, a letter was dashed off to Jane, now Mrs Marshall of Leeds, a bride of a month. Christopher has been on an all too brief visit: 'The calls of Duty were not to be resisted.' They were, as Dorothy was to learn, to be less and less so, leading in an undeviating line to high and inhuman places. Meanwhile 'I am going now to tell you what is for your own . . . ears alone . . . I need say no more . . . to insure your most careful secrecy. Know then that I am going to live in Dorsetshire. Let me, however, methodically state the whole plan'. This she proceeds to do. Mr Montagu will pay fifty pounds a year for Basil's board; there will also be a companion for Basil, a girl aged about three or four, the natural child of a cousin, and coming from India 'by the first ships'. There will be the garden produce, is already a cow; and she means to keep one maid who 'must be a strong girl and cook plain victuals tolerably well', since Montagu and the Pinneys will stay at times. 'I shall have to join William at Bristol and proceed thence in a chaise with Basil to Racedown, it is 50 miles. I have received a very polite invitation from the Pinneys to stay at their house on my road.' If she had, why all the secrecy? Aunt Rawson approved the scheme. The answer was she must first obtain her formal release from Forncett and could not, without this, consider herself free.

William, however, confident, had gone on ahead to Bristol and was busy charming the wealthy sugar merchant, Pinney *père*, who ascribed his wealth to meticulous business methods and—devoted father though he was—both let Racedown to John, the eldest son, for fifty pounds a year and continued to retain control of it. More in William's own line of business was his meeting with two young poets, Southey and Coleridge by name, formerly friends but recently made enemies by the defection of Southey in the matter of Pantisocracy. This was a scheme for setting up a Utopian colony composed of twelve young men, equipped with wives, on the banks of the Susquehanna, the whereabouts of which seemed somewhat vague (as did the shipping arrangements, acquiring of ploughs and so forth). The voyage, however, was now off. But unluckily wives had already been enlisted, three in one family. And if schemes could be scrapped, the Fricker girls could not. It is doubtful if any of this was known to William in Bristol, since, deeply impressed though he had been by Coleridge—'his talent appears to me very great'—he saw 'but little of him. I wished indeed,' he wrote, 'to have seen more'.

One could wish he had seen more; and had had Dorothy with him. As it was, by the time she passed through Bristol, in haste to set eyes on her new home, it was already too late. By 4 October she had been for a week mistress of Racedown Lodge and Sara Fricker was Mrs S. T. Coleridge.

VIII

And the Spring comes slowly up this way

Coleridge, *Christabel*

1795–1797

'WE ARE NOW surrounded by winter prospects without doors, and within have only winter occupations, books, solitude and the fireside, yet I may safely say we are never dull.' There are innumerable pleasant walks, and, a great advantage, the roads are sandy and almost always dry. She can see the sea 150 yards or so from the door; the trees are warped and twisted by the sea blasts. But all around are proper woods, and 'hills which seen from a distance almost take the character of mountains'. Some are cultivated, but those covered with furze and broom best please her, since they recall 'our native wilds'. Their 'common parlour is the prettiest little room that can be; with very neat furniture, a large book [case?] on each side the fire, a marble chimney piece, bath stove, and an oil cloth for the floor. The other parlour is rather larger, has a good carpet, side boards in the recesses on each side the fire, and has upon the whole a smart appearance, but we do not like it half so well as our little breakfast room.'

There are no shades of Dorothy's oilcloth at Racedown today and those in search of her are well advised to do as she did, to lift up their eyes unto the hills—and keep outside the opulent wrought-iron gates. The later encrustations of yellow stone porch and mullions, stripped now of ivy, and an unfortunate clash with the old red brick, give a heaviness that make it hard to recover Dorothy's simple sash-windowed hunting lodge. Gone are the ghosts, the broken-down fences that kept Joseph Gill in a constant state of agonized frustration, since nothing he said would induce the gardener to mend them; but nor could he get Perkins' cattle to lay off the vegetables, nor 'old Jnᵒ Hitchcock's' yearlings out of the roses. If and when he did manage to call in a husbandman, the fences were no sooner up than gone. And no wonder, with such poverty all around. William, who had seen and described such things, was depressed enough by the hovels they saw on their walks, 'shapeless structures (I may almost say) of wood and clay', Dorothy wrote, such as one might expect 'in savage life'; and lived in by little better than savages. If to Dorothy, after Forncett's poor, this came as an eye-opener, it must also have opened her eyes to much of what so preyed on William's mind.

And then there was Joseph Gill himself, the Pinneys' strange poor relation, who—uncouth and perhaps slightly simple—both had charge of the brick kiln near by and of the attics at Racedown, to which he alone possessed the key. To these, it seemed, Dorothy must resort when there were guests for such glass, silver and linen as were needed. But as yet, by December, there had been no guests, only books, solitude and the fireside. The nearest neighbours had called but had 'not much conversation' and did not promise to be any great acquisition.

For herself she did not mind this. She has only, after being 'a whole month without servant', got a maid; and has as much as she wants, or means to allow, to occupy her. The little girl unfortunately has not materialized, but there is Basil's confidence to be won and nice new clothes to be made for him, bright-coloured and warm, that will cheer the little fearful shivering boy; as well as 'putting my brothers into order'. For the rest she is highly organized: 'everything goes on with the utmost regularity'. The wash will be monthly only. She has hired a woman to do this for ninepence a day. There must then be two days of drying and ironing; but this is 'the only time in which I have any thing to do in the house'.

Nowhere in her letters does Dorothy mention her main task, or hint that books, solitude and the fireside, even with her, are not sufficient for William. 'We are . . . both as happy as people can be who live in perfect solitude. We do not see a soul', was his moody version of Dorothy's picture of their life to Jane. He was constantly writing to London, urging his friends to come. And it must at first have hurt and bewildered her that, together at last in the gilded cottage, William patently was far from happy.

There were, however, plenty of reasons why he should be as he was. And if these explained his longing for distraction, there was a further factor—that for over two years he had written nothing, and feared to try. Everything now hung upon his gift; if this proved lacking, the gilded cottage must prove a pinchbeck toy. Such a sense was enough to paralyse one. If only he would write something confidence would return. But to do so confidence was needed. And lacking this, without pausing, he had on their arrival done the very worst thing possible—plunged into revising the poem she had copied at Windy Brow and which he had then said he might want to alter.

She was perhaps herself quite as relieved as William when in January she had, for the first time, to climb to the attics with Joseph Gill and stand upon the threshold while he fossicked about in his treasure trove taking an age, and making a note in his diary of each item she required. In the event, it might be as well that, if glasses got chipped or broken, their first guests would be the Pinneys themselves, though William might have preferred to see London friends. And in fact the round-faced brothers proved a good investment, quite as fond of books as the sporting life. 'We have read a good deal while they were with us . . . ,' Dorothy reported. 'When the weather was fine they were out . . . all the morning, walking sometimes; *then* I went with them frequently.' When they went riding she did not go and when coursing kept well away. Though Wordsworth, as Azariah or Aza reported, 'relaxed the rigour of his philosophic nerves so much as to go a-coursing several times' and, poet though he was, Aza noted, devoured the hares with a relish not precluded by having been in at the death.

And it did relax William's 'philosophic nerves'. There was also the fact that even a poet must eat. The vegetables on which Dorothy had reckoned were grown for a hunting lodge, scanty in winter and shared with the Perkins cows. Raisley's legacy was trickling through at last, but would do so more and more slowly, to be paid in full only in August 1798. Of the first instalment Wordsworth had lent Montagu £300, but the interest would be high, ten per cent. When by Christmas some further £200 came in, he decided to invest in the same way with a friend of Montagu's. Even so this meant they could count only on fifty pounds a year. There was, of course, Basil's fifty pounds. But the lack of the little girl had thrown things out badly. And then William felt it impossible that when the Pinneys came they should provide the house—and the hares—and pay for board and lodging. And they did provide the hares and as well chop wood, this last 'a very desirable employment', since the coal which came by sea to Lyme was abnormally dear—'You would be surprised . . .' Dorothy wrote, 'what a small cart full we get for three or four and twenty shillings.' Joseph Gill marvelled that she could get it at all, marvelled enough to enter in his diary that J. Hitchcock went for it 'with less difficulty than was expected as his wife said he should not go'.

Poor Gill lodged *chez* Hitchcock six miles down the road, where life was as thorny as the subject of hedges. And the grounds for his hate of J. Hitchcock may have contributed to his easy acceptance of the Words-worths, who had evidently like himself gone down in the world, were hard up and treated him as human. From time to time he lent Dorothy small sums of money; and did such shopping as she required. One entry in his diary-account book reads rather pathetically, 'Miss Words likd the things'.

Miss Words evidently could charm even a Hitchcock. She was less successful with Azariah Pinney, perhaps because, although liking both brothers, she preferred the elder, John, just down from Oxford. And perhaps because Aza—in business at Bristol and his father's favourite— was young enough to wish to appear older, young enough to write of his lodger-cum-hostess: 'Miss Wordsworth has undoubted claims to good humour, but does not possess, in my opinion, that *je ne sais quoi* so necessary to sweeten the sour draught of human misfortune'. Rich young Aza was evidently going through the Werther phase, which would explain Dorothy's preference for John.

It was none the less Aza who provided red-hot news of, if not London, lively doings in Bristol, where, after a Marie Antoinette-like incident in October when a mob had surrounded the King's coach shouting 'Peace' and 'Bread', feelings had run high over the Government's swift repressive measures. William's new friend Coleridge, it seemed, was in the thick of things. Altogether the week was a lively one. And if Dorothy lacked *je ne sais quoi*, it did not deter the Pinneys from returning for close on a month in February. They might provide hares and hew wood, but it nevertheless entailed buying in such luxuries as tea, when—Peggy the maid apart— they were living, or trying to live, almost as frugally as at Windy Brow.

But perhaps this was as well, since William had long finished revising what proved indeed less an altered version than a new poem, so changed and extended as to bear little resemblance to the one she had written out at Windy Brow. Since then, for almost three months now, he had done nothing but Euclid. But if this too—as he said it did—relaxed his philosophic nerves, she must be thankful for it, and never let him feel she was watching or waiting. And he had read parts of the poem to the Pinneys, who pressed him to let them take it to the publisher they and William knew in Bristol. This he could not bring himself to do. They had none the less fired him sufficiently to write the day after they left to the publisher in question, Joseph Cottle; and Mr Cottle was eager to see the work. There matters stood, would perhaps have remained, had not the Pinneys returned to the attack; returned for, this time, in Dorothy's eyes, a somewhat overlong visit. And with two young men accustomed to a daily change of linen, back dirty and ravenous after hunting, the wash can scarcely have been kept a monthly one, nor the meals confined to Dorothy's budget.

But the Pinneys were not too rich to be imaginative, and were too generous to accept William's terms. Besides they were familiar with poets' problems. There was poor Coleridge in what he called 'a quickset hedge of embarrassments', struggling to support his wife's family, with, as he put it, 'five mouths opening and shutting'. But this was one more reason for Wordsworth to publish. Cottle, they knew, was waiting for the poem. They would deliver it. And at length William's philosophic nerves relaxed, or stiffened, sufficiently to agree. On 6 March, with the poem in their baggage, the Pinneys left, having attained their—but even more Dorothy's—object.

It was medicine, however, not money that most concerned Dorothy. For publication must surely be the best, if not the only, cure for loss of confidence. The degree to which William needed one was further illustrated by his doing a thing he would never have done in the past, insisting that before the Pinneys submitted the poem to Cottle it should go first to Coleridge for his opinion.

Even believing as she did in William's poetic powers, she could hardly have failed to regret this, to be fearful that Mr Coleridge might only put him back, not forward. For that the least thing might do so Mr Coleridge could not know; on the other hand perhaps he did, since he and William now wrote regularly. But then how delicate was Mr Coleridge? From all that she had gathered and what William read out of his letters, he was himself harassed to death, had been rushing half round England trying to raise subscriptions for a periodical, *The Watchman*—a desperate remedy for the five mouths opening and shutting—but notwithstanding, made lively matter of it. His tale of the Birmingham tallow chandler had made even William smile:

'And what, Sir, [asks the chandler] might the cost be?' . . . 'Only FOURPENCE . . ., only fourpence Sir, . . . to be published on every eighth day'—'That comes to a deal of money at the end of a year. And how much did you say there was for the money?'—'Thirty-two pages, Sir, . . . octavo, closely printed.'—'I'm as great a one as any . . . in Brummagen, Sir! for liberty and truth and all them sort of things, but bless me! That's more than I . . . reads, Sir, all the year round!'

But William's poem was no laughing matter, and in itself none, with the man who met the woman on Salisbury Plain himself invested with a fearful history. Transformed into a sailor, press-ganged, paid to fight and kill, inured to carnage and his own misdeeds, rich and released, then defrauded of all that was rightfully his, he now committed a crime on his own account. Returning empty-handed to his wife and children, nearing home he robbed and killed a man—and fled to live henceforward a tormented vagrant. 'From that day forth no place could be to him / So lonely but that there might come a pang.' But then he fell in with the woman, whose story, too, had grown in horror since the first version. It was none the less she who uttered words of comfort,

. . . his peace of mind endeavoured to restore.
'Come let us be', she said, 'of better heart.'
Thus often-times the woman did implore
And still the more he grieved she loved him still the more.

Copying this, Dorothy could not but reap her own comfort from it. And then there were other touches that spoke to her, as when the woman described her love for her betrothed: 'And I in truth did love him like a brother.' Was not this an odd way to love one's future husband? Dorothy could not feel it to be so; nor William, it seemed, 'For never could I hope to meet with such another'.

This grim poem then, too, was in her part hers, but as she—if imperfectly—must have grasped, above all William's own; less an indictment as he claimed of the penal system, than a loaded indictment nearer home. For had not he likewise defrauded of all that was rightfully his, pursued a headstrong course that led to crime, the crime of an act thoughtlessly committed; and now of no longer wishing to marry Annette? Of loving and betraying, but not only this, of being betrayed by what is false within?

But what afflicts my soul with keenest ruth
Is that I have my inner self abused,
Foregone the home delights of constant truth
And clear and open soul so prized in fearless youth.

That Dorothy had herself no knowledge of such states constituted her power as a talisman, the thread that 'Through the weary labyrinth / Conducted me again to common day'.

But that day was still far off, had Dorothy known how far her heart surely must have quailed within her. In the interval there was nothing to do but wait for a letter from Bristol. But then, almost immediately, came not a letter but reassurance in another form, a first volume of poems by Mr Coleridge himself and containing a glowing tribute to William: 'The expression "green radiance" is borrowed from Mr Wordsworth, a Poet whose versification is occasionally harsh and his diction too frequently obscure; but whom I deem unrivalled among the writers of the day in manly sentiment, novel imagery and vivid colouring.' If she needed any further reassurance (on the score of Mr Coleridge, critic) she now had it: the author of *Religious Musings* had proved himself serious, if nothing else.

Meanwhile the volume kept William stimulated, and then came a copy of *The Watchman* and William buried his nose in this and termed Coleridge a very brave man indeed. Did she realize he was risking the Tower in writing as he did? Coleridge was making himself heard. This must mean he would do so in the matter of William's poems. And when at the end of March the letter from Bristol came, not it was true from Coleridge but from John Pinney, it seemed that she was right. Coleridge, Pinney was given to understand, had read the poem with the greatest care, interleaving the page with white paper in order 'to mark down whatever may strike him as worthy of your notice and intends forwarding it to you in this form'. Nor was this all: William had thought he might need to raise subscriptions, but Coleridge felt, wrote Pinney, 'so lively an interest to bring forward so valuable a poem (as he terms it) that he assures me that through his Bookseller he can secure you from every Expense'.

It was wonderful news and almost certainly all of it hot air, apart from Coleridge's laudable intentions, genuine but (with thirty-two pages, octavo, closely printed, to be written weekly) impractical. Coleridge was not his own most accurate reporter, but is himself later on record as saying, 'I shall hardly forget the sudden effect produced on my mind' by hearing the poem read by Wordsworth four months later! At all events no manuscript interleaved with even the blankest sheets of white paper returned to Racedown. It was next heard of in London, where Coleridge had sent it on to one Charles Lamb, lately out of a madhouse.

But it was spring at last, and even Joseph Gill, whose Racedown duties did not extend to gardening, actually entered in his diary: 'Amusing myself in the Garden . . . the weather being tolerably mild. Planted one bed Cabbage plants, 1 Bed pease.' But if Gill's activities meant everything to Dorothy, they seemed only to depress William. 'We plant cabbages,' he wrote gloomily, 'and if retirement in its full perfection be as powerful . . . as one of Ovid's gods, you may perhaps suspect that into cabbages we shall be transformed.' Only Basil bloomed for her: 'he is my perpetual pleasure . . . metamorphosed from a shivering half starved plant, to a lusty, blooming fearless boy'.

The change effected in Basil, however, was not enough. With by May no improvement in William and no poems, she could not have failed to feel increasingly worried. Copying the revised *Salisbury Plain*, she may well have come on a fragment, 'Incipient Madness'—some lines about a broken pane of a glass in a ruined cottage to which, it seemed, night after night William returned, obsessed by the pane glittering in the moon. Was not melancholy often the prelude to madness? But now William said he must go to London; must try to get the legacy finally paid over and matters with Montagu put on a proper footing.

Perhaps if he did this would ease his mind, or at least take his mind from brooding. It was nevertheless her turn to be restless, with all arranged to run on oiled wheels without her. Barbarous as were the locals she could not ramble about this country on foot, and for the post must go seven miles to Crewkerne. 'The greatest inconvenience we suffer here', she had written, 'is in being so far from the post office.' She can never, however, have felt the inconvenience as she now did walking to Crewkerne with Joseph Gill, whom she persuaded to make three journeys with her. Would there be letters from William and if so what would his news be? Still no progress with the legacy, but that he was seeing Godwin, had met a man called Stoddart, got his poem sent back by the man Lamb, who— no longer mad but too ill to deliver it in person—wrote he had read it 'not without delight'; and that he planned to return with this via Bristol, there see Coleridge and himself deposit the poem with Cottle.

The time would soon pass, she would make it pass, would work harder than ever at Italian, had finished Ariosto—that would surprise William —and might perhaps embark on Boccaccio. The trouble was she read so fast; now that her French was fluent even this could not slow her up. As for English, with *Tristram Shandy* and travel works she might in a hunting-lodge have been left far worse off. And then when William returned from London in the summer to a sea shimmering in the distance, to all green and flowering—it must strike him freshly, must force him into poetry despite himself. And when he walked in on a day full of the scent of new-mown hay, she was certain of it: the summer would work a cure.

But then, it would happen, rain set in for a fortnight. And the poem had not been left with Cottle; perhaps because 'the sudden effect produced on' Coleridge's 'mind' the latter did forget or, at least, misdate—the incident could relate to the following spring. For if William returned by Bristol, he could still there have missed both Coleridge and his enthusiasm (removed to Somerset, or even to Derbyshire where Coleridge had a chance of a tutorship). *The Watchman* had watched in vain, expiring in mid-May, when

Mrs Fricker also promised to do so, but failed in her promise. With Sara expecting a child and wanting baby clothes, his brother-in-law dying in agony, and he himself—as Southey some years later said of him—of necessity 'spawning plans like a herring', it would hardly be surprising if Coleridge later in life retained a confused picture of this period.

With publication as a cure, for whatever the reason, out, Dorothy had now to pin her hopes on herself and the summer season. For that a cure was still needed was quickly apparent. William had returned, if anything, gloomier than ever. Godwin this time clearly had done him no good. The former's beliefs—in the perfectibility of man, in education—which once had meant much to William, he now dismissed as hopelessly naive. She had long, in fact, had on her hands a man who had lost far more than belief in his own poetic powers, who,

> Dragging all passions, notions, shapes of faith
> Like culprits to the bar suspiciously
> .   .   .   .
> With impulse, motive, right and wrong, the ground
> Of moral obligations, what the rule
> And what the sanction; till demanding proof
> And seeking it in everything I lost
> All feeling of conviction and, in fine,
> Sick, wearied out with contrarieties,
> Yielded up moral questions in despair.

That such problems in themselves were non-existent for Dorothy gives us her measure better than anything else. There is no more difficult, self-denying task than to understand where we do not understand, to grant that what to us seems simple is for others complex. In Dorothy's case it was doubly hard, perceiving him as she did 'Sick wearied out with contrarieties'; and by these kept from his true calling. All this would fall away if he would only look about him. But it seemed as if he had lost the power to look; or could look only inwards. What did he see? Dreadful things, to judge by the nightmares he owned to in the morning when she asked how he had slept. The Reign of Terror in France had been over for two years, but in William's dreams the heads still rolled. The nightmare he most dreaded was the recurrent one of standing himself before 'an unjust tribunal', unable to get his words out, to remember what he must say— accused but, worst of all, justly so; confounded 'with a sense of treacherous desertion / In the last place of refuge, my own soul'. It seemed as if the horrors he had witnessed in France had deranged him. This feeling that he had betrayed his Girondist friends—what good could it have done had he thrown in his lot with them, and gone to the guillotine? Would he feel better dead? She did not question or reason, did not fully understand more than that he must learn to live in the present; must exert himself to do so, that she understood. And at times, as when on their walks she drew his attention to something that drew her own, he barely glanced at it, it did— she could not help it—make her sharp.

That no letters survive from either of them between the March and October of this year, 1796, is probably accidental; but may indicate the depression that reigned at Racedown during that long hot summer. Hot enough for Joseph Gill to do the outside painting, and, as far as the gardener went, give up the struggle; 'my saying anything to him this long time has been as useless as it would be to sing psalms to a dead horse'. Dorothy might have echoed this, toiling the hills with William. And she had at Christmas herself acquired a diary. 'Dec. 24th Miss Ws Diary 10^{d.}, Joseph Gill had itemized in his. Would she ever, she must have wondered, be able to write, as he now did, 'The garden produces everything we have sown and planted in it very well this year'?

If no letters or diary survive, there survives what is both the proof that she would be able to write so of *her* garden, and also a picture of Dorothy at this time, of 'the beloved woman' who

> . . . now speaking in a voice
> Of sudden admonition like a brook
> That did but *cross* a lonely road, and now
> Seen, heard and felt, and caught at every turn,
> Companion never lost through many a league,
> Maintained for me a saving intercourse
> With my true self . . .
> [who]   In the midst of all preserved me still
> A Poet, made me seek beneath that name
> My office upon earth and nowhere else.

The measure—if not as yet of her success—of her power to make him seek his office there, exists in the scrap that mysteriously (almost miraculously) survives of her first extant letter since March. To write it she had to wait till 24 October. That it reaches us in the form it does—as the smallest fragment of any letter we have of hers, seems, if accidental, typical of her. Sufficient, distilled, her triumph flames: '[William is] now ardent in the composition of a tragedy'.

This in a sense was all she knew and all we need to know. That Wordsworth in his tragedy *The Borderers* was still obsessed with criminal types mattered, or matters, little more than that much of it is unreadable. It acted as a catharsis, and, if masochistic, he faced in it more than the Robespierres of this world. His own essay on the play is, however, illuminating. In this he wrote: 'In works of imagination we see the motive and the end. In real life we rarely see either. . . . We are lulled asleep . . . and betrayed before we know that an attempt is made to betray us.' In the case of most people it is the fact that a wrong act was deliberate, the end foreseen, that counts. Wordsworth's conscience was more sensitive, the unwitting crime the greater in his eyes. It behoves us to know what we do and the real crime consists in not knowing. Guilt so pervasive may well prove incurable.

Meanwhile if, in contrast to their first mild winter, a cruel one now set in, Dorothy was happy to be snowbound—with William beside her writing at last in their common parlour. Basil, also her product, was sturdy enough to play for hours outside in the biting wind, build his first snowman and come in glowing. What if they did live on air, on the essence of carrots, cabbages, even parsley, since William could joke about it; and have, at the end of February 1797, his tragedy finished. Her only worry by March, apart from the rising costs (when they could not afford now even to frank their letters but must depend for this, too, on the charity of the recipients), was that Richard's shirts had not got done. But neither had the cloth come through, nor Richard's measurements. Happily, since he required twelve and was 'in great want of them', she had on hand someone to help her with these; Mary Hutchinson had come for a much-needed change. For Peggy, laughter-loving Peggy, had the previous spring, at Dorothy's age, died of a rapid consumption. That Mary's choice of change of scene was not wholly Dorothy's work, nor solely due to the fact that she had an escort in her sailor brother Henry, on his way to Plymouth, cannot but gleam through Henry's execrable 'Cantos' in late life:

> For she had long a great desire
> To visit friends in Dorsetshire,
> Friends now well known to fame,
> A sister and a brother dear,
> A bard whom all good men revere,
> And Mary did the same,
>
> .   .   .   .   .
>
> But now an obstacle arose
> Dear Mary was in want
> Of many necessary clothes
> Her wardrobe being scant
> So 'twas agreed that we should ride
> To Stockton upon Tees;
> We went and got her well supplied
> Which set her heart at ease. . . .

If Mary's want was 'necessary clothes', this is hardly likely to have been a synonym for sensible shoes. The necessity was, however, indubitable when meeting a man who, if he had once seemed lover-like in his attentions, had left one severely alone now for eight years.

For Dorothy, the company of a close woman friend, at last, was exactly the holiday she needed. And now a visitor, hitherto a stranger to Dorothy, but later indirectly to play a small but painful role in her life, 'came upon us unexpectedly before we were risen'. This was Basil's father, handsome Montagu, who, if his mode of arrival was typical—Wordsworth later, though still without the hideous hindsight that followed, called him 'the arrantest Mar-plan that ever lived'—could scarcely fail to win Dorothy's heart. Not only did he possess great charm and show his appreciation of the miracle she had wrought in Basil; he did not conceal the fact that he loved and looked up to William—he was, indeed, always to do so—above all men. But then Montagu bore William off for a fortnight to Bristol and Bath, and Jane 'cannot imagine how dull we feel and what a vacuum his loss has occasioned'; for Jane may not think it, having met him when she did, but William 'is the life of the whole house'.

He was back by early April, having returned via Coleridge who had overlapped with him in Bristol, but was now living in Somerset in a village called Nether Stowey, and 'in a depression too dreadful to be described'. This had been brought on by a lodger and acolyte, Charles Lloyd, whose epileptic seizures night after night Coleridge had had to restrain by main force. 'Wordsworth's conversation, etc', he wrote, 'rouzed me somewhat.' Coleridge, in fact, encouraged by Sheridan, had himself on hand a drama for the stage. William's had been written to be read, but Coleridge persuaded him to alter his too for production. And this, no laggard now, he set about doing. But then the whole household went down with illness; Dorothy, from what William could see, was after a fortnight no better and Basil so ill that she feared 'we should have lost him'. By 7 May, however, still with a hacking cough, she and Mary got down to Richard's shirts. They must have sewn like maniacs, for before the end of May she could report to Richard that six were ready. William, meanwhile, with a streaming cold, has his tragedy nearly redrafted and 'good hopes of getting shewn to Sheridan'. She does not mention what is all-important: that not only is there a tragedy. Mary and she, working as seamstresses, cannot, as copyists, keep up with William's flow. From now on, except at rare intervals, this was never to cease. If later Dorothy was to write of Racedown, 'I think it is the place dearest to my recollections upon the surface of the whole island', she had by her own sustained faith and effort, now triumphantly justified, made it so. Meanwhile, she contented herself with writing to Richard: 'The country is now delightful. It has burst into beauty at once after the coldest spring I ever remember.'

On 5 June Mary left with Richard's shirts in her baggage. But the next day Dorothy with William was outside on the watch for yet another visitor who might not easily recognize the place. She was thus able to witness, and never to forget, his novel mode of approach—how, to cut off an angle, 'he did not keep to the High Road' but 'leapt over a gate and bounded down a . . . field' into her life.

IX

And all should cry, Beware! Beware
His flashing eyes, his floating hair!

Coleridge, *Kubla Khan*

1797

'AT FIRST', SHE admits, 'I thought him very plain, that is, for about three minutes: he is pale and thin'—pale perhaps, but only due to illness can he this once go on record as thin—'has a wide mouth, thick lips, and not very good teeth, longish loose-growing half curling rough black hair. But if you hear him speak for five minutes you think no more of them. His eye is large and full, not dark but grey.' In short, it is like her own, very like: 'it speaks every emotion of his animated mind.' But here she, too, in her turn must fall back on poetry: 'it has more of the "poet's eye in a fine frenzy rolling"' than she, a poet's sister, has ever witnessed.

There was, in fact, everything to appeal to her in this man, at twenty-five a year younger than herself, who to the last remained—and if in this lay his weakness, here also lay his greatness—more child than man:

> Noisy he was and gamesome as a boy;
> His limbs would toss about him with delight,
> Like branches when strong winds the trees annoy.
> Nor lacked his calmer hours device or toy
> To banish listlessness and irksome care;
> He would have taught you how you might employ
> Yourself; and many did to him repair—
> And certes not in vain; he had inventions rare.
>
> Expedients, too, of simplest sort he tried:
> Long blades of grass, plucked round him as he lay
> Made, to his ear attentively applied,
> A pipe on which the wind would deftly play;
> Glasses he had that little things display,
> The beetle panoplied in gems and gold,
> A mailèd angel on a battle-day;
> The mysteries that cups of flowers enfold
> And all the gorgeous sights which fairies do behold.

Such was the boy, magician, rapt observer of nature, who put everything under the microscope—himself not excluded—and saw wonders none had seen before; but who, more to Dorothy's present purpose, openly marvelled at William and now entered her life in search of him.

Within hours that same day they were at it: 'The first thing that was read after he came was William's new poem . . . with which he was much delighted; and after tea he repeated to us two acts and a half of his tragedy.' Not the least remarkable thing perhaps about this last performance was that it *was* 'repeated', that is, recited, in part perhaps improvised. At all events, within no time the description quoted above had gone off to a recipient, presumably Mary: 'You had a great loss in not seeing Coleridge.' He is already not 'Mr'. And already, 'He is a wonderful man'.

Did Dorothy fall in love with Coleridge? My feeling is that she did. The main argument for her not doing so rests on the fact that in her letters and journals, she made no attempt to conceal her love for him. But guile, as we have seen, came hard to Dorothy, who, moreover, as De Quincey says, was 'liberated from that false shame, which in so many persons accompanies all expressions of natural emotions'.

On Coleridge's side, it has been argued that whereas at Stowey 'Wordsworth's conversation rouzed' him 'somewhat', it was only somewhat, and was the meeting with Dorothy that clinched things. There is a case for Dorothy providing a link between them. But that she did so at this stage seems unlikely. If Coleridge stayed three weeks and not as he had intended a few nights, the two men had much to talk about; and already for Coleridge writing letters from Racedown, if not before this, Wordsworth 'is a great man'. My hunch would be that it took him a considerable time to do more than register that there was an oddish sister. He did not expect women to say anything of interest and he did not expect them to look like Dorothy. To conventional charms he was highly susceptible; had Dorothy, as was a woman's role, looked and dressed as Sara did, he would have noticed her at once. As it was, I suspect, her qualities dawned on him only slowly. He was still physically happily married to Sara, who as a mental companion had palled as early as on his honeymoon, as must almost any woman have done; but who, teamed with his friend, Poole—Poole's arbour and library in the daytime—was all that a man could wish for after nightfall. Tom Poole was the man to whom he had felt himself closest, a thinking man and one of advanced ideas. But he was not Wordsworth—had he not, when he met the latter, named Wordsworth the greatest man he had ever met?

Three weeks was not long enough, and at the end of these Coleridge only tore himself away to fetch a cart and bear his friends back on a visit to Stowey. William could have gone and Dorothy stayed at Racedown. Or if William did not wish to leave her, Dorothy must have pleaded she too could walk. But Coleridge wanted both Wordsworths, and Dorothy was in his eyes, by this time, woman enough to need a cart.

Dorothy must herself have looked forward to a new friendship, to meeting the wife of this wonderful man. And the shock of Sara Fricker must have been great. For surely the conditions with which Sara was grappling in the diminutive, dark, damp, thatched cottage—without an oven and with a baby—must have shocked Dorothy into sympathy? Poole had considered it an unthinkable place, and Coleridge himself had dismissed it out of hand, his heart set on a beautiful farmhouse in a wooded coombe. But as hopes of this dwindled, anything, any loophole where a man might write and earn, might think in peace (words not in the Fricker vocabulary) and with Sara now with a baby—anywhere was not anywhere. It was the cottage in Lime Street with one and a half acres where he could grow vegetables, raise corn, keep two pigs on the refuse, earn forty pounds a year at the least reviewing; and Sara manage, she said, on sixteen shillings a week. 'And pray what does your Lordship know about farming?' Charles Lamb enquired. And already by July— they had moved at Christmas—there was, as Dorothy must have seen, no trace of vegetables, let alone corn, and no sign of a pig; nothing but weeds without and within doors smoke. And from Dorothy, now and later, nothing but silence, as Sara coped with the visitors, hastening to the baker's with anything that required to be cooked in an oven, and then— just as Hartley's napkin needed changing—remembering it was time to fetch it back. No wonder that on the second day 'dear Sara accidentally emptied a skillet of boiling milk' over Samuel's foot, thus confining him to Poole's arbour and the necessity of leaving his guests to explore alone. No wonder that, with the following week another guest added, she had at the end of the month a miscarriage.

The wonder is that Dorothy did not see it. If she did, no word of sympathy would fall from her pen in the year ahead for this girl who, to the end of their interlocked lives, was 'Mrs Coleridge', never 'Sara', to her. Later, with the marriage unhappy and Coleridge made miserable by it, such silence might seem discreet and explicable. But now what did it mean—simply the shock of discovering that Mrs Coleridge was thoroughly commonplace? But many great men have been happy with, and indeed preferred, such wives. And Coleridge with his arm round Sara's waist, if not a napkin on his knee, was at this stage both obviously happy and eager to show off his beautiful wife and child. Dorothy was neither an intellectual nor a social snob; and if she did not suffer fools gladly, Sara Fricker was far from being a fool. Any cultivated man of means might have moulded her into a woman who adorned his dinner table with distinction. This had, in fact, been what she assumed she would do. She had married a brilliant man, as yet without means, but who would undoubtedly rise fast. Her parents' marriage had not been a happy one, and there was small advantage when Mr Fricker, a tin manufacturer, gave up the ghost, leaving his wife bankrupt with five children. Not only could Sara not remember a time when anxiety had not been the dominant note of the household; she had witnessed her mother's struggle and it is hardly surprising if she lived in dread of a similar fate.

But the two women had more than an insecure background in common. If to Sara, who had never lived in a Racedown, the keeping up of appearances was of paramount importance as a means of rising in the world; if she was chock-full of feminine wiles, she was—she could not help it—utterly transparent, in her lesser way too a *coeur simple*. And one might have thought that Dorothy would have taken her as such—if lightly, as not worthy of her powder. The antipathy on both sides is on Sara's explicable. But on Dorothy's? Was it not inspired less by the fact that Coleridge's wife was extremely commonplace, than that she was extremely bedworthy?

I am not suggesting on Dorothy's part anything as simple as ordinary jealousy—rather the reverse. Dorothy, if passionate, was essentially virginal. But the origins of her attitude to Sara can only, it seems to me, be sought in the stay at Stowey; in the fact that she had at Racedown been swept off her feet, swept safely, as it seemed, further than she knew by the buoyancy and verve of this young married man. Wrapped up though she was in William, she was not above falling in love, indeed she would seem to have been created to do so. But this was the first man she had met who could compete with William, a lovable man whom one could not fail to love. There was nothing wrong in such feelings—until she came to Stowey. There they suffered an abrupt check. Not that she had ever thought of Coleridge as other than married, as in any sense a potential lover. But if the nature of his relationship with Sara was to bring out a puritan side in Coleridge (as lust without respect perversely to make him regard the marriage tie, however unhappy, as binding, since in this way only could it be purified), must not Dorothy, quick and herself chaste, have been before him—in recognizing that Sara was far from being, as he put it, 'a wife in the purest holiest sense of the word'? Must not the sight of Coleridge with his arm round Sara's waist, their clearly purely sexual relationship, both have repelled her in this man of whom she thought so highly and hurt her in herself, in her pride? Not only would she have felt lowered by it, she must have felt pain: this is something men want which I am not.

And it may have been more than her critical acumen that now led Dorothy to take Coleridge down a peg or two. When, in his own words, he read out 'some half a score or more of reviews' 'I thought clever & epigrammatic & devilishly severe: but a Remark made by Miss Wordsworth to whom I had, in full expectation of gaining a laugh of applause, read one of my judgements occasioned my committing the whole batch to the fire'. However disturbed Dorothy's feelings, Sara, without the vegetables and with her pittance the fruit of such reviews, could hardly have taken the holocaust in Coleridge's debonair spirit. Nor welcomed the descent of a further guest; who, however, proved someone she could like. And it says much for Sara that Coleridge's boon companion when he had been on the run from marriage with her, could write in his bread-and-butter letter of 'you and your dear Sara—to me also very dear because very kind'.

Charles Lamb during this visit stood in great need of kindness. Nine months before his adored sister, Mary, had in his presence, in a fit of insanity, stabbed their mother to death and was now in a madhouse. 'The young lady had been', as the coroner put it, 'once before deranged from the harassing fatigues of too much business'. Mary, in fact, eleven years older than Charles, had as a mantua-maker been for years the mainstay of the family. The father was senile; added to this she had latterly been kept night and day in attendance on her mother, who had lost the use of her limbs and who, although Mary loved her, had never shown her daughter a crumb of affection.

Lamb, his apprenticeship over, was at last able to earn; and, employed as a clerk at the East India House, was anxious now to get Mary, sane, released. He would be answerable for her. But part of the year of the tragedy 'your very humble servant', as Lamb then wrote, had himself 'spent very agreeably in a madhouse at Hoxton'. This had been brought about by his rejection as a suitor on the grounds of insanity in the family. Lamb, could he only have known it, was to prove the sanest, as well as one of the most endearing of men. But at Stowey he could not know it, and 'could not', he wrote, 'talk much, while I was with you . . . but, in truth, disuse has made me awkward at it . . . company and converse are strange to me'.

For Dorothy even this subdued young man of twenty-two—to become an increasingly close, life-long friend—served, perhaps, no less than for Sara to relieve the tension. That there were other ways of doing this is, however, plain from a letter dashed off to Mary Hutchinson:

> . . . There is everything here; sea, woods wild as fancy ever painted, brooks clear and pebbly as in Cumberland, villages so romantic; and William and I, in a wander by ourselves, found out a sequestered water-fall in a dell formed by steep hills covered with full-grown . . . trees. The woods are as fine as . . . at Lowther, and the country more romantic; it has the character of the less grand parts . . . of the Lakes.

'Romantic' is not a word with which Dorothy is lavish, but here it tumbles out twice in quick succession. But nor is the letter in her usual purely descriptive vein. It is heightened in tone, the letter of one in love? With the countryside, if with nothing else; this, at least, is all that Coleridge's country should be. And that same day, tearing themselves from the dell, they had wandered on and seen a large mansion in a park. This we know from her next letter to Mary. Little had she then dreamt that when six weeks later she wrote this her address would have been for a month Alfoxden House.

But some scheme for their removal must have been mooted early, before the arrival, surely, even of Lamb, whom they now took off with them, leaving the crippled Coleridge to fret and write *This Lime-tree Bower My Prison*; to picture them at the waterfall, then emerging to look down, as one may still do today, through the Alfoxden beeches to the sea at Kilve, blue and, as he wrote of it, streaked with purple; and to proceed with his madly mistaken concept of Lamb, of all the three glad walkers,

> Thou most glad
> My gentlehearted Charles! For Thou has pined
> And hungered after nature many a year
> In the great City pent . . .

Not only did Lamb not hunger after nature, but loved and preferred every nook and cranny of London: 'For God's sake', he exploded '. . . don't make me rediculous any more by terming me gentle-hearted in print, or do it in better verses.' If another edition is called for 'please to . . . substitute drunken dog, ragged head, seld-shaven, odd-eyed, stuttering or any other epithet which truly . . . belongs to the gentleman in question'.

Meanwhile if Dorothy failed to sell the beauties of nature to Lamb, she helped, it would seem, to give him something else—encouragement, confidence, the power on his return to seek and find distraction in literary work. Like Lamb Dorothy stammered, and in her relation with William he could see reflected his with Mary. He would soon be writing to her. And when three years later he wrote a play, Coleridge was commissioned to transmit a copy of this not to Wordsworth but to 'Wordsworth and his sister'.

But the bulk of the talk during Lamb's stay must have gone on in Poole's arbour. Tom Poole owned a tanyard in Nether Stowey. An autodidact, unlike his brother denied an education, as hot for learning as for liberty, he had taken himself off from his gouty, sneering father to work as a common tanner in Wantage. At thirty-two Poole was very much the gentleman, but still in reaction against his snobbish relations and—crossed in love for his cousin Penelope—his devotion to Coleridge knew no bounds. If Coleridge wanted the Wordsworths near, it fell to him, Poole, to arrange this. And he did, within twelve days of their arrival; standing security for Wordsworth—by 14 July the tenant of the mansion, the dell, the waterfall.

Two days later Coleridge and Sara went to see them in, with transport doubtless, too, laid on by Poole, since Coleridge was still too lame to walk 'further than a furlong'. The next day Sara returned home early, alone, for the Monday wash, while Coleridge, who remained 'for a change of air', presumably meaning a change from smoke, sat down and wrote triumphantly to Southey that he had brought Wordsworth and 'his sister back with me [from Racedown] & here I [!] have *settled them*. By a combination of curious circumstances a gentleman's seat, with a park and woods, elegantly & completely *furnished*—with 9 *lodging-rooms*, three parlours & a Hall, in a most romantic and beautiful situation by the seaside—four miles from Stowey—this we have got for Wordsworth at a rent of £23 *a year, taxes included!*' Southey must come—a three-week break in 'country so divine and wild' must increase his stock of images—and Wordsworth will offer him and Edith Southey 'a suit of rooms', and 'is very solicitous to know you'; while Miss Wordsworth is, for the second time, 'a most exquisite young woman', though specifically, 'in her mind and heart'.

One may wonder how Miss Wordsworth herself had come so readily to abandon 'the first home I had', the place that was to be 'I think dearest to my recollections upon the whole surface of the island'. But Racedown was and remains a very lonely place. If in her task of raising a poet from the dead she could feel she had been successful, to complete it she needed help, not isolation. Their 'principal inducement', in short 'was Coleridge's society'—Coleridge's vast esoteric knowledge which, with his uncanny memory, made him throw out in five minutes more ideas than a man might hit on in years; Coleridge the perfect stimulant. And not only this; but who now—quite as much to Dorothy's purpose—as she and William explored their new territory, actually sat in one of the three parlours writing, 'Wordsworth is a very great man'; adding with more conceit than tact, 'the only man to whom *at all times & in all modes of excellence* I feel myself inferior', 'the London Literati' being 'little potatoes'.

It is hardly surprising if Southey failed to turn up on the doorstep. But if Coleridge's lack of humility seems obnoxious, this, as will be seen, was a strangely acute case of diffidence as the other side of the coin. Meanwhile one can hardly grudge him such youthful insouciance, nor quarrel, indeed, with his estimate of himself—on the brink of writing two of the greatest poems in the English language, *Kubla Khan* and *The Ancient Mariner*.

Sara's mood, returning alone from the splendours of Alfoxden to cope with the problems of the wash in her hole of a kitchen, must have been a good deal less triumphant. Nor, had she known that by evening she would be instrumental in terminating the lease so newly signed, would this have made any difference, have procured her—would anything do so?—a gentleman's seat with elegant furnishings. But at least she did not have to compete with the wash entirely alone. The Coleridges, poor as they were, had a young girl, Nanny, who had looked after the baby, Hartley, while she was away. If Sara—to whom in troubled times Coleridge could still write, 'In one thing, my dear Love! I do prefer you to any woman I ever knew. I have the most unbounded confidence in your discretion'—did not stoop to confiding her blues to Nanny, Nanny had, with all Stowey, formed her own view of the Wordsworths, with their dark skins, foreign accents and gypsy ways. Coleridge, as Wordsworth had never done, had published treasonable matter, and Poole had circulated *The Watchman* in Stowey. But Coleridge spoke as a Devon man—he pronounced the *l* in 'talk'—whereas, it is comical to learn, when Wordsworth wrote, 'I heard a thousand blended notes', 'notes' for him did actually rhyme with 'thoughts'—as is proved by his slip in a letter about a 'nought' for twenty pounds—no laughing matter in Stowey in time of war.

There still exist country folk hostile to what they term 'incomers'. One who, as Sara was up to her eyes in the suds, was something a great deal worse—acquitted admittedly of high treason but nevertheless a known political agitator—now knocked on the door of the thatched cottage in Lime Street. This, to Sara's consternation on quite a different score, was none other than Samuel's friend, Mr Thelwall; who, however, quickly made it plain that he found her as pretty as she undoubtedly was, flushed from the wash-tub, and who 'slept', as he wrote to his wife, 'at Coleridge's 'cot'.

The next morning Sara had him up 'by times' and walked to Alfoxden, in 'time enough to call Samuel and his friend Wordsworth up to breakfast'. Dorothy went with them when, after three days, 'the enthusiastic group', as Thelwall termed them, returned to a less than enthusiastic Stowey. 'Alfoxden House is let to one of the fraternity. To what are we coming?'—Poole's waspish cousin, Charlotte, for once, in her diary, voiced something more than her own philistine snobbery, an already growing note of rustic alarm.

By the Saturday they were back, having taken, Coleridge wrote to jog Poole's memory, 'a fore-quarter of lamb from your mother, which you will be so kind, according to your word, . . . to send over to The Foxes . . . by a boy'. Poole himelf is, if possible, to come by eleven, 'that we may have Wordsworth's tragedy read under the trees'.

There were, as the charmed Thelwall noticed, no servants at The Foxes, and, as the reading went on under the trees to an audience swelled by Poole's friends, Dorothy must have felt the want of Peggy. Fourteen people sat down to the forequarter of lamb, and it had seemed a piece of luck that one, Jones, had been found to come in and wait at this, Dorothy's first dinner party. That the bulk of the guests were local, however, and brought by Poole who—whatever the friends he imported from away—was in Stowey loved and respected, could not make the occasion a suitable one for the Alfoxden dining room. Jones not only asked 'To what are we coming?' He was frankly terrified, in particular by 'a little Stout Man with dark cropt Hair', who 'wore a White Hat and Glasses and . . . got up and talked so loud and was in such a passion' that Jones 'did not like to go near them since'.

A former Alfoxden servant, with the promising name of Mogg, visiting Bath hastened to tell his friend, the ex-Alfoxden cook now employed in Bath, of the carryings-on at the Great House. These she passed on to her new employer—who, without delay, passed them on to the Home Secretary:

11th Aug. My Lord Duke—On the 8th instant I took the liberty to acquaint your grace with a very suspicious business concerning an emigrant family who have contrived to get possession of a Mansion House at Alfoxton . . . under Quantock Hills. I am since informed that the Master of the house has no wife with him, but only a woman who passes for his Sister. The man has Camp Stools which he and his visitors take about with them when they go about the country upon their nocturnal or diurnal excursions and have also a Portfolio in which they enter their observations which they have been heard to say were almost finished. They have been heard to say that they should be rewarded for them, and were very attentive to the River near them. . . . These people may *possibly* be under-agents to some principal in Bristol.

The 'observations' were concerned with a long philosophical poem Coleridge was meditating, called *The Brook*. And matters were not improved when 'the French people' (William and Dorothy) asked Christopher Trickie, who lived at the Alfoxden gates, 'whether the brook was Navigable to the Sea . . . and were afterwards seen examining the Brook quite down to the Sea'. If any further proof was needed of their being dangerous foreigners, Dorothy washed and mended 'cloaths all Sunday'.

The Home Office wasted no time, or rather wasted too much. By 13 August, if not before, a detective, Walsh, had been dispatched and installed in the pub at Stowey, where he quickly learnt of Thelwall's visit; that one Mr Coldridge had a printing press in his house, that the French people were English but highly dangerous. Led by a man named Wordsworth, they were protected by a tanner, a gentleman but one who held violent views and ran a Poor Man's Club from which at any time he could muster his own private army.

'After', wrote Coleridge, 'three weeks truly Indian perseverance in tracking us (for we were commonly together)', they were wholly unconscious of being followed. Mr Walsh had a sensitive spot, however, a 'Bardolph nose'. And 'at first . . . fancied we were aware of our danger, for he often heard me talk of one Spy Nozy'. (Can this really have been how Coleridge pronounced Spinoza?)

Meanwhile, as Mr Walsh concealed this 'remarkable feature' as best he could behind 'a bank at the seaside (our favourite seat)', the trembling Jones, fortified by a shilling, was sent to weed the garden at Alfoxden. Here he learnt from the equally innocent Peggy (who had devotedly followed with Basil from Racedown) nothing more useful than that Dorothy had again had visitors, one 'a great Counsellor from London' (presumably Montagu who could counsel no one) and 'a Gentleman from Bristol' (one of the Pinneys?). After taking a stroll, in the guise of a traveller with strong Jacobite views, with Coleridge himself and being made to eat humble pie, Walsh signed off, though not without giving the landlord a last going over: Did not 'Coldridge' distribute pamphlets and harangue the people in knots and clusters—'"What are you grinning at, Sir?" "Beg your Honour's pardon! But . . . if what I have heard to be true, your Honour! they would not have understood a word he said."' What exactly had he heard? '"Why, folks do say, your Honour! as how that he is a *Poet*, and that he is going to put Quantock and all about here in print; and as they be so much together, I suppose the strange gentleman has some *concarn* in the business."'

Thelwall's objective had been to forgo future spells in the Tower, settle near Coleridge and himself turn poet. And perhaps he hoped the lines he enclosed in a letter would forward matters not only at Stowey but at Alfoxden, that its

> . . . musing tenant and the maid
> Of ardent eye who with fraternal love
> Sweetens his solitude . . .

would sweeten things.

This, in fact, was the last quarter to which he could look for help. By September, had it been legally possible, the Wordsworths would themselves have been out on their ear. Ignorant as they still were of the spy business, they could not be so of Mrs St Albyn's wrath, now unleashed on the head of the luckless Poole, who as usual rose to the occasion. The Wordsworths, he wrote, came of a highly respected family—the former vicar of Stowey had known their uncle, a Canon of Windsor—and were, as a small household with one excellent maid, much to be preferred to 'a large family—full of careless servants, a run of idle company, hunting, breaking down fences etc.' Wordsworth was of retired habits and entertained little. As for Thelwall's visit, 'No person at Stowey or Mr Wordsworth knew of his coming.' And no one at Stowey could have done more than Poole, who 'will pledge himself in every respect' that Mrs St Albyn 'will have no cause to complain of Mr Wordsworth'.

Poole in his letter to Mrs St Albyn does not mention Miss Wordsworth. And the truth was, as Samuel's Sara knew, that Dorothy's 'notable' aunt was right—such people always are. What might be forgiven a man could never pass in a woman. And Dorothy's wild ways—her washing on Sunday, above all her rambling about the country on foot, her tan deepening with the summer days, if not alone, in the company of her so-called brother—did quite as much if not far more damage than Thelwall. For that the relation was not one of brother and sister the people of Quantock were not in doubt. This suggests that Dorothy did not look like William, that any clear family resemblance was lacking. Since rife as was the gossip (William, among other things, was believed to keep a whisky still), openly loving as they were seen to be, one rumour Sara did not have to support— or perhaps incest was not a word in the Stowey vocabulary. Or possibly Dorothy was too clearly a loose woman, as often as not out upon the heights alone with a married man, or, if with the two men—with Mrs Coleridge conspicuous by her absence. Stowey's sympathies were all with Sara, who, after her miscarriage in July, was now pregnant again, and increasingly dropped out of expeditions for which she had no taste.

But if going to the Coombe for eggs, as Dorothy constantly did, was not the pleasant business it might have been, if she and William felt the hostility keenly enough to decide against ever returning to the district, they did not now allow this to depress them. The truth was nothing could depress 'three persons and one soul', Coleridge's reputed designation, 'the buoyant spirits that were our daily portion [Dorothy's too] when we first . . . wantoned in wild poesy'.

X

*The slender notes of a redbreast, which sang at intervals
on the outskirts of the southern side of the wood.*

—Alfoxden Journal

1797–1798

THERE HAD, IN fact, by November been no poesy wild or sober out of
William since moving in early July; and to Dorothy Coleridge's society
might well have come to seem strikingly like an inducement to talk about
rather than write it. On and on it flowed, the talk and the laughter,
whether out on the hills or in Tom Poole's arbour. But Dorothy knew
better than to deplore this. For that, despite the buoyant spirits which
were their daily nectar, William was still far from in the clear must have
been plain to her even had she not been shown a poem that did now find
its way into his notebook:

> Away, away, it is the air
>   That stirs among the withered leaves:
> Away, away, it is not there,
> Go, hunt among the harvest sheaves.
> It is a bed in shape as plain
> As from a hare or lion's lair
> It is the bed where we have lain
> In anguish and despair.
>
> Away, and take the eagle's eyes
>   the tyger's smell,
> Ears that can hear the agonies
> And murmurings of hell;
> And when you there have stood
> By that same bed of pain,
> The groans are gone, the tears remain.
> Then tell me if the thing be clear,
>   The difference betwixt a tear
> Of water and of blood.

But if William needed distraction, to talk rather than write, the talk
between two poets in the *annus mirabilis* was quite as vital to poetry as the

writing of this, and Dorothy, too, a member of 'the Concern'. Naturally gay and gregarious, she herself needed the break, and was happy now to walk, listen and look, the more so since Coleridge had been converted from Miltonic musings to share the vision which William had had at Hawkshead. This was the more easily done since it here lay all about them; as they talked, she could point it out—the extraordinariness of the ordinary if one only looked, or, as Coleridge later summarized it, 'the sudden charm which accidents of light and shade . . . moonlight or sunset cast over known or familiar things'. This was her field as much as theirs, a bond now with Coleridge as much as it had always been with William. And then she was happy since clearly the medicine was working; since William, as Coleridge could not fail to observe, was talkative and lighthearted with him as with no one else, as Dorothy herself had never seen him. Hitherto William had been close only to her. Now she had every reason to be thankful that he had found a friend who did not come between them, who had not taken William away from her, but made it plain that he wished her to go with them on their walks and listened to her quite as William did.

Meanwhile September had brought yet more visitors. A rich delicate young philanthropist, Tom Wedgwood, of the famous pottery family, had heard of William from Montagu, not as a poet but reformer, and wanted him to start an 'advanced school'. In this the walls would be painted grey, with one or two 'vivid objects', and 'hard bodies' hung about the children which would 'continually . . . irritate their palms'; the pupils were never to be allowed out of doors, or out, indeed, of their separate grey apartments. There had also been the tall, clumsy, pitiful epileptic, Charles Lloyd, whom Coleridge had looked after, and who, added to his tragic disease, had lately on the grounds of this been refused as a suitor by the family of the girl he loved. Lloyd, who appeared to be in a highly nervous state, declared himself deeply hurt by Coleridge whom he loved and revered above all men, but who never now wrote to him or, he complained, answered his letters.

But Coleridge by now, plainly, was himself far from well. Dorothy must have got over the first shock of seeing him on a walk fling himself to the ground and lie there writhing like a worm. At first it seemed this violent pain was rheumatic in origin, a relic perhaps of the ague brought on as a child—when after a fight with his brother over some toasted cheese and expecting a flogging from his mother, he had run off, and (in the hope of waking more maternal feelings?) lain out all one night in late October. At school he had been dangerously ill with rheumatic fever. But at times it seemed the pain was dysentery. In both cases, however, his sufferings were relieved by the only palliative then available—laudanum.

Whether determined to be quit of a dysentery, or of his tragedy (still incomplete) or both, he now briefly took himself off to his favourite haunts round Porlock and there put up in an isolated farmhouse. With him he had a book, Purchas's *Pilgrimages* and an 'anodyne' that sent him to sleep in his chair at the moment he was reading, 'How the Khan Kubla commanded a palace to be built'. And dreamed in his sleep a poem which perhaps on his return he read out at The Foxes as a joke-poem. Dorothy seems fondly to have thought of it as such and it would not be heard of again till, in 1816, Sara wailed: 'He has been so unwise as to publish his fragments of "Christabel" and "Koula Khan" . . . the price is 4s.6d.'

The only fruit for Dorothy of Coleridge's going off to Porlock may well have seemed his declared determination to go back, taking herself and William to see what they too must see, in its full perfection, now, before winter set in:

> The hanging woods that touched by autumn seemed
> As they were blossoming hues of fire and gold,
> The hanging woods most lovely in decay,
> The many clouds, the sea, the rocks, the sands.

At all events they went; and from Porlock, as Dorothy wrote, 'kept close to the shore about four miles . . . through wood, rising almost perpendicularly from the sea, with views of the opposite mountains of Wales: thence we came by twilight to Lynmouth, in Devonshire'. The next morning Coleridge 'guided' them 'to a valley at the top of one of those immense hills which open at each end to the sea, and is from its rocky appearance called the Valley of Stones. We mounted a cliff at the end of the valley, and looked from it immediately on to the sea.'

She would not for two months keep a journal, but from this simple description, bare even of any note of colour, to Mary, one may catch the drama of the impression. And there can have existed no one more rewarding than Dorothy with whom to share, to show one's chosen land, who never failed to take one's point and often took in more. She was the freer to do so since the expenses of this jaunt were to be defrayed by a long poem, written by William and Coleridge jointly, but the whole scheme of which Coleridge had already worked out in detail. The subject would be *The Wanderings of Cain* and the epic dispatched in a night, William in one room, Coleridge in another.

Had the guide, impresario, joker, laid them under a spell? Was poetry to be the party game of a night? The episode which terminated the Lynton–Porlock tour could still after thirty years make Coleridge smile; and may still 180 years on carry us back to Alfoxden on a night in November 1797. With Dorothy's poets shut each in his parlour with his allotted canto (William's the first and Coleridge's the second) whoever got through quickest was to set about the last. Outline: 'midnight on the Euphrates—Cedars, palms, pines. Cain is discovered sitting on . . . ragged rock . . . his soliloquy. Beasts are out on the ramp . . . The screams of a woman and children surrounded by tygers. Cain makes a soliloquy debating whether to save the woman' etc. Coleridge, his task dispatched 'at full finger-speed' hastes to his fellow bard, to meet a look of comic despondency fixed on a sheet of all but blank paper, a 'silent mock-piteous admission of failure struggling with the sense of the exceeding ridiculousness of the whole scheme—which broke up in a laugh. And the Ancient Mariner was written instead.'

It was not quite as simple as that, or rather it was simpler. The tour had been too enjoyable not to repeat, and within the week they were off again, acting, perhaps, on the impulse of the moment, for they did not, wrote Dorothy, set out till half-past four, and that on an evening 'dark and cloudy: we went eight miles, William and Coleridge employing themselves in laying the plan of a ballad, to be published with some pieces of William's'.

'Much of the greatest part of the story', according to the latter, 'was Mr Coleridge's invention; but certain parts I myself suggested. For example some crime was to be committed which should bring upon the Old Navigator, as Coleridge . . . delighted to call him, the spectral persecution . . . and his own wanderings.' That Wordsworth was fresh from reading in Shelvock's *Voyages* about albatrosses is, perhaps, of less interest than his unconscious motivation here. '"Suppose", I said, "you represent him as having killed one of these birds on entering the South Sea, and that the tutelary Spirits of these regions take upon them to avenge the crime?"'

Coleridge, in short, supplied the idea of persecution; in *Cain* he had supplied the idea of guilt. Now Wordsworth came up with a crime the consequences of which the Mariner would only afterwards realize. Dorothy, with 'guilt . . . a thing impossible in her', evidently confined herself to listening. On their return her two poets retired once more to their separate parlours. But this time the produce of these partners in crime 'proved', said Wordsworth, 'so widely different that I withdrew from an undertaking upon which I would only have been a clog'.

Their manner of dealing with guilt was indeed to prove widely different and to provide, I suggest, the rock on which they split—and on which Dorothy's ship, in an essential sense, went down with both her poets on board.

The Ancient Mariner, meanwhile, was to be no mere work of a night; nor the remaking of nine of Richard's shirts—the original batch, one hopes, and not a fresh order. Dorothy could nevertheless bring herself to write, 'If you wish to have the wrists altered pray let me know as it will be very expensive for you to get it done in London'. She had 'abided exactly by the measure which you sent' but 'was so much astonished at its shortness' that 'I should . . . have written for a second measurement, if I had not so much confidence in your exactness'. One wonders why she had since, if Richard was exact about money to the point of meanness, they were still at this moment being harassed about the Whitehaven debt which Richard had said he would meet four years back. And now there was Montagu broke—unable to pay for Basil let alone the interest on William's loan; or even to keep himself, it seemed, since he arrived and stayed for some eight weeks. Dorothy, however, kept both her head and Basil, and somehow kept within their meagre income. So that the following June she would write with pride: 'Notwithstanding Mr Montagu . . . we are not a farthing poorer than when we began house-keeping'.

Initially she must have been helped by astonishing news from London. William's own tragedy, *The Borderers*, had been sent to Covent Garden in mid-October. 'We have not the faintest expectation that it will be accepted,' Dorothy wrote on 20 November. This letter must almost have crossed with one from the theatre, saying that one of the chief actors there had read the play with 'great approbation' and 'advised William strongly to go to London to make some alterations'. By 8 December not only was William in London and Dorothy with him, but the changes in the play made. They had now to wait on the manager's decision. By the 13th they had this: after their hopes had been raised and the expense of the journey —a negative one. If Dorothy, writing on the 20th, was brief, her disappointment rings through her brevity: 'our business was the play; and the play is rejected.' It is doubtful if she greatly enjoyed the visit. Mary Lamb had again gone mad—this time in lodgings—and Lamb, in despair, was not in circulation. Southey, to whom she took an instant dislike, was, as was Charles Lloyd, now living with him.

One wonders why they saw so much of Southey, whether perhaps Coleridge had asked William to mediate in the matter of three facetious sonnets signed 'Nehemiah Higginbottom'. In these he had satirized not Southey, but himself; but also tactlessly Charles Lloyd and Lamb, neither of whom was in any condition to take it. Lloyd now tried to enlist Dorothy's sympathy; and it is hard to believe that had the sonnets been read, like the 'devilishly clever' reviews, to the gentle electrometer, these would not have followed them into the fire. Southey, though not a butt, thought himself one; and met Dorothy, for the first time, on delicate terrain for both—Coleridge ground.

Southey at thirty-seven, meeting Shelley aged nineteen, could write, 'Here is a man . . . who acts upon me as my own ghost would do. He is just what I was in 1794'—that is, as unconventional and enthusiastic, less elegant and remote than he later appeared. But if, in 1798, Dorothy met not a Shelley, but 'a young man of rigidly virtuous habits', she for once failed to divine what lay behind these, to divine what Southey had, it would seem, himself already discovered—that 'though some persons . . . suppose I have no nerves . . . if it were not for a strict intellectual regimen [incessant work, but with several kinds on hand] I should very soon be in a deplorable state of what is called nervous disease'. 'A clear handsome piece of Water in a park' would be Coleridge's way of disposing of the man who had led to Sara Fricker, and for whom his feelings were always to be ambivalent. That Dorothy anticipated this estimate is, perhaps, one yardstick of her love for Coleridge.

At the beginning of January she was back at Alfoxden, having stayed on the way for some ten days at Bristol, possibly at her anxious insistence that William see Cottle and try getting published, if not performed. Her fears, if natural, were unnecessary. With *The Borderers* put behind him, William was suddenly freed, by March free to flow in a very different vein.

We owe much, perhaps, to the failure of the London visit. Was it the sheer ecstasy of being back, the eye, each sense, so sharpened that to look about one was to see as one had never seen before, that now drove Dorothy herself to write—a journal? Or did she start this only at William's request, to recall for him exactly what they, or she, had seen? Her aunt and her cousins in Halifax were under the impression that the tragedy had been a joint work, that the pair of them wrote poetry and worked as collaborators. This false impression was now to become true. Her first entry was, as has been said, not lost on William, though he may not always have taken from the journal but freshly at the time from Dorothy's lips; just as having a poet on hand it would hardly be surprising if her language at times echoed his. But we know that when at Dove Cottage she read him her account of an incident he wanted for a poem, 'an unlucky thing it was, for he could not escape from those very words, and so could not write the poem'.

It is, in fact, extraordinarily hard to escape from Dorothy's words, so simple and all sufficient are they. Thus on 25 January she wrote:

> Went to Poole's after tea. The sky spread over with one continuous cloud, whitened by the light of the moon, which, though her dim shape was seen, did not throw forth so strong a light as to chequer the earth with shadows. At once the clouds seemed to cleave asunder, and left her in the centre of a black-blue vault. She sailed along, followed by multitudes of stars, small, and bright, and sharp. Their brightness seemed concentrated (half-moon).

It is hard to improve on this, and I am not sure Wordsworth does in 'A Night-Piece', composed, he specifically says, 'extempore', 'on the road between Nether Stowey and Alfoxden'—owing nothing, then, to Dorothy's journal. If not, how closely their minds worked, how much in unison, is nevertheless shown by his construction:

> The sky is overcast
> With a continuous cloud of texture close,
> Heavy and wan, all whitened by the Moon,
> Which through that veil is indistinctly seen,
> A dull, contracted circle, yielding light
> So feebly spread that not a shadow falls,
> Chequering the ground—from rock, plant, tree, or tower.

This, less compressed, to my mind lacks the force of Dorothy's. Nor, when his 'clouds are split / Asunder', does she sink to 'The clear Moon, and the glory of the heavens'.

> There, in a black-blue vault she sails along,
> Followed by multitudes of stars, that, small
> And sharp, and bright, along the dark abyss
> Drive as she drives: how fast they wheel away . . .

Gathering strength and outsoaring Dorothy here, one may still prefer her exact notation—as simpler and more original, closer, as yet, than Words-worth to what he himself was aiming at. From both one may understand how he came to write of one 'Whom I have loved / With such communion, that no place on earth / Can ever be a solitude to me'.

Dorothy from now on came into her own. Not only was William's poetic output enormous, she was and was to remain closely involved with it. Whether or not she or William was the first to remark, 'The moss rubbed from the pailings by the sheep, that leave locks of wool, and the red marks with which they are spotted, upon the wood', in it went to the poem as into the journal. By this time, 4 February 1798, the second day only* since Coleridge, too, had got back after being away, there was much to hear. His tragedy had likewise—and more cruelly—been rejected, to the tune of much laughter in the green room, as Sheridan read out the line about water in a cavern, '"'Drip, drip, drip'—There's nothing here but Dripping!"' He had fared somewhat better in Shrewsbury, where he had been offered the post of Unitarian Minister; and 'for three weeks held that good town . . . in delightful suspense', according to a youth, William Hazlitt, who, rising before daylight, walked ten miles through the mud 'to hear this celebrated person preach'. It was, in fact, staying overnight in the house of this farouche lad, the son of the Minister at Wem, and for whom no mutton had ever tasted so good as it did that evening, that Coleridge decided against the Ministry. Here the next morning he had received an offer, three times refused, of a pension from Tom and Josiah Wedgwood, the former of whom now wished to exchange grey walls and prickly pears for enlightenment in the form of S.T.C. 'Coleridge seemed to make up his mind to close with the proposal in the act of tying on one of his shoes.' Hazlitt was here not describing decision but doubt, the almost uncanny self-prophetic powers of one now writing *The Ancient Mariner* and who would indeed as he feared, and as the Mariner did, 'slay the bird / That caused the breeze to blow'. With so much to hear it is doubtful if the three who, that morning, left the redbreasts singing in the garden, touched on Dorothy's having started a journal. But certainly within days Coleridge had access to this and was steeping himself in her observations.

Meanwhile if William had put an albatross round his friend's neck, the

---

* For the questionable dating of these entries in the Alfoxden Journal, see *Journals of Dorothy Wordsworth*, 2nd edn. (1971) p. 4, n. 4.

friend had more than returned the compliment in the shape of his own long philosophic poem. Even renamed *The Recluse*, the always fatal *Brook* would definitely not prove 'Navigable . . . to the sea'. 'I know not anything', William wrote manfully in March, 'which will not come within the scope of my plan'. This might sound like the death-knell of Dorothy, no philosopher. But the truth of it was, no more was this William's line. And if there needed no excuse for the daily to-ing and fro-ing that went on between Stowey and The Foxes, this was doubtless in great part entailed by Coleridge supplying the wherewithal, including his belief that 'the Giant Wordsworth—God love him—is writing a blank verse superior . . . to anything in our language which any way resembles it'.

Coleridge's failure to understand where Wordsworth's true gifts lay was only to be paralleled by the latter's failure to grasp the greatness of poetry so far removed from his own. But in 1798–9, all things were possible, in all things—in the conjunction of opposites, in poetry, in Dorothy—everything to bind and stimulate 'three persons and one soul'. And if William, bent to his great philosophic task, could make no present use of Dorothy's journal, her role was the more needful and obvious. William, in fact, required no prompting to escape; he knew where the cure for the pains of philosophy lay, and was in no way lost to her. One might indeed wonder when the work got done, if one did not know the answer—out of doors, in the course of their walks together. If he has not been with her, he will want to know what she has seen, and if he has been present but composing, muttering as he went, then, too, he will want to know what he has missed.

And so her notes flow on: and as we read through the Alfoxden Journal, impersonal as this is, we come to know her. As she sits in the wood 'The breeze rose gently; its path distinctly marked, till it came to the very spot where we were'. It is almost as if she is part of the woods, as if, because she has followed the course of the breeze but also sat there so gently, the breeze has come to her as naturally as might a deer or a bird. Her ear is, if possible, more sensitive than her eye, sensitive above all not to silence—for nothing so empty as silence exists for her; what she hears is a stillness 'undisturbed except by the occasional dropping of the snow from the holly boughs; no other sound but that of the water, and the slender notes of a redbreast . . . at intervals on . . . the southern side of the wood'. In the quietness that surrounds her one learns her need for this. But when 'the trees almost *roared*' in a gale, she picks up a second rustling sound 'distinct from that of the trees', made by the dead leaves lifting off the ground. We here, however, learn at first-hand more than her gentleness, more than her powers of discrimination. She not only describes things, but conveys her own sensations without ever directly referring to these. Even when it is simply, after the snows have melted, 'the turnips of a lively fresh green', her robust epithets both perfectly fit turnips and convey how glad she is to see green again. Robustness—but also delicacy:

The shapes of the mist, slowly moving along, exquisitely beautiful; passing over the sheep they almost seemed to have more of life than those quiet creatures. The unseen birds singing in the mist.

Two days after writing this she went to the shoemaker: 'William lay under the trees till my return'. It was warm enough and time enough, and in short enough was enough of a blank verse however superior. Perhaps it was on this day that Dorothy, busy indoors, was brought a poem-cum-summons from William by Basil:

To My Sister

It is the first mild day of March:
Each minute sweeter than before
The redbreast sings from the tall larch
That stands beside our door.

There is a blessing in the air,
Which seems a sense of joy to yield
To the bare trees and mountains bare,
And grass in the green field.

My sister! ('tis a wish of mine)
Now that our morning meal is done,
Make haste, your morning task resign;
Come forth and feel the sun.
.   .   .   .   .

No joyless forms shall regulate
Our living calendar:
We from today, my Friend, will date
The opening of the year.
.   .   .   .   .

And from the blessed power that rolls
About, below, above,
We'll frame the measure of our souls:
They shall be tuned to love.

Then come, my Sister! come, I pray
With speed put on your Woodland Dress;
And bring no book: for this one day
We'll give to idleness.

Dorothy was never to allow 'joyless forms' to 'regulate' mealtimes, bedtime or anything else, and always ready to don her 'Woodland Dress' —evidently, since she was urged to accomplish this with speed, old clothes and not merely a cloak. Nor, to judge from the outcrop of short

88

poems which followed, was one day only given to 'idleness'. The recalcitrant *philosophe* had the bit between his teeth, and Coleridge must make the best of such heresy.

But Coleridge for once was absent, had been two whole days missing, was ill, on 6 March 'very ill', as Dorothy, having hastened alone that evening to Stowey, reported. The bad teeth she had observed were the cause—and of more than his present illness. Why had he not had the poisoned stump extracted? He had tried, or rather the dentist had, and failed in anything except increasing the pain to agony. He would rather, Coleridge said, 'put my hand in a lion's mouth than put my mouth in that man's hands'. There was nothing for it but laudanum. When Dorothy, like everyone else, took this anodyne for the same complaint, there is nothing to indicate that she found in it the enchantment Coleridge did, 'a green spot of fountains & flowers & trees in the very heart of a waste of sands', as he was able to write by 10 March—adding, 'God be praised the matter has been absorbed'.

He was writing from Alfoxden, where he had gone to convalesce, accompanied for once by Sara and Hartley. Dorothy's way of recording their arrival is curious, comic and significant: '*9th March*. A clear sunny morning, went to meet Mr [!] and Mrs Coleridge.' The visit lasted nine days. One entry, for 14 March, may have been deleted in the journal, but having kept this daily between the 9th and 13th, on the 15th she resumes inaccurately and with, for good measure, a *non sequitur*: 'I have neglected to set down the occurrences of this week, so I do not recollect how we disposed of ourselves to-day.' On the 17th she writes, 'I do not remember this day.' On the next she could enter, 'The Coleridges left us'.

Nowhere else in the Alfoxden Journal does she lose track of a week, or rather think she has; and nowhere else does 'not remember this day'. But then nowhere else had the protuberance of Sara's stomach been as noticeable as it was now. At Stowey Sara was always busy and a background figure, and then the rooms were so dark one could hardly see. Whereas here, as she reclined in a chair in the high light rooms of The Foxes, her condition was all too much *en évidence*. That Dorothy steeled herself in advance and was from the outset on guard is surely clear from the entry of 'Mr' Coleridge—of Coleridge, that is, in the guise of a husband. For the rest of the visit admittedly he reverts to being Coleridge, but then he is never coupled with Mrs Coleridge, who may stroll in the park but does not walk, and of whom, in fact, after her coming, there occurs in nine days no single mention. The truth would seem to be that Coleridge was in the habit of living as much at The Foxes as at Stowey; that for most of the time Dorothy could forget there was a wife—except as a thing convenient to remember. And taboos are extremely useful things. That one existed in Coleridge's case, if it blocked her path, also allowed her feelings to flow more freely, allowed her to feel that she loved Coleridge as one might a brother—which allowed one to love a very great deal indeed. Jealousy and malice were, as will be seen, emotions of which she was almost incapable, even when it came to sharing William. But Sara as an invisible *carte blanche* was one thing, her proximity, which destroyed this, quite another.

De Quincey, conjuring up Sara's difficulties, says that 'bitter' as it must be 'to a young married woman to sustain any sort of competition with a female of her own age for any part of her husband's regard, or any share of his company', Sara could comfort herself with two things—that her rival 'was always attended by her brother' and that 'she had no personal charms'. He is almost certainly inaccurate on both counts. Dorothy was often unchaperoned. As for her charms, when De Quincey met her she had literally aged out of all recognition since 1798. In Coleridge's one mention of her looks in a letter to Cottle—'if you expected to see a pretty woman you would think her rather ordinary; if you expected . . . an ordinary woman . . . pretty'—he is far from saying that her looks are against her, that she is what she is despite these; rather does he seem to suggest that these are hard to pin down, so changeful is her expression—and fascinating. When one recalls that Dorothy cared not a straw about looks or dress, this from Sara's husband is no mean tribute. He is aware of her looks. But had not mentioned them the second time round, in his letter to Southey; why? Because Southey was like himself married and to Sara's sister, was his brother-in-law, and not like Cottle a bachelor? Because he was by this time himself on guard? Because her looks have merged with what she is? There is no way of knowing, no shred of evidence that Coleridge was ever in love with Dorothy. But there are, I suggest, grounds for thinking that, had he been free to marry, Coleridge might have married Dorothy Wordsworth.

As it was, not only was there a Mrs Coleridge; on Dorothy's side, too, there were taboos. She was herself both virginal and William's property. The position suited Coleridge down to the ground. He too could love Dorothy without feeling immoral; he did not want sex, he wanted love. In fact he wanted exactly what William had—a sister. And the more he saw in Dorothy a woman one could respect, the more did he find his relation with Sara degrading. Dorothy did for years hold the first place in his heart as a woman. When at last she was displaced it was by one who, unlike Dorothy, *was* described as plain; but of her exact height and colouring; who did differ from her, but chiefly in being free—for him.

Dorothy's journal for 9–18 March reads the more oddly when one knows what was being discussed during the visit. Alfoxden would soon, as they had long known it must, be lost to them, let to more desirable tenants. But they have 'a delightful scheme in agitation': have come, wrote William, by 11 March 'to a resolution' of going all four to Germany to learn the language and study natural science. Their plan is to settle for two years, 'if possible in a village near a University, in a pleasant, and, if we can a mountainous, country'.

It seems likely that Coleridge came up with the scheme or with the itch to learn German as a means to reading German philosophy. With the

Wedgwood pension this was now possible, and made it almost incumbent on him to do so. William, too, 'thinks it will be a great advantage . . . to be acquainted with the German language', Dorothy wrote to Richard, 'besides that translation is the most profitable of all works'. The journey will cost between twenty and twenty-five guineas, but 'we have reason to think we can live cheaper in Germany than in England'. Even so, with no money like the Wedgwoods' behind them, the project was far beyond their purse. Thus was hatched the idea of *Lyrical Ballads*. Poetry must pay. The simplicity of this ethic is somehow epitomized in Dorothy's journal: '*22nd March*. I spent the morning in starching and hanging out linen'. The next day 'Coleridge . . . brought his ballad* finished'.

William had already almost too many wares and Dorcas, in the shape of Cottle, was willing to bring these out in two volumes. 'He is to have twenty guineas for one', wrote Dorothy proudly in April, and 'expects more than twice as much for another which is nearly ready for publishing'. This should make Richard sit up. To Mary she had written eight weeks before that her ship had come home at last: 'His faculties seem to expand every day, he composes with much more facility than he did . . . and his ideas flow faster than he can express them.' So fast that Dorothy must have found it hard to keep up as the copyist; and been shaken when William changed his mind. He would publish not in two volumes or under his own name, but in a slim selection shared with Coleridge—and all her haste to get done (*The Ruined Cottage* alone had run to 900 lines) rendered pointless. The leavings, despite Cottle's protests, would come out anonymously. 'Wordsworth's name means nothing' Coleridge wrote oddly of the Giant, with curious lack of logic, '& mine stinks'.

If Dorothy was briefly cast down, William stuck to his guns, and these would always swiftly become hers. And even when written separately the poems were, as he said, a joint work still (if not a triple one). In both cases the subject was predominantly the same, one she had constantly heard discussed between them—the effect of a curse laid on an innocent person. A joint work cementing their friendship might be a less paying project, but emotionally there seemed everything to gain.

Meanwhile it still went on. Coleridge was there for tea, and while they waited for William (not yet back from composing in the grove), he talked of his new ballad, *Christabel*, and—as Dorothy sewed—sat leafing through her journal. William came in at last and read them his poem finished, but for the first line which must rhyme with 'limb'. He should relax and enjoy his tea the more if this were got. How must it begin? 'A simple child . . .'. 'A simple child, dear brother Jem,' Coleridge threw off gaily. Thirsty as he was, William could not swallow this one; but then they 'all enjoyed the joke of hitching in our friend James Tobin . . . who was familiarly called Jem'.

Laughter was their daily portion and even a portion of poetry. In *Peter*

* *The Ancient Mariner.*

Bell, the last poem which Dorothy copied, the joke was on Coleridge, flying high in a moon-boat and wishing one who preferred the earth to do so:

> There's something in a flying horse,
> There's something in a huge balloon;
> But through the clouds I'll never float
> Until I have a little Boat
> Shaped like the crescent-moon.

It was long, and light as a feather; it was also, as Dorothy happily could not know, prophetically near the bone:

> My little vagrant Form of light,
> My gay and beautiful Canoe,
> Well have you played your friendly part;
> As kindly take what from my heart
> Experience forces—then adieu!
> . . . . .
> Go—(but the world's a sleepy world,
> And 'tis, I fear, an age too late)
> Take with you some ambitious Youth!
> For, restless Wanderer! I, in truth,
> Am all unfit to be your mate.

Meanwhile by the end of March the entries in Dorothy's journal suggest that she was still oddly disturbed: '28th. Hung out the linen.' '29th. Coleridge dined with us.' '30th. Walked I know not where.' '31st. Walked.' '1st April. Walked by moonlight', even by moonlight joylessly still it would seem.

And fully employed as she was at this time as a member of 'the Concern', this hardly accounts for the bleakness of these entries; if for their brevity, certainly not for 'walked I know not where', a feat of which she was almost incapable. Later, in the Grasmere Journals, she admits to, and has cause for, depression, agitation and, once, prostration. But at Alfoxden this disturbed note occurs only once elsewhere—during the visit of 'Mr' and Mrs Coleridge. There may, of course, be quite other explanations, but the only one which seems to offer itself is that she did not relish being closeted in a carriage with Mrs Coleridge suckling Samuel's child.

And there we must leave the mystery, and, even were it not one, more profitably go with her to 'Crookham' (Crowcombe), to walk with her 'about the squire's grounds', where Dorothy saw 'Nature . . . very successfully striving to make beautiful what art had deformed', 'quaint waterfalls', 'ruins, hermitages'. Nature has today won the battle at Crowcombe, which, its formal garden and follies erased, stands beautiful, derelict; but still the site of Dorothy's cry of relief, 'Happily we cannot shape the huge hills, or carve out the valleys according to our fancy'.

Early in May a parcel of books arrived at The Foxes from Cottle, among them a novel, *Edmund Oliver*. This was by Charles Lloyd. William had not, he wrote, read the novel as yet; but Dorothy has and 'thinks it contains a great deal a *very* great deal of excellent matter'. In other words, she had totally failed to recognize the hero, even from his physical description. But how should she possibly recognize one who described himself as having 'at all times a strange dreaminess about me . . . with that dreaminess I have gone on . . . if any time thought troubled, I have swallowed some spirits, or had recourse to my laudanum'? Whoever opened her eyes, whether Coleridge or Lloyd himself, it failed to open either hers or William's—to anything more than the malice of Lloyd, much of whose material Coleridge had supplied him by his own fireside: such as the escapade of one S.T.C. who, beset by his creditors at Cambridge, had disappeared into the ranks of His Majesty's Forces re-christened Silas Tomkyn Comberbache. As told by Coleridge the feats of this gentleman must have made Dorothy laugh. But she could not laugh at the letter she now had from Lloyd, terming Coleridge a villain; and, on the strength of his talk with her in London, somehow assuming that Dorothy thought him one. She rushed across, in tears, with the letter, to Stowey. 'I laughed at it,' Coleridge wrote. And no doubt he did—for Dorothy's sake. He was nevertheless cut to the core, though hurt most of all by Lamb his oldest friend, to whom the novel was dedicated and who he now learnt from Dorothy intended to have no more to do with him.

But Lamb and Lloyd had lately been deeply hurt by Coleridge, who— the facetious sonnets apart—had in his neglect of them laid himself wide open. This warning bell went unheeded by Dorothy and William; the more easily so since Coleridge himself desired only to make it up with 'poor Lloyd' who had been 'the instrument of another man's darker passions' (Southey's). Such charity, however, did not mean that Sara, delivered of a second philosopher, Berkeley, might not two days later be abandoned, having as Coleridge said had 'a remarkably good time'. It meant, as once before, two successive walking tours. On the first 'Coleridge, William and myself set forward to the Chedder rocks; slept at Bridgewater'. The tour, once again repeated within the week,—'Walked to Chedder. Slept at Cross'—meant something more, the end of the Alfoxden Journal.

Their 'main business' (though not the sole excuse for this last tour) was to catch 'poor Lloyd' in Bristol, a mission for which in the last resort it seems to have been decided that William would be the fittest ambassador. Lloyd, it transpired, had left. Whether or not Dorothy returned with Coleridge to Stowey or went with William, she arrived home in Cottle's gig complete with William and Coleridge—but not complete: without the large cheese which had been laid on at Bristol, without the brandy which now fell out and smashed, and *with* the head collar on the horse for life it seemed. Coleridge declared the horse's head had grown—he suggested gout. Peggy had it off as if by magic. There was bread in the house, but no salt, and lettuces in the garden. No wonder Dorothy kept the bills within bounds.

The battle about the two volumes versus a single joint one was unresolved when Cottle, who liked his comforts, left; to be pursued by William back to Bristol. Coleridge, unaware of this move, now descended on Dorothy with a visitor, a youth who had walked from Shropshire. William Hazlitt had last seen Coleridge at Wem, and despaired when he there accepted the Wedgwood pension. 'For instead of living at ten miles distant [as a minister] he was henceforth to inhabit the Hill of Parnassus. Alas', the boy 'knew not the way thither'. But then this god among men had given him an address, and said he would be glad to see him at Stowey. Since then he had lived through the winter in a fever, surely a dream: '*I was to visit Coleridge in the spring*'. He now met Miss Wordsworth, who, with her brother absent, was not above putting up two men for the night. The next morning, sitting outside on the trunk of an old tree, Hazlitt heard the great Coleridge read not his own poems but those, he was made to understand, of a yet greater man, Miss Wordsworth's brother. Back at Stowey he met the greater man and the next evening, after a day at The Foxes, walking to Stowey got with him into a metaphysical muddle. Coleridge meanwhile was talking to Dorothy. Of what did he talk to her? For once, it is rare, we overhear their talk: he is explaining the notes of the nightingale.

And so it draws to an end, the *annus mirabilis*. For Dorothy it has not yet quite come to an end. But Basil cannot be fitted into the German scheme, nor Peggy who would have followed them to the world's end. And then she must part with The Foxes itself, 'that dear and beautiful place', with the deer in the park, the Tor of Glastonbury which, 'wherever we go, keeping about fifteen yards above the house' has for so long made 'a part of our prospect'. But part with it she must; and on 14 June wrote urgently to Richard, the family banker, who has still not sent the money William had asked for: 'We have expected daily to hear from you. I am now obliged to write to you again, as we shall leave Allfoxden on . . . the 23rd of this month. William is already gone to Bristol. . . . I have the rent to pay, our servant's wages, and several other things before I can quit this place . . . I write in haste.'

William in fact, returned, and on Monday 25th they together left 'that dear and beautiful place', to stay for a week—waiting on Richard's payment?—in Lime Street with Himself away.

They then set out on foot for Bristol where their business was to see *Lyrical Ballads* through the press. 'But a city in feeling, sound and prospect is hateful', Dorothy wrote; after The Foxes unendurable. They *must* get away. And out they got, over the hills and a great way off in Wales, a great way certainly for Dorothy, but not too great to see where William had so often come along the Wye to visit Robert Jones; the last time five years ago in 1793. And he had, he wrote, then come 'more like a man / Flying from something that he dreads than one / Who sought the thing he loved'. But he had also come earlier, at an age when nature

> (The coarser pleasures of my boyish days
> And their glad animal movements all gone by)
> To me was all in all—I cannot paint
> What then I was. The sounding cataract
> Haunted me like a passion: the tall rock,
> The mountain, and the deep and gloomy wood,
> .   .   .   .   .   .
> . . . That time is past,
> And all its aching joys are now no more
> And all its dizzy raptures . . .

For him, perhaps; but not for Dorothy. For what dizzier rapture could there be than to stand by this huge stream, under its bending trees, with the sense that this is William's offering to her? William says that he does not mourn his own youthful rapture, but that in any case he would not do so,

> For thou art with me here upon the banks
> Of this fair river; thou my dearest Friend,
> My dear, dear Friend; and in thy voice I catch
> The language of my former heart, and read
> My former pleasure in the shooting lights
> Of thy wild eyes. Oh! yet a little while
> May I behold in thee what I was once. . . .

As she walked back into Bristol with William still composing, she could glory in something more than her faith fulfilled, in the sense that William relied on her at the deepest level of all—to revive 'the language of his former heart'.

95

XI

Home Thoughts from Abroad

1798–1799

AT THIS POINT, it has lately been said, Dorothy and William, 'dropped out of reach and out of cognizance like two ravens locked in love embrace dropping out of the sky'.* Where they actually fell was into their separate cabins, Dorothy heaving even before the anchor, to emerge still green only when, two days later, the Yarmouth packet entered the mouth of the Elbe. 'The sea', according to Coleridge, had 'rolled rather high'. 'I was surprised to find,' Dorothy wrote, 'when I came upon deck, that we could not see the shores, though we were in the river'; she might have said 'shaken'.

And might surely—being Dorothy—have done better had she, like Coleridge, weathered her first qualms and stayed on deck, where he was 'gay as a lark', and 'dressed . . . all in black, with large shoes and black worsted stockings' nicknamed 'Dr Teology' by a tipsy Dane whose talk he noted down at the time: '(Dane) "Vat imagination! vat language! vat fast science! vat eyes!—vat a milk vite forehead!—O my Heafen! You are a Got!—Oh me! if you should tink I flatter you—no, no, no—I haf ten tousand a year—yes ten tousand . . . vell, vat dhat? . . . you are a Got! I a mere man. But my dear Friend! . . . Is I not speak English very fine? Is I not very eloquent?" (S.T.C.) "Admirably, Sir, most admirably! . . ." (Dane squeezing my hand most vehemently) "My *dear* Friend! vat an affection and *fidelity* we have for each other!—But tell me, do tell me—Is I not now and den speak some fault? Is I not in some wrong?"' etc. Vat, we can only tink, poor Dorothy missed.

One thing, below in her cabin, however, she must have missed with pleasure: Mrs Coleridge and her progeny. Coleridge had decided to stay away three or four months only—'in which time I shall at least have learnt the langauge', and then, 'if all is well [i.e. financially], to fetch over my family—if not to return'.

Mrs Coleridge had been replaced by a youth from Stowey, Chester, who hung upon Coleridge's every word without, according to Hazlitt, understanding one. With Chester, now, on landing at Hamburg, Dorothy

* Molly Lefebure, *Samuel Taylor Coleridge: A Bondage of Opium.*

guarded the luggage, which included 'a sort of travelling furniture and toilet—all of silver and gold', the property of a French emigré whose baggage, perhaps, since he meant to settle near Hamburg, included some German. With him, at all events, William went to seek lodgings; while Coleridge, who had letters of recommendation, 'dashed into the town', to deliver them.

Dorothy, meanwhile, stood riveted by the life which eddied around her:

> . . . the Dutch women with immense straw bonnets, with flat crowns and rims in the shape of an oyster . . . and literally as large as a small umbrella. Hamburgher girls with white caps, with broad overhung borders, crimped and stiff, with long lappets of ribband . . . Fruit-women, with large straw hats in the shape of an inverted bowl, or white handkerchiefs tied . . . like a bishop's mitre. Jackets the most common . . . ladies without hats . . . Soldiers in dull . . . red coats with . . . immense cocked hats. The men little differing from the English, except that they generally have a pipe in their mouths.

Hamburg, on closer inspection, proved less picturesque. The party met up at Der Wilder Mann, approached by Dorothy through 'narrow, ill-paved, dirty, stinking streets', and itself pronounced by the impenitent Coleridge 'an hotel not of the genteelest Class.—But Wordsworth & the Emigrant had trudged [not dashed] over and over the City—every House was *full*! However they were drinking some excellent Claret, & I joined them with no small glee.' The floor of Dorothy's room had been washed, but this she could see had only 'spread or plastered the coating of dirt'. And Coleridge, already over the claret, declared it 'a foul city . . . Huddle and Ugliness, Stink and Stagnation'. Dorothy's room, like Coleridge and Chester's, looked on the market-place, where even the church, as Coleridge said, was ugly, with its 'Wens and Warts, or rather unseemly Corns'. But most unseemly of all were the prices; and William not only emerged from the baker's next morning without any rolls, but a shilling the poorer.

Coleridge, wasting no time, hastened back to the least unpromising of his introductions, whose partner he there met, old 'Young Klopstock'—young, that is, in comparison with his famous brother, the then Grand Old Man of German poetry. Young Klopstock knew no English, but with William fetched spoke French, if 'with a glorious havoc of Gender & Syntax'. He recommended Ratzeburg as a beautiful place on a lake, and presumably Altona, adjoining Hamburg, but where, being higher, the air was pleasanter. The two poets accordingly set off; Coleridge, the richer, allotted Ratzeburg, and William Altona, the name of which derived from All-zu-nah. And All-zu-nah (all-too-near) in price and all else it proved, as Dorothy the next day saw for herself; everyone rooked you, and to get with their baggage across the sands would take—and cost—a carriage with four horses. She 'lay down till Coleridge's return from Ratzeberg, a beautiful place, but very dear'.

Dorothy's mouth must have watered for Ratzeburg, actually on an island in the lake, seven and a half miles long. Coleridge had been enchanted by it. The lake, or rather two lakes joined by a little bridge, had winding shores with perpetually varying views and was fringed by magnificent groves. But to live—as to learn the language one must—*en pension*, in a family, was prohibitive; in English money sixty pounds a year each, and this excluding laundry, wine or tea. 'The cheapness of Germany was a Hum.' And they were all, he wrote, 'in a state of doubt and oscillation as to whether we should proceed to Weimar', but then were frightened at the expenses of travelling. In the end he could not resist, and could just afford, Ratzeburg. For the Wordsworths it was simply not on the cards. Cottle had paid William only ten of the thirty pounds owed him for his share of *Lyrical Ballads*, and to come at all they had borrowed from the Wedgwoods. 'Wordsworth & his sister have determined to travel on into Saxony to seek cheaper places', Coleridge wrote on 28 September to Poole, adding, 'God knows whether he will succeed'.

On the 30th he and Chester left. And on 3 October Dorothy for the second time embarked on a journey which, thanks to German roads and transport, made her again violently ill. It took them two days and sleepless nights of travel to reach Brunswick, 'an old, silent, dull-looking place'. Where should they go from here? A diligence left for Goslar at eight in the morning. Where might Goslar be? At the foot of the Harz Mountains. Their hearts must have leapt at the word 'mountains'. And Dorothy sounds more cheerful the next morning, when William 'went in search of a baker's shop' and 'brought me his pockets stuffed full of apples . . . and some excellent bread. Upon these I breakfasted and carried Kubla [a lovingly christened jug or mug, not the poem] to a fountain . . . and drank some excellent water. It was on Saturday the 6th of October when we arrived at Goslar [26 miles] . . . between 5 and 6 in the evening.'

What at this point, unhappily, did drop out of reach and out of cognizance was Dorothy's Journal. And by 8 November Coleridge had no word from them 'to my great Anxiety & inexpressible Astonishment. Where they are, or why they are silent, I cannot even guess'. Within a week of this, however, he had heard; and William's excuse—a hatred of letter-writing—would not now prevent Coleridge hearing from them, 'as often as letters can go back & forward in a country where 50 miles in a day and a night is *expeditious* Travelling'; one of his, Dorothy said, took eleven days.

Always admitting that Dorothy's short-lived Hamburgh Journal *is* impersonal, and that it is slightly unfair to set against this the tone of Coleridge's, written in letter form to Sara and Poole, one cannot help being struck by his note of exuberance—and bear in mind that William did not find his brush with the baker tragi-comic as Coleridge would have done. There was nothing, as an impoverished northerner, funny in being cheated, and the cheapness of Germany *was* a Hum. The Wordsworths' predicament was a very real one; and if they delayed in writing to Coleridge from Goslar, we have seen Coleridge's power to wound and be unaware of this. Had he, unlike them, arriving in Hamburg elated by the voyage, his mood at the opposite pole from William's, in his enchantment with Ratzeburg seemed a shade insensitive, heartless in the manner of his departure?

This would not be uncharacteristic. There is also the fact that they had vainly tried to live in a family, and instead been obliged merely to go into lodgings. But that Goslar, 'once the residence of Emperors', was now as William wrote, exclusively that of 'Grocers and Linen-drapers, who are, I say it with . . . sorrow, a wretched race; the flesh, blood, and bone of their minds being . . . knavery and low falsehood', was a lesson that could not be learnt without trial. Their silence, in short, could at first have been simply the fruit of a debate, renewed each day, whether to stay or move— and then of a more unexpected development. In the letter which Coleridge at last received, Dorothy, as Coleridge reported to Poole, 'says "William works hard, but not very much at the German" — this is strange'.

It was both as strange and as little strange as to find Coleridge—while Dorothy, on deck at the mouth of the Elbe, 'drank tea . . . by the light of the moon' — writing to Sara and asking the question only lovers ask: 'Over what place does the Moon hang to your eye, my dearest Sara? To me it hangs over the left bank of the Elbe . . .' His letters to Sara are, initially, disconcertingly loving. True his marriage is not yet on the rocks. But once the disorientating effects of travel wear off, once, as he swiftly does, he has mastered German, once he is in his element his homesickness is transformed into a callousness hard to credit in him.

'Coleridge is in a very different world', Dorothy wrote, 'from what we stir in, he is all in high life, among Barons counts and countesses.' In Goslar, with its grocers, the Wordsworths' situation was different indeed. Dorothy, with a dictionary, did 'work . . . at the German'. But William was restless and less adaptable. His sense of disorientation did not diminish but grew—to find its natural, only possible, outlet. So that already by 14 December, Dorothy, writing jointly with William to Coleridge, copying out long passages, could speak of these as selected 'from the mass of what William has written'.

What was selected? The famous school-time skating (thirty lines), the no less well-known stealing of the boat and the terror inspired by the cliff (forty-nine lines). 'I will now transcribe a nutting scene (I think I shall not tire you). It is like the rest, laid in the North of England, whither wherever we finally settle you must come to us. . . .' They would explore that romantic country together; and she 'would once more follow at your heels, and hear your dear voices again'.

It is Dorothy's own voice— 'I think I shall not tire you' —that suddenly addresses us from Goslar, gentle, unaffectedly open; the voice of the alert, unobtrusive figure that darts along always behind the other two and whose concept of happiness it is to walk so—free to look while listening to the oddly mingled strains of the two voices dearest to her.

Fittingly her voice now. For the lines she has been copying are not from what she would know as 'The Poem to Coleridge'. They belong to the 'Two-part' *Prelude*, a work which, though recently published, is still known largely only to scholars. It is, however, no accident that the lines copied for Coleridge are among those we know best from the longer poem: an undiluted rendering of childhood, the poet without the prophet, youth without moral age, William without Coleridge—with Dorothy. Not only did she make it possible. In this poem, miraculously pieced together often from the stubs of torn-out pages (and from these we learn the fate of Dorothy's Hamburgh Journal), that she is the one addressed is not in doubt—the 'dearest maiden on whose lap I rest / My head', and who, in lines left incomplete, is not to 'deem . . . these . . . idle sympathies'.

William's tone in the letter enclosing Dorothy's extracts perhaps better than anything explains the silence Coleridge found inexplicable. The passages being sent him are 'a few descriptions'; Coleridge is to read them 'at your leisure', i.e., they are no great matter. Dorothy will also copy for him 'two or three little Rhyme poems which I hope will amuse you. As I have had no books I have been obliged', he adds by way of excuse, 'to write in self-defence'. An excuse for what he is sending *is* needed—to Coleridge; as is plain when the poem becomes one addressed to him, and not to the 'gentle maiden':

> Need I dread from thee
> Harsh judgements if I am so loth to quit
> Those recollected hours that have the charm
> Of visionary things . . .

The answer is from Coleridge, yes, he must dread it. Only the great philosophical poem will do. Instead, he is writing now on and of home ground—the country which he shares with Dorothy. For this, William's country and that of Windy Brow, is as his native land her adopted one, only different in being for her no recollected thing but ever on hand, ever ready to flame. And so it is that in Goslar, in a room with a big black stove, but in fact in a world of their own creating, Dorothy, at his elbow, allows him to write as himself—and not as Coleridge wishes him to be. Allows him to write short poems, if such is his inclination—a lapse of which Coleridge can never approve—which, if short, he cannot but think are good, and are therefore sent to the maestro, but only as 'little Rhyme poems' which may amuse him.

It is doubtful if Coleridge split his sides over the little rhyme poems, among the most perfect lyrics in the language. His reaction to only one of the five is known, 'A slumber did my spirit seal'; this, 'a most sublime Epitaph', he copied and sent to Poole, adding, 'whether it had any reality,

I cannot say. Most probably, in some gloomier moment he [Wordsworth] had fancied the moment in which his Sister might die'.

This is not a shot in the dark since he had already seen the poem 'Strange fits of passion have I known', of which Dorothy, copying for him, wrote, 'The next poem is a favorite of mine—i.e. of me Dorothy'. The poem, as Coleridge who knew the approach to Racedown would realize, exactly described William's returning there, at nightfall to Dorothy; and ends (in its published form):

> My horse moved on; hoof after hoof
> He raised, and never stopped:
> When down behind the cottage roof,
> At once, the bright moon dropped.
>
> What fond and wayward thoughts will slide
> Into a lover's head!
> 'O mercy!' to myself I cried,
> 'If Lucy should be dead!'

Are we then to take it that Dorothy was Lucy, this whole cycle of love poems addressed to her? One, however, is not a love poem, but about a child who perished in the snow; not Dorothy, who herself supplied the tale from her Halifax memories, but one who yet is christened 'Lucy Gray'. Dorothy did not live and die 'beside the springs of Dove'. And why, if Dorothy, is she always dead?

Poems are complex growths, one will inspire another, and Wordsworth melted such strange matter together, as when he christened the woman in *The Thorn* 'Martha Ray'—the murdered actress mistress of Montagu's father. (Basil is Edward; Dorothy, when it suits, Emmeline or Emma, and place names are recklessly transposed.) A more promising line to pursue may be a cancelled stanza, one which, in the letter to Coleridge, followed 'If Lucy should be dead!'

> I told her this; her laughter light
> Is ringing in my ears
> And when I think upon that night
> My eyes are dim with tears.

The cycle could have been touched off by one who did die young, Mary's sister, Peggy Hutchinson. 'I travelled among unknown men', 'She dwelt among the untrodden ways', the rejected stanza of Dorothy's favourite poem—with all these it would fit, always allowing for poetic licence: not merely that the Tees is not the Dove (though there is, in fact, a stream near Sockburn named the Dove, and the ways round Sockburn are nothing if not 'untrodden') but that William was at Penrith lightly in love with both sisters, Peggy as well as Mary. And that Coleridge did, perhaps, put his finger on it. There is no doubt where William's deepest love lay.

And, one more theory: that in killing off Lucy he was symbolically killing off an incestuous passion.

One thing is certain—that Annette has been killed off, or more appropriately, her ghost laid. French, townbred, she could never be Lucy; and, William might safely feel, would cherish now no hankering for the role.

Coleridge, meanwhile, was indeed in a very different world—where they danced, in his eyes, 'a most infamous dance called the Walzen', in which the couples 'embrace . . . arms round waists and knees almost touching, and then whirl round and round . . . to lascivious music'! He was, in fact, working as no one would ever believe that he did work— though it has been said that four years at Göttingen whither he was to proceed and excel, would, with his powers of absorption, have made him the most learned man in the world.

But Dorothy knew only, it seems, that he was 'all in high life'; and learning, which might surely have pleased her, to skate. Her voice, as, it seems to me, happens in the case only of Coleridge, comes over, at times, as less gentle than tart:

> You speak in raptures of the pleasures of skaiting—it must be a delightful exercise, and in the North of England amongst the mountains whither we wish to decoy you, you might enjoy it with every . . . advantage. A race with William upon his native lakes would leave to the heart and the imagination something more . . . valuable than the gay sight of Ladies and countesses whirling along the lake of Ratzeberg.

By 14 December she is writing still from Goslar, when they had planned to leave by the end of November. But—and it may be that this explains her tone—the coldest winter for half a century has trapped them. The cold on Christmas day, she wrote, 'was so excessive that when we left the room where we sit [with the stove] we were obliged to wrap ourselves up in great coats . . . though we only went into the next room . . . for a few minutes'. Such was the first snowfall that 'the whole town was in commotion, traineaus [sledges] everywhere!' 'No wonder then', as she said, 'that we were afraid of travelling all night in an open cart!' And the diligence would be little warmer, being German little better if not worse, since it followed a circuitous route, adding in thirty-five miles twenty more of needless expense and nausea. They walk, however, every day, suitably attired, 'at least an hour . . . often much more. William has a green gown, lined . . . with Fox's skin, and I wrap myself up in furs that defy the cold.'

As far as learning German went, they were confined to the household— by William's 'unseeking manners', Coleridge thinks. And then, as he wrote to William, 'You have two things against you; your not loving smoke, and your sister'; 'Sister here', he explains to Sara, being 'only a name for Mistress [Goslar, it seems, has something in common with Stowey]. Still however *male* acquaintance he might have had—& had I

been in Goslar, I *would* have had them—but W., God love him! seems to
have lost his spirits & almost his inclination for it.'

Perhaps W. has. But if Coleridge, as on the packet, could briefly have
amused himself in Goslar, it is doubtful if he would have continued to seek
out its Grocers and Linen-drapers much more assiduously than William
did. As for the latter's inclinations, these would seem to have been
abnormally normal, to judge from a letter: 'We should be perfectly
contented if we could find a house where there were . . . young people
some of whom might perhaps be always at leisure to converse'. The nigger
is in another part of the woodpile: they 'are every hour more convinced'
they cannot afford to enter 'high or even literary german society . . . but
should both be highly delighted to be chattering and chatter'd to, through
the whole day'.

As it is, he and Dorothy have only 'one dear and kind creature . . . so
deaf that we could only play . . . games of cross-purposes', who 'likewise
labours under . . . the loss of teeth, so that what with . . . bad hearing, and
bad utterance you will imagine we have had very pretty dialogues'. So far
from William, as Coleridge claims, having 'lost his spirits', these seem in
the circumstances in miraculous shape; the more so when one considers
that writing 'in self-defence' can be resorted to only in small doses. He
'should have written five times as much' had he not, he wrote, been
'prevented by an uneasiness at my stomach and side, and a dull pain
about my heart'. This, brought on by writing, 'renders writing unpleasant', and would always make Dorothy's role an anxious one. So that
if we ask how she herself filled the days at Goslar, the answer is in the
main by filling his, relieving him where she could, writing his letters for
him. Cribbed and confined by the cold to the room with the stove, with
William 'consumed', as he said, 'by thinking and feeling'—'his mind is
always active; indeed too much so', Dorothy confirmed—she must know
when, and when not, to suggest a walk. But the ramparts of Goslar could
not replace being free to range the hills, the vital outlet of physical
exertion. And, his head in her lap, she could only strive to stroke away
thought, and, with it, the uneasiness in his side.

In all this she had her reward not only in being needed and supplying a
place no one else could fill. The man she cherished was still the man
described in her letters at Forncett, one who loved more than the common
run of men and in whom love took a form all too rare, that of an extreme
awareness of Dorothy's needs, her moods, her expression as she sat,
perhaps, writing to Mary. It is not only she who describes this. It is
there in poem after poem. Even one of the worst poems he wrote at Goslar,
predictably of things not distanced but present—a fly in the room—and
as bad as 'the coldest day of the century' could make it, contained, if she
needed any, its tribute to her:

> No brother, no mate has he near him—while I
> Can draw warmth from the cheek of my love

As blest and as glad, in this desolate gloom
As if green summer grass were the floor of my room
And woodbines were hanging above.

The words of one who is 'the most affectionate of brothers'—or the key to a tragedy in Dorothy's life?

Whatever the answer, their bags have been packed, unpacked, repacked for weeks; and Dorothy's happiness is not in doubt as, with these sent on ahead, they on 23 February made good their escape at last and 'were saluted by the song of a lark, a pair of larks, a sweet liquid and heavenly melody heard for the first time after so long'.

XII

In England Now

1799

ONE IS NOW, as they climbed among tiny waterfalls alias 'kittenracts' (since as William says they are to cataracts what a kitten is to a full-grown tiger) brought up against the map—and an odd fact: that they did not head straight for Göttingen, where Coleridge had been for a fortnight, as the crow flies some thirty miles from Goslar. Instead, there were letters, *poste restante*, from him at Nordhausen, south-east of Göttingen and twice as far, which they had reached in four, if not three, days. And Dorothy did not scruple to write back that she 'burst open the seals and could almost have kissed them in the presence of the post-master'. William, however, wrote that they 'think of staying here two or three days', and, weather permitting, are then 'resolved . . . to saunter about for a fortnight or three weeks at the end of which time you may be prepared to see us in Göttingen. I will not say to tarry long there for I do not think it would suit our plan, but to have the pleasure of seeing and conversing with you . . .'

At Ratzeburg, briefly laid up with a stye, out of the social whirl, and unable to read or write anything down, Coleridge had composed some hexameters. Such fragments as he remembered he sent to Goslar, as metrical experiments, but also for 'the truth of the sentiment':

William, my head and my heart! dear Poet that feelest and thinkest!
Dorothy, eager of soul, my most affectionate sister!
.   .   .   .   .

O! what a life is the eye! What a fine and inscrutable essence!
.   .   .   .   .

Sure, it has thoughts of its own, and to see is only a language.

There was a great deal more, which I have omitted, and a great deal more which Coleridge had forgotten. But the last lines he wrote he remembered:

William my head and my heart! dear William and dear Dorothea!
You have all in each other; but I am lonely, and want you!

William's German, was, he owned, 'as dust in the balance', but Coleridge's, with 'a hideous pronunciation', was he claimed so fluent 'that it must be a torture for a German to be in my company'. He was now, at

Göttingen, laying his hands at last on philosophy (as well as 'the Gothic and Theotiscan languages') and where the professors pay him 'the most *flattering* attention'—no wonder; never can they have had such a pupil. 'Dear William, my head and my heart! . . . I am lonely and want you', could hardly here apply in the same way.

But on Dorothy and William's side how explain the delay? By the fact that Göttingen was, according to Coleridge, 'a most emphatically ugly Town in a plain surrounded by naked Hills, that are neither high nor interesting'? Was a town at all? That on getting out of Goslar, Dorothy found 'the brilliant green of the earth-moss . . . made our eyes ache after the snow'? That both needed a blood transfusion—of green? Perhaps. And perhaps because William, who walking through the lichened pine trees wrote yet another little rhyme poem—'Three years she grew in sun and shower'—felt himself still in the grip of an afflatus the fruits of which Coleridge could never approve.

Their reply from Nordhausen was loving and gay, however:

We intend to import into England a new invention for washing. Among other advantages which our patent will set forth we shall . . . insist upon the immense saving which must result from our discovery which will render only one washing bason necessary for the largest family in the kingdom. We dare not trust this communication to a letter, but you shall be a partner, Chester likewise. Adieu. God bless you, Dorothy's best and kindest love. We shall soon be with you.

This joint epistle was to be Dorothy's last from Germany, or the last that survives. We have only Coleridge to go by, but the day she spent at Göttingen would seem to have been a fiasco for reasons illumined by Sara's pathetic letter, written to Poole from Bristol on 11 February.

Oh! my dear Mr Poole, I have lost my dear dear child! at one o'clock on Sunday Morning a violent convulsive fit put an end to his painful existance . . . I wish I had not seen it, for I am sure it will never leave my memory; sweet babe! what will thy Father feel when he shall hear of thy sufferings and death! I am perfectly aware of everything you have said on the subject in your letter; I shall not yet write to Coleridge, and when I do—I will pass over all disagreeable subjects with the greatest care, for I well know their violent effect on him—but I account myself most unfortunate in being at a distance from him at this time, wanting his consolation as I do, and feeling my griefs almost too much to support with fortitude . . . Southey has undertaken the business of my babe's interment and in a few days we shall remove to his house at Westbury which I shall be rejoiced to do for this house at present is quite hateful to me . . . I suppose you will have received from Coleridge the promised letter for me. I long for it—for I am very miserable!!!

Coleridge was so far considered that the news was broken to him only around 5 or 6 April. By this time, when he had 'Sara's lively account of the miseries which herself and the infant had undergone, all was over & well —there was nothing to *think* of . . . and I was made to suffer it over again . . . I cannot truly say that I grieve—I am perplexed—I am sad—and . . . a very trifle would make me weep; but for the death of the Baby I have *not* wept'. This last is honest and understandable; he cannot, absent, grieve for the death of an infant he scarcely knows. But by 8 April he is able to write to Poole of housing at Stowey, that, 'with regard to myself I am very busy, very busy indeed'; to elaborate on this, not just with no mention of Berkeley—this again would be understandable—but no mention of Sara, no thought, it seems, of her, no trace of identification with her sufferings. True, he writes to Sara herself on the same day, but not to pour out support and tenderness, a sermon instead which might have graced a Unitarian pulpit, much of which must have been above her head—and cold comfort, ending as it does: 'We are well my dear Sara—I hope to be home at the end of ten or eleven weeks'.

It is even possible to understand his need to complete his work, that he felt and wrapped up his guilt in a web of words. But already one feels an unreality born of complexity, which, if it does not reflect, anticipates the fatal effects of opium. A further letter from Sara imploring his early return unhappily exactly coincided with the Wordsworths' reaching Göttingen. It is from his exasperated reply to 'My dear Sara', that on 23 April we learn of their visit:

'Surely', he opens, 'it is unnecessary for me to say, how infinitely I languish to be in my native Country . . . and had I followed my impulses I should have packed up & gone with Wordsworth & his Sister, who passed thro', & only passed thro' . . . two or three days ago. If they burn with such impatience to return to their native Country, they who are all to each other, what must I feel . . . ?'

By 6 May, bearing in mind that he is writing to Poole, who would always feel Wordsworth as a threat, we learn the rest of what little more can be known of the day Dorothy spent in Göttingen. For that it was only a day Coleridge testifies, and that he 'walked with them 5 english miles'. 'They', Dorothy, too, it would seem, 'were melancholy & hypp'd'. 'W.', twice in the same letter, was

. . . affected to tears at the thought of not being near me, wished me of course to live in the North . . . I told him plainly, that *you* had been the man in whom *first* . . . and . . . alone, I had felt an *anchor*! . . . My Resolve is fixed, *not to leave you till you leave me* . . . & I think it highly probable, that where I live, there he will live . . . My many weaknesses are of some advantage to me; they unite me more with . . . my fellow-beings—but dear Wordsworth appears to me to have hurtfully segregated & isolated his Being. Doubtless, his delights are more deep and sublime; but he has likewise more hours, that prey on his flesh & blood.

There is no recognition of facts, the ugly fact of money, that one cannot borrow what one cannot repay, that isolation has been enforced, not desired, no sympathy for it stoically endured. As for the fruits of William's 'hurtfully' isolating his being, clear these are entirely lost on him. If William and Dorothy were 'melancholy & hypp'd', the progenitor of these states seems obvious. And one can only be thankful for small mercies; that dreading the crossing from Hamburg as she must have done she had this time 'an excellent passage to England'.

That the scheme of their now living temporarily at Sockburn was Dorothy's there can be little doubt, or rather that it was strongly urged by Mary, become, since Jane Pollard's marriage, Dorothy's closest friend; but almost certainly still, in another sense, 'close'. Had she not been so, Dorothy could hardly have resorted with William to Sockburn at this juncture. 'Observe', William was to write of 1800 in 1805, 'this was . . . when I had no thoughts of marrying. . . .' Nor was this merely a question of means; Coleridge, who joined them at Sockburn in October, records that he 'did not then know Mary's and William's attachment'; that is, was not only not told of but scented none.

If then to Mary the Wordsworths' arrival was agitating, she was quite capable of concealing this, of hastening out of the front door to greet them, if more warmly, in much the same 'winning way' that would charm De Quincey, 'presenting her hand with so frank an air that all embarrassment . . . fled . . . before the native goodness of her manner'. De Quincey did not meet Mary until she was thirty-seven, when he described her as 'a tallish young woman' and 'believed her to be twenty-eight'. To be taken in those days as young at thirty was something of an achievement. But her 'exultant outside look of youth' did Mary well, still blooming for De Quincey in a skin which, reflecting her inner repose, took long to line. She can only at twenty-nine, have endorsed the rest of his portrait; the 'considerable obliquity of vision . . . much beyond that slight obliquity . . . often supposed an attractive foible in the countenance' which 'ought to have been displeasing . . . yet . . . was not'. Mary, in fact, furnished 'a remarkable proof' that 'a woman . . . generally pronounced very plain' may 'exercise all the . . . fascinations of beauty, through the mere compensatory charms of sweetness all but angelic, of simplicity the most entire . . .'. Such was the figure who greeted them, Dorothy's closest friend. As for Dorothy, after foreign lands, the endless travelling and haggling, William, writing to Kit, speaks for them both: 'We are right glad to find ourselves in England, for we have learnt to know its value.'

And nowhere, perhaps, would England be so felt as safe harbour at last as at Sockburn, among Hutchinsons; with their balance, their understatement, their wry salty humour; with the fields in May still dotted with ewes and lambs. But coming back from abroad to England is not all ewes and lambs. Letters that today lie in wait from solicitors and the bank were rolled in one in communications from Richard. Douglas, Montagu's friend, in whom William had invested, had absconded—with William's money—to the West Indies. Montagu was head over heels in debt, his desire to pay William taking the form of fury that John Pinney would not do so for him. Richard was threatening Montagu with gaol. Meanwhile there was their own debt of a hundred pounds to the Wedgwoods and no possible means of settling this. Cottle was going out of business, and had sold *Lyrical Ballads* to a London firm one had never heard of, Arch. Worry and trying to work had made William ill. And it must have needed all Mary's calm to keep Dorothy off the boil when she, like William, had read Southey's review of *Lyrical Ballads*—the bulk described as 'destitute of all merit'. Southey knew William had published only 'as it would help him to pudding'; and if he could not praise should not have reviewed them. Meanwhile, there were other reviews and William became convinced that the trouble was *The Ancient Mariner*. No one had a good word to say for it (or no one but Lamb, who, in Coleridge's lifetime remained, with De Quincey, almost its sole protagonist).

From one person—'astonished' by their six weeks' silence in Goslar—they had in two and a half months heard nothing. And Dorothy now applied to the rival camp: '. . . We are very anxious to hear from Coleridge —he promised to write to us from Göttingen, and though we have written twice we have heard nothing of him . . .' To this she added some strange humble pie: 'We are yet quite undetermined where we shall reside . . . If you hear of any place in your neighbourhood [Poole's] . . . likely to suit us we shall be much obliged to you if you will take the trouble of writing to us.'

What has become of their fixed determination to live in the North? Still more pertinently, it might be asked, why had the 'two-part' *Prelude*, addressed to Dorothy, become what she would know as 'the Poem to Coleridge'? Coleridge had seen the 'few descriptions' she had copied in Goslar, and presumably, taking these, too, for short poems, shown his lack of interest too clearly to see more. Since he did not, it seems, learn of the poem's existence till this October, it had not been discussed, even mentioned, in Göttingen.

The explanation would seem to be that a long poem did exist, that William was now confident of its value, and determined that Coleridge be made to recognize this. It was not what Coleridge clamoured for, the great philosophical work, but nevertheless embodied his own declared aim in *Lyrical Ballads*. The more, when one thinks of their differences, does it seem a mystery that 'the Concern' had ever come into being. For what could be more unlikely than close friendship between a man who believed that everything should be simple and one who knew that everything was complex?

Dorothy, perhaps, provides the best clue. If she did fall in love with Coleridge, she partly did so because there was great affinity—and no one, surely, was so fitted as she to understand what he meant by 'O! What a life is the eye!'—and partly because she did not understand him. Where

109

Coleridge ranged she could never follow—her bent was still less speculative than William's; though the probability is that she would have sought to follow had her love, in this form, not suffered an early check. William, on the other hand, she loved for the opposite reason—that she understood him absolutely.

Under William bent on simplicity in fact lay William complex, if not in Coleridge's metaphysical sense; but as he himself put it, 'having two natures in me, joy the one the other melancholy . . .' That this was the price was a lesson Coleridge had yet to learn, and he would drink of it deeper than Wordsworth did. Meanwhile, not for nothing did he tactlessly repeat to Poole what was still in Göttingen circles applicable. 'W. . . . is the only one whom in *all* things I feel my Superior'; and Poole will believe him when he says, 'I have few feelings more pleasurable than to find myself in intellectual Faculties an Inferior'. Wordsworth's intellect is too easily forgotten, because he did not think its place was poetry, and kept it out—perhaps, as for his contemporaries, too much at times for our modern cerebral tastes:

> Two voices are there, one is of the deep,
> And one is of an old half-witted sheep
> Which bleats articulate monotony,
> And, Wordsworth, both are thine.

To this late-Victorian parody Wordsworth would lay himself open. But Coleridge offers a salutary reminder that intellectually Wordsworth towered above his fellows, and that the condition is a lonely one.

Epitomized as was the simple life as led at Sockburn—but also spiced with the wit and intelligence of Jack from Stockton, of George and Sara farming at Bishop Middleham—one element, here lay its strength, was missing. Stress, if not actually laughed out of court, was conspicuously absent from the Hutchinson metabolism. Surrounded by people untroubled by creation, William felt proportionately cut off—and proportionately aware of the need for Coleridge. Here poor Mary could not compete with Dorothy, who—not only poetically vital to William—was herself impelled to capture the evanescent in words, and understood the difference implicit in doing so; the difference between the thing itself and the thing written. And more and more, as William's pain in his side grew worse and worse, understood that the only medicine was Coleridge.

And so, if necessary, they would abandon the North, but first make a bid for decoying Coleridge there. By the end of July he was back but otherwise engaged, thick—as Dorothy learnt with outrage—with Southey. But Coleridge could scarcely do less than be reconciled with a brother-in-law who had stepped into his own absent shoes at the time of Berkeley's death. And staying with Southey, he at least wrote letters—even two to Richard Wordsworth, who bothered him 'with ungentleman-like Importunacy' about 'a damned old Shirt', left behind by Dorothy at Stowey. This Coleridge had got, or rather failed to get, an acquaintance of Poole's, one Stutfield, to deliver. And to Poole he now wrote 'on the spur or . . . Sting of the moment' that he could almost wish some incubus would get into Stutfield's bed 'and blow with a bellows the Wind of *cold* colic against *his* Posteriors'. He writes also that he has heard from Wordsworth, 'he is ill—& seems not happy . . . he renounces Alfoxden altogether'. 'Renounces' seems only to mean in favour of Coleridge, who is himself 'very anxious to have it'. With Southey as an example in punctiliousness, in fact facing him across the desk, he also wrote on 10 September to William, 'I do entreat you to go on with *The Recluse* . . . for in my present [ever-present] mood I am wholly against . . . short poems.'

And then no sooner are he and Sara back at Stowey than Hartley has, or seems to have, the Itch. The place reeks of sulphur; Hartley, aged four, covered with brimstone, alone enjoys it: 'I be a Funny fellow / And my name is Brimstonello'; Coleridge and Sara don Mercurial Girdles, but Coleridge throws his off: 'I would rather have old Scratch himself'. Instead he has violent rheumatics. Then there is everything to be washed—sheets, blankets, clothes—and buried, *and* in pouring rain; and finally the house itself scoured: 'Our little Hovel is almost afloat—poor Sara tired off her legs', with no servant. 'And by way of a Clincher', he is 'almost certain that Hartley has not had the Itch'.

By 12 October, however, he has learnt of the long poem, the copying of which is now employing the greater part of both Mary's and Dorothy's time. He has learnt that it is dedicated to him; and the lure, combined with the horrors of Lime Street, works. On the pretext of tracing a box, still missing, of German books, he had already got himself out to Bristol, where Cottle, invited to Sockburn, now offered him the luxury of travelling north at his expense in a post-chaise. To Sara, 'tired off her legs', the Itch proved fatal. Coleridge never returned to Lime Street, and it was not till December that she finally learnt of his whereabouts.

For Dorothy matters at last moved fast. If for Mary the very thing she stood for, normality, had failed her and only made William restless not happy, she could at least savour the small triumph of seeing her charms palpably not lost upon his friend. A lively evening followed, triggered off by Cottle who, improving on the informal atmosphere, asked Mary, 'immediately after tea, on our arrival, "Pray what do you think of Mr Coleridge's first appearance?"' While Coleridge, digesting Mary and the Print of the Blackwall Ox, winced at hearing Dorothy called Dolly.

Next morning the three men left them, Cottle, his rheumatic legs swathed in bandages, astride Lily or, as he would insist on calling her, Violet. Despite Lily–Violet, Cottle, liking *confort cossu* and not liking the sound of what lay ahead, defaulted as early as at Greta Bridge. It was well that he did so. Having accomplished the journey, no corner of the Lakes was left unexplored.

They set off on 27 October and not till 8 November was a joint letter despatched to Dorothy. It was worth waiting for. John has been with them and Coleridge has been greatly taken with him—'he is one of you; a man who hath solitary usings of his own Intellect, deep in feeling, with a subtle Tact, a swift instinct of Truth & Beauty. He interests me much'. Nor, satisfactorily, could he express his delight in 'scenery absolutely new to me'. This was not all. John had come from Newbiggin, where he had been for the funeral of Uncle Kit; and Dorothy had been left a hundred pounds. 'Nobody else is named in his Will', William wrote bitterly, but irrationally on his own behalf. This, however, was still not the main meat of the letter. 'Coleridge enchanted with Grasmere and Rydal', was in particular 'struck with Grasmere and its neighbourhood and I have much to say to you, you will think my plan a mad one, but I have thought of building a house there by the Lakeside'. John would give forty pounds to buy the ground, 'and for £250' William is confident he 'could build one as good as we can wish . . . There is a small house at Grasmere empty which perhaps we may take . . . but of this we will speak . . . I shall write again . . .'

XIII

A Passion for the Particular

1799–1800

MAY 14TH, 1800. Wm and John set off into Yorkshire after dinner at ½ past 2 o'clock, cold pork in their pockets. I left them at the turning of the Low-wood bay under the trees. My heart was so full that I could hardly speak to W. when I gave him a farewell kiss. I sate a long time upon a stone at the margin of the lake, and after a flood of tears my heart was easier . . . I walked as long as I could amongst the stones of the shore. The wood rich in flowers. A beautiful yellow, palish yellow flower, that looked thick round and double, and smelt very sweet—I supposed it was a ranunculus—Crowfoot, the grassy-leaved Rabbit-toothed white flower, strawberries, geranium—scentless violet . . . the crab coming out as a low shrub. Met a blind man, driving a very large beautiful Bull and a cow—he walked with two sticks. Came home by Clappersgate. The valley very green, many sweet views up to Rydale head when I could juggle away the fine houses; but they disturbed me even more than when I have been happier . . . I resolved to write a journal of the time till W. and J. return, and I set about keeping my resolve because I will not quarrel with myself, and beause I shall give Wm Pleasure by it when he comes home again . . . Arrived at home with a bad head-ach, set some slips of privett . . . had a fire—my face now flame-coloured. It is nine o'clock. I shall soon go to bed. A young woman begged at the door—she had come from Manchester on Sunday morn with two shillings and a slip of paper which she supposed a Bank note—it was a cheat. She had buried her husband and three children within a year and a half—all in one grave—burying very dear . . . 20 shillings paid for as much ground as will bury a man . . . Oh! that I had a letter from William!

She is writing not in the house which William had thought of building—for where should they raise £250? the plan was indeed a mad one—but in 'the small house at Grasmere empty which', he had written, 'perhaps we may take'.

It was not, however, Dove Cottage. Had you enquired for this from Dorothy, she would have said she did not know it; it could not be near by, since she herself lived there at Town-End. Nor was this the name of her house, she headed her letters 'Grasmere'. Dorothy, in fact, lived in a pub —or what had once been one, the Dove and Olive Branch; shedding its name with its function, it had never acquired another since, in a few cottages outside the village proper, it needed none.

What it needed, all it needed she had, to William's amusement, instantly decided, to be perfect was 'a seat with a summer shed on the highest platform in this our little domestic slip of mountain. The spot commands a view . . . of . . . two thirds of the vale'. Though she could, as it was, look from the house straight across the fields and watch the moon shining on the lake and on Silver How, the fell beyond, with nothing to intervene but their yew tree and the roof of the Ashburners' cottage.

William had moved fast, so fast that despite her impatience to see him she had not, in November 1799, been at Sockburn when he returned, but away on a jaunt with Sara at Bishop Middleham. 'I was sadly disappointed in not finding Dorothy,' William sat writing to Coleridge on Christmas Eve. 'Mary was a solitary housekeeper and overjoyed to see me.' *Over*joyed is indeed the word; for though Mary must have rejoiced in the timing, it seems too much to hope that William concealed his disappointment. And if Dorothy could not wait to see the cottage that William described, trying to play down the pretty latticed windows and stress its limitations, he, too, clearly could not wait to leave—to escape with Dorothy from routine and regular meals to the life and land of the imagination.

Their joint elation speaks for itself as early as on the journey, from the moment when, at sunset in Wensleydale—William parting from Lily-Violet and Dorothy from her 'double horse' shared with 'that good creature, George'—they took to the road, on foot and alone at last. The leitmotif from now on was happiness, not haste. With 'twenty one miles to perform in a short winter's day' and snow threatening, they constantly 'turned aside' for waterfalls which they left 'with reluctance but highly exhilarated'. The wonder is that they ever reached Town-End. But they did—in a post-chaise from Kendal, presumably laden with some of the furnishings bought in a hectic day's shopping out of Dorothy's money from Uncle Kit.

An old woman, Molly Fisher, who lived across the road and had kept a fire going in the house for a fortnight, affords an as always tantalizing glimpse of Dorothy on her entry into the gilded cottage; in the wainscotted room, already dark in the late cold afternoon, pausing to warm herself before the fire which Molly, typically, had let get low. 'It was a miserable dark chimney', Dorothy recalled, 'with a handful of reddish cinders in it.' Old Molly was to remember Dorothy. 'Aye,' she would say, 'I mun never forget t'laal striped gown and t'laal straw bonnet as ye stood here.'

Not surprisingly they have both, wrote William on Christmas Eve, caught 'troublesome colds in our almost empty house'. On top of this, 'D.

is now sitting beside me racked with the tooth-ache . . . a grievous misfortune as she has so much work for her needle among the bedcurtains etc. that she is absolutely buried in it'. They have also, of necessity, lit fires in every room, and been for two days buried in smoke. Here an ominous note makes its first brief appearance, that of the famous Wordsworth smoking chimneys—famous in that no chimneys have so smoked before or since, none surely caused such human havoc. For the present, however, the poltergeist is confined to William's bedroom; from the rest he expects only '*puffs* of *inconvenience*'.

Not only were there bed- but also window-curtains, not only sheets (always made not bought), 'We have been overhead in confusion, painting the rooms,' wrote William, 'mending the doors and heaven knows what!' William's 'we' must here be taken with a grain of salt. He was no sort of hand at mending doors, and the extent of his contribution almost certainly consisted in digesting the state of being overhead in confusion. '. . . a small low unceilinged room I have papered with newspapers', Dorothy wrote, describing the house to Jane Marshall. But it is William who, after only 'four days in our new abode', on Christmas Eve gives the game away: 'The weather since our arrival has been a keen frost'; he has been anxiously watching the ice on the lake and does not intend to be caught unprepared, has 'procured a pair of skates', and 'tomorrow'—with the ice on Rydal 'clear as polished steel'—'mean to give my body to the wind'.

Meanwhile, there were other things still than walls and curtains: 'as to the Tragedy and Peter Bell,' William wrote to Coleridge, 'D. will do all in her power to put them forward'. This appalling fate she seems to have been spared. But in four days 'overhead in confusion' she has somehow already provided what no other woman, surely, would or could— conditions for William to write. To embark on a poem about which his one fear is it may be too long, but which he hopes to enclose in his next letter! They are 'looking for John every day'; though 'it will be a pity, if he should come, that D. is so much engaged, she has scarcely been out'.

In this he was wrong. If anyone was what Dorothy needed now it was John, handy as only sailors are; who seemed to see at once why the door would not shut, and as if he should not rest until it did. He did not seem to like being talked to while he worked, nor called her when the thing was done; but only when she found it for herself up and closed, came and opened it and—she could feel—took a pleasure in the way it swung. Though she soon learnt, too, that anything makeshift or slapdash could rouse an unexpected shortness of temper, depths of frustration, a degree of impotent rage that seemed, but were not, perhaps, inexplicable. All this, however—and it was much, since it meant the place being shipshape in no time and as she could never had made it—was the least of what she learnt. How blind they had been to what Coleridge had seen at once. But then how few people could know what John was—when he had twice approached the door of the cottage, been too shy to knock, returned to Robert Newton's inn and from there sent word that he was come. 'John', as William said, '. . . being accustomed to live with Men with whom he had little sympathy and who did not value or understand what he valued . . . lived . . . with the deepest part of his nature shut up within himself'; 'not a tenth part of his worth . . . his taste, Genius and intellectual merits was known to anybody but ourselves and Coleridge'.

Making his home now with Dorothy and William for nine months, 'he paced over this floor', Dorothy wrote, 'in pride . . . exulting . . . that his Father's Children had once again a home together'; planting the garden with shrubs, 'so that I daresay', Mary was to write, 'there is not one but when it was [afterwards] put in the ground dear John was not in the mind of the Planter'. Coleridge's name for John was 'the silent poet'. As William and Dorothy did their first exploring, it was John who 'was continually pointing out something which perhaps would have escaped our observation, for he had so fine an eye that no distinction was unnoticed by him'. Nor did the bond with Dorothy end here. 'Many a time', she wrote, 'has he called me out . . . to look at the moon or stars, or a cloudy sky, or this vale in the quiet moonlight—but the stars and the moon were his chief delight,—he made of them his companions . . . when . . . at sea'. His sense of subordination to William, too, had gone, matured into open loving admiration. Hating the sordid foreign ports at which shore leave might be had, it had long been his practice to stay on board and read. In future it would be William's poems that formed his favourite reading. And his goal was henceforward clear: ' "I will work for you", was his language, "and you shall attempt to do something for the world" '.

No wonder Dorothy utterly lost her heart to this new brother. Mary, perhaps, came near to losing hers. She arrived at the end of February for a stay of six weeks, 'during which John', she was to remember, 'was the first who led me to everything in the neighbourhood that I love'. Dorothy, too, remembered: 'John walked with her everywhere, and they were exceedingly attached . . .' John, not William. The sting and the palliative. But were they not perfectly matched—in silence even? Was not John *like* William, but also more kin to herself, one who did not (as Sara, her sister, would say) give himself 'a vast of plague' and pains in the side writing, with his mind no more on marriage than earning a living, a man who made her no sign—was it not John in William for whom she had been all these years waiting? John thought it was; and could see in William no bar to making a bid for Mary, once financially in a position to do so, a position which now that he was to sail, and trade, as a Captain might be achieved in a single voyage.

Meanwhile Mary left, and Coleridge came from London. He had last seen Dorothy at Sockburn, whither he had returned a week ahead of William (a letter having caught up with him at Keswick, offering work on the *Morning Post* which, in debt to Wedgwood and Poole, he had no choice but to accept). Doubtless he then brought Dorothy William's second promised letter, and, doubtless full of its contents and burning questions, she had failed—would in any case have failed—to see anything odd in his delaying at Sockburn for a week. And the probability is that, knowing Hutchinson ways and Coleridge spirits, there was nothing to see, nothing of what Coleridge three years later read into the last night of his stay. That Mary's spell was still the one he felt most seems likely; and that in 1803 he remembered this. Copying and extending the entry recording his first meeting with her, Mary retains her place beside 'Asra',* 'curiosity of true love / respectfulness yet eager look of kindness—& when turned away to do anything . . . a relief to the strong feelings which sitting & vis à vis the respect due to a stranger made it necessary to repress and chasten.—O dear Mary [. . .] never [. . .]† shall I forget your manners'.

Not till 1803 did he record an incident of which, unlike his earlier meeting with Mary, he took at the time no note: 'Conundrums & Puns & Stories & Laughter—with Jack Hutchinson—stood up round the fire . . .' The rest is in Latin and translated reads: 'And pressed Sara's hand a long time behind her back, and then for the first time, love pricked me with its light arrow, poisoned, alas! and hopeless.' By 1803 much tragic water had flowed under the bridge; his marriage was in ruins, and his love affair with 'Asra' itself unhappy. The arrow flew in not in Dorothy's presence but in retrospect, poisoned and by 1803 hopeless.

The arrival now in April of Coleridge at Town-End could only for Dorothy be a gala occasion. And there can be little doubt that she showed this openly, reached up and threw her arms about his neck and—hanging as familiarly upon his arm as William's—proudly showed him over their little domain. And only just in time remembered the pike in the oven, which she had stuffed with particular care, and flew to look at this, then back upstairs to the living-room where she could hear shouts of laughter. Coleridge had come from Lamb's where, with Sara and Hartley away, he had been living for the past month. One could not keep up a quarrel with Lamb whose sympathies, it was natural, should have lain with the unstable Lloyd, but who had since learnt to know Lloyd better. As for Coleridge, '"The rogue has given me potions to make me love him"', and Lamb had been 'living in a continuous feast', a feast it was now Dorothy's turn to enjoy.

But she had other reasons for happiness in the visit. A second edition of *Lyrical Ballads* was called for; that the first had been sold out was largely due to Coleridge. 'Take no pains to contradict the story that the L.B. are entirely yours. Such a rumour is the best thing that can befall them,' William had written oddly, it would seem, on Christmas Eve, oddly in the light of his conviction that *The Ancient Mariner* had been the fly in the ointment. But S.T.C., journalist, had inside a month, proved a brilliant performer in the field; had between then and now written forty political leaders, besides drudging at Schiller's *Wallenstein*, a translation—'but for

* The anagram Coleridge made of Sara Hutchinson's name, and used to distinguish her from Sara Coleridge.
† 'Asra' obliterated. 'Dear' also could be read as 'Asra'.

5 pounds! Never, never, never again . . . Newspaper work is comparative ecstacy'. He had indeed, as he said, worked 'from I-rise till I-set'—and been offered half-shares in two papers, the *Morning Post* and the *Courier*, to the tune of two thousand pounds a year. This was close to what Sara supposed she had married. But were he to live in London, he 'should be dried up wholly'. Poole was doing all in his power to find him a house, had indeed found several, 'but that . . . which suits me does not suit my wife'. With Sara pregnant again, however, a house they must have, and one where a man with a family could be 'in quietness'.

But they—Dorothy was perhaps the one to stammer out what she had all this time been waiting to tell him—had found the very thing, a most beautiful place at Keswick, which looked as if it should go at a very low rent. And off they all tramped the twelve miles over Dunmail Raise; and Coleridge was, it seemed, instantly wooed and won by the house alone on its eminence, as grand as Sara could wish, with close below the for her all-vital town. While for him from the very windows, 'my god!—what a scene—!' not only two lakes (Keswick and Bassenthwaite) but 'a great Camp of . . . mountains . . . the most fantastic mountains that ever earthquake made in sport'. Should he live there 'so sublime . . . will be . . . my visual existence', 'I shall have a tendency to become a God'.

But if today one could wish, with Poole, he had never set eyes on this pleasure dome, he did not immediately commit himself. He had not asked the Wordsworths to house-hunt for him and he had asked Poole, Poole whom he had sworn never to leave, Poole who had waited in the wings when *The Watchman* failed and since come forward in every sort of crisis; Poole, who, unlike the Wordsworths was a friend to Sara, a lonely man to whom he was all in all.

For Dorothy much now hung upon the outcome, the more so since Coleridge had dropped his long obsession, and *The Recluse*—with the greater toll sustained work took of William—as such passed temporarily out of Dorothy's life. This despite the fact that only six months ago Coleridge had been 'wholly against . . . short poems'; '*The Recluse* . . . of nothing but *The Recluse* can I hear'. His change of heart can only be ascribed to Dorothy's fruits, to the walking tour taken in November, to the fact that 'in a world of scenery wholly new to me' he had recognized a new poetic truth—in William's world William's truth, fostered by Dorothy, her faith and intuitive sense of where this lay. At all events he was eager now to read and discuss poems regardless of length, a new *Lyrical Ballads*, to be brought out not anonymously, under the banner of his prestige, but under the name W. Wordsworth. On 4 May he left for Poole's, to house-hunt as far as Porlock and arrange for the printing of the poems in Bristol.

If Dorothy seems in all this to disappear from view, she is now about to step out of the shadows, to speak to us not indirectly, as in the Alfoxden Journal, but directly of her days in all their detail.

Dorothy, *c.* 1800. Silhouette by artist unknown

Above: Alfoxden House

Below: Racedown, Dorset

William Wordsworth by H. Edridge, 1805

Left: Sara Hutchinson (Asra) *c.* 1815. Silhouette by artist unknown

Below: Greta Hall, Keswick

Samuel Taylor Coleridge in 1795, by P. Vandyke

Left: Mary Wordsworth, watercolour on ivory by Margaret Gillies

Below: Rydal Mount

A page from Dorothy's Journal showing the entry for 16th November 1801

Dove Cottage, Grasmere, today

Meanwhile, there is Molly, who if Coleridge has christened her 'that drollery belonging to the cottage', Dorothy during these first few months found anything but droll. 'She was very ignorant, very foolish, and very difficult to teach so that I once almost despaired of her.' Why then had they ever engaged or kept her? 'Partly out of charity', Molly was bent on the job, desperate for a few pence she could call her own; but chiefly bent on escape from Agnes, her sister-in-law, who was as avaricious as she was clever.

Initially they had taken her because without Basil and in a cottage the size of a handkerchief, with no prospect of any income from Douglas or Montagu, they had decided to do without a servant. They will merely give Molly two shillings a week to come in for two or three hours a day to light fires, wash dishes, etc. When on Saturdays she scours, as when there are visitors and she is needed more, 'she will have her victuals'. For this they could have paid eighteen pence, but have added the sixpence, since 'the poor woman . . . is made happy by it'. That to employ anyone for two or three hours a day was then considered a breadline minimum is a reminder of all the things, inconceivable to us, which had then to be done in a frugal household. Among countless jobs Dorothy took for granted, and does not mention, there were all the candles to be made.

What they had not considered when taking Molly on was how seldom there would not be guests, that Dorothy's work was William—copying, acting as critic, watching his health, being always at his disposal. Molly had therefore somehow to be taught, if not to cook, at least to watch what was in the oven, and did at length learn to prepare and boil vegetables. Meanwhile William reports the results of her being consulted about the baking of a pepper cake: 'The oven must be hot, perfectly hot said Molly the experienced, so into a piping red-hot oven it went, and came out . . . black as a genuine child of the coal-hole', having 'died of a very common malady, bad advice'.

But at least Dorothy need only help to iron 'at the great washes about once in 5 weeks'; the weekly minimum-iron one Molly can manage, and 'this she does so quietly in a place apart from the house as makes it very comfortable'. That is, made Dorothy comfortable, since quiet was essential to William. Added to this she was cheerful, 'blithe as a Lark', and 'sleeps at home which is a great convenience'—not to say vital, if she was not to choose between sharing a bed with Dorothy, William, or 'Maister John'. If Dorothy almost despaired of her, one could do with more of Molly: 'Aye Mistress them 'ats Low laid would have been a proud creature could they but have [seen] where I is now fra what they thought mud be my doom'. For Hazlitt she was 'the woman who had never heard of the French Revolution ten years after it had happened'.

Molly, in fact, had risen higher than she could know, rocketed into the literary firmament as, on 14 May, Dorothy, alone and desolate, turned back at Low Wood Bay under the trees. In the three weeks ahead 'poor old Molly', Dorothy was to write, 'did but ill supply to me the place of our good and dear Peggy'. Heartless as it may sound, this was as well. Since she could not with Peggy have felt the same need to take the measures she did against what she rightly foresaw as the enemy.

She comes to us in a mood that is both as uncharacteristic as her situation, and characteristic. She has never before been thrown on herself as now: 'I felt myself very lonely; while I was within doors'. She is lonely, however, specifically indoors, and cannot contain her irritation when, returning from Ambleside late one night, she was accompanied by the postmistress: 'This was very kind, but God be thanked I want not society by a moonlight lake'.

Her first day alone was, needless to say, 'a coldish dull morning—hoed the first row of peas, weeded etc. etc., sat hard to mending till evening. The rain which had threatened all day came on just when I was going to walk'. But the following one she was off, noting that the woods have, in May, an 'autumnal variety and softness'. As she was starting out she had 'met a half crazy old man. He shewed me a pincushion and begged a pin, afterwards a halfpenny. He began in a kind of indistinct voice in this manner: "Mathew Jobson's lost a cow, Tom Nichol has two good horses strayed. Jim Jones's cow's brokken her horn etc"'. He quitted her at last for Aggy's (parsimonious Agnes), leaving Dorothy to go on her way, 'Oh! that we had a book of botany. All flowers now are gay and deliciously sweet'. Continuing round the lake under Loughrigg fell, she was kept amused by a pair of stonechats, 'Their restless voices' as, pursuing each other, they skimmed the water 'their shadows under them. . . . After dinner Aggy weeded onions and carrots. I helped for a little', and now, perhaps, learnt from Aggy that the crazy old man had 'persuaded her to give him some whey and let him boil some porridge'. Aggy 'declares he ate two quarts'. She then 'wrote to Mary Hutchinson—washed my head—worked. After tea went to Ambleside . . . Rydale was very beautiful with spear-shaped streaks of [an echo of William?] polished steel. No letters! . . . I returned by Clappersgate. Grasmere was very solemn in the last glimpse of twilight it calls home the heart to quietness'. Hers needed it. 'I had been very melancholy in my walk back. I had many of my saddest thoughts and I could not keep the tears within me. But when I came to Grasmere I felt that it did me good.' And she sat herself down to finish 'my letter to M.H. Ate hasty pudding, and went to bed'.

'Incessant rain from morning till night' kept her the next day a prisoner. But she 'Worked hard' (this will often mean copying), 'and read Midsummer Night's Dream, Ballads', and the coals came. But then she could stand it no longer; out she must go. And 'sauntered a little in the garden. The Skobby* sate quietly in its nest rocked by the winds, and [like Dorothy] beaten by the rain'.

Meanwhile it goes on, the long wait for the letter she has wanted since

* Chaffinch.

William left five days before. On Monday she 'bound carpets, mended old clothes. Read Timon of Athens. Dried linen. Molly weeded the turnips, John [Fisher] stuck the peas'. And then she made the mistake of walking in Easedale, one of their favourite haunts—and could not take it; 'the quietness and still seclusion of the valley', that for which they prized it, now 'producing the deepest melancholy. I forced myself from it'. And the next day went as usual to Ambleside. 'It was a sweet morning', so sweet there must be a letter; but no, there is none and she goes to bed with a headache.

When after four more days she at last had her reward, she records it for some reason joylessly. And goes to bed with this time 'a bad head-ache'. Is it that William has mentioned being troubled with 'the tooth-ach'? Or that letters are easily misconstrued: 'When you are writing to France say all that is affectionate to A. and all that is fatherly to C.' Does this suddenly seem a renewed threat? Or is it that John in Yorkshire is courting Mary; that whatever William may say, he will be sure some day to marry also? And then it rushes upon her, with as dreadful a certainty as if the wedding day were already fixed, that he *will* be sure to, that it will one day be so, that on that day she will lose him; will cease to be loved or needed and must somewhere live out her days in the desolate fashion she now does, alone.

But this is the very state she has sought to keep at bay, by setting herself the task of keeping a journal—that is, giving herself the means of giving pleasure to William and holding at bay what cannot be pleasing to him. And perhaps the very strength of his love prevents William divining the true source of her saddest thoughts: the degree to which insecurity has built itself into her being, how new and exquisite happiness is to her, and in proportion precarious—how with William away, unable to reassure her, the void to which she might return returns.

For why does he not write more often? Because not for a moment being able to conceive of life without her, he pictures her as by 1 June she is, lying on a warm evening 'upon the steep of Loughrigg my heart dissolved in what I saw', and 'not startled but re-called from my reverie by a noise as of a child paddling without shoes'. A lamb has come to examine her and Dorothy does not move. This is how William knows her and what he expects.

But by now one does not need to be told what is in the wind, and her journal is far from being all she has to show. Few days have passed when she has not been out with her basket, not only to dig up 'Lockety Goldings' (the Globe flower). She has been to Jenny Dockray's and 'got white and yellow lilies, periwinkle, etc., which I planted'; and then, on the Friday that she had gone to Ambleside—'forgetting that the post does not come till the evening. How was I grieved when I was so informed . . .—planted London Pride upon the well and many things on the Borders', and that same day got John Fisher to sod the wall so that they might sit upon it, a thing they could not do on upright flagstones. (This was the wall they had had put up between the house and the road, on which from now on Dorothy constantly 'sate making my shoes' or 'mending my shifts until I could see no longer'.) Finally from 'the Blind man' she had 'got such a load [of plants] I was obliged to leave my Basket in the Road and send Molly for it'. That she did send sixty-year-old Molly is a pictorial reminder of Dorothy's small stature and slight build.

In fact it is not, up till the last moment, final, though she will not 'go far from home, expecting my Brothers'; and planting lemon thyme by moonlight, 'lingered out of doors in the hope of hearing my Brothers tread'.

She does not know that William will come alone, ahead of John. But on 3 June there is 'no letter, no William'; and when on the evening of the 6th she does go to Ambleside it is as if in the hope that her absence will bring him—and again 'No William! I slackened my pace as I came near home fearing to hear that he was not come' and 'listened till after one o'clock to every barking dog'. That her revelation is wholly unconscious is clear. For the next day after going only as far as the lake to take 'up orchises etc. . . . I did not leave home in the expectation of Wm and John, and sitting at work till after 11 o'clock I heard a foot go to the front of the house, turn round, and open the gate. It was William—After our first joy was over, we got some tea. We did not go to bed till 4 o'clock . . . so he had an opportunity of seeing our improvements. The birds were singing, and all looked fresh, though not gay. There was a greyness on earth and sky. We did not rise till near 10 in the morning'.

There was much then to talk about. Montagu's friend, Douglas, had paid back William's money, including the interest. This was part of their slender capital. But the debt to the Wedgwoods must, and could only, be met by this. More important was Dorothy's news that Coleridge had failed round Stowey and definitely decided on Greta Hall. She had been in touch with Mr Jackson, the owner, about rent, but the house will not be ready till late July and Coleridge cannot wait so long. He has asked her to find lodgings in Ambleside. This she has so far failed to do, but they cannot afford to delay, since he talks of being upon them in ten days. William, meanwhile, has seized on her journal, but wishes to know more, every detail of her days during his absence; and then—as they go to Ambleside about the lodgings for Coleridge—she is reminded of something she did not put down and William is so much interested that at his particular wish she writes it out for him now on 10 June:

> On Tuesday, May 27th, a very tall woman, tall much beyond the measure of tall women, called at the door. She had on a very long brown cloak, and a very white cap without Bonnet—her face was excessively brown, but it had plainly once been fair. She led a little bare-footed child about 2 years old by the hand and said her husband who was a tinker was gone before with the other children. I gave her a piece of Bread. Afterwards on my road to Ambleside, beside the Bridge at

Rydale, I saw her husband sitting by the roadside, his two asses feeding beside him, and the two young children at play upon the grass. The man did not beg. I passed on and about ¼ of a mile further I saw two boys before me . . . one about 10 the other about 8 years old at play chasing a butterfly. They were wild figures, not very ragged, but without shoes and stockings; the hat of the elder was wreathed round with yellow flowers, the younger whose hat was only a rimless crown, had stuck it round with laurel leaves. They continued to play till I drew very near and then they addressed me with the Beggars' cant and the whining voice of sorrow. I said I served your mother this morning. (The Boys were so like the woman who had called at the door that I could not be mistaken.) O! says the elder, you could not serve my mother for she's dead, and my father's on at the next town—he's a potter. I persisted in my assertion and that I would give them nothing. Says the elder Come, let's away, and away they flew like lightning. They had however sauntered so long in their road that they did not reach Ambleside before me, and I saw them go up to Matthew Harrison's house with their wallet upon the elder's shoulder, and creeping with a Beggar's complaining foot. On my return through Ambleside I met in the street the mother driving her asses; in the two panniers of one of which were the two little children whom she was chiding and threatening with a wand which she used to drive on her asses, while the little things hung in wantonness over the Pannier's edge. The woman had told me in the morning that she was of Scotland, which her accent fully proved, but that she had lived (I think at Wigton), that they could not keep a house and so they travelled.

This entry gives us Dorothy's power to compress and capture essentials, and reminds one that, for her, few days passed without some such episode. This one is so vivid not only the scene but the words stick in the memory; they are, in fact, those that lodged themselves in William's, so that when he wished to use these for a poem he could not do so, 'for he could not escape from those very words'.

And perhaps it was as well that she waited to write it now in the mood restored to her by William's return. From now on the whole tone of the journal changes. We may hear of her being tired or unwell or the heat may give her a headache, but there will be no more melancholy; nor, it must be said, many pertinent facts. They boat, fish for and live on pike, plant spinach and kidney beans, Dorothy irons till dinner, sews till near dark, pulls peas, boils and picks yet more gooseberries. They walk to Brathay and meet 'near Skelleth a pretty little Boy' who 'was going to "late" a lock of meal* . . . When . . . asked . . . if he got enough to eat he looked surprized and said "Nay". He was 7 years old but seemed not more than 5'. There is 'a gloom almost terrible over Grasmere water and vale . . . No

* Beg a measure (dialect)

Coleridge whom we fully expected'. William has his tooth drawn and replaced. Then, ten days behind schedule, on 29 June, 'Mr and Mrs Coleridge and Hartley came. The day was very warm. We sailed to the foot of Loughrigg. They staid with us three weeks', and four days. 'On the Friday preceding their departure we drank tea at the island. The weather very delightful . . .' Can this be all?

Not quite all. With the weather still hotter, the 'house was a hot oven but yet we could not bake the pies'. The men bathe, but no woman can bathe without a bathing box; and she is 'obliged to lie down . . . from . . . heat and headach'. But 'the Evening excessively beautiful—a rich reflection of the moon . . . and from the Rays gap a huge rainbow pillar'.

She can, however, boat with the men in the cool of the evening and hear 'a strange sound in the Bainriggs wood . . . it *seemed* in the wood', but proved to be a raven very high '—it called out and the Dome of the sky seemed to echo the sound—it called again and again as it flew onwards, and the mountains gave back the sound, seeming as if from their centre a musical answering to the bird's hoarse voice'. Can and must, when Coleridge comes 'very hot', sit in the breeze and the shade by the lake altering William's poems for the new volume. She is now copying these, also planting honeysuckle, also nailing up the runner beans, which, scant as is their plot of ground, she has had the inspiration of growing all over the house itself. So that if we are to picture her cottage we must do so as comically smothered 'with green leaves and scarlet flowers'—and beans. These in her eyes, however, are 'exceedingly beautiful', and 'useful, since their produce is immense'.

By August, however, as she continues to nail up the scarlet beans, stuff the pike, pull peas and boil gooseberries—'N.B. 2lb of sugar in the first panful, 3 quarts all good measure—' we may feel that we know her not better but less well; or feel, at least, that we have here a poor exchange for 'Venus almost like another moon. Lost to us at Alfoxden long before she goes down the large white sea'.

And now, on 3 August, with William at Keswick with Coleridge she does not respond to his urgent request that she join them. John goes but she stays behind, ties up the Scarlet beans, helps Molly spread the linen, irons and sews. This has nothing to do with the heat, it is briefly rainy and cold. And finally William returns himself to fetch her. Even so, it takes him a day to decoy her from gooseberry jam, and cart her off for a week to Greta Hall. She does not explain her reluctance or her reasons for going— unless the first is self-explanatory: she cannot leave the gooseberries; if she does they will be wasted, and never before have they had enough to eat. Never before has she made a garden, planted for the future or planted to 'give Wm pleasure by it'. Neither at Racedown nor Alfoxden could she make the bed-curtains, herself sow peas and, entranced, watch these come up. Her prosaic entries, in short, are those of a bride. It is under three months since, in May, she started to keep a journal, and for close on one month she had no time to keep it. She has 'almost despaired' of Molly, must paper William's room, is making but has not finished the 'mattrass' for Keswick; and has, in fact, grown too many peas. These must still be picked to be given away. The heat by July has knocked her up. She is happy but whacked, and when not actually 'too much tired to walk', too tired to record her impressions while fresh in her mind. Even, and only, such facts as these can, supplemented, be extracted from her entries at this time. For the rest it is useless, or practically so, to apply at this stage to her journal for more than the faintest clue to what is going on.

It is not, however, for this that one does apply to her, but for what has always been her matter—a passion for the particular, that now includes a passion for the particulars of keeping house for William, of days too miraculous still to let slip by. But as Molly improves, as she herself masters the mysteries of gooseberry jam, she is free to write of what, too, she cannot let pass. There is no need to wax poetical, only to be precise: 'The moon shone like herrings in the water'.

XIV

O the mind, mind has mountains; cliffs of fall

Gerard Manley Hopkins, *Sonnet*

1800–1801

NEVERTHELESS IT BECOMES essential to know what is going on. And the answer is the first act of a tragedy. Though I cannot agree that the Wordsworths initiated this in now making unscrupulous use of Coleridge.

The Coleridges had been put up, somehow squeezed in and catered for, for three days short of a month at Town-End. They presumably slept in Dorothy's room, where 'the bed, though only a camp bed is large enough', Dorothy wrote, 'for two people', she herself sleeping in what Molly called 'Maister John's room', the cubby hole she had papered with newspapers, while John had the second bed in William's room. Not only this, Coleridge arrived with a cold, he said, 'caught from wet', which 'at Grasmere became rheumatic fever almost'; and for the first ten days was 'more unwell than I have ever been since I left school'.

Dorothy mentions none of this, nor explains the endless fishing. Coleridge, however, does: Wordsworth's 'health is such as to preclude all possibility of writing. . . .' In fact, so worried is he that, while himself still ill, he writes a full description of William's state to Dr Beddoes of the Pneumatic Institute in Bristol. But William will have no truck with Dr Beddoes: 'I saw his countenance darken, and all his hopes vanish; his *scepticism* concerning medicines!'

Coleridge recovered, he and Dorothy together shouldered the copying and tedious correspondence with the printers concerning the order, changed order and alteration of poems entailed by William's forthcoming publication. This work fell largely within a month which included—and explains—the visit Dorothy paid to Greta Hall. Even then it was far from being full-time, or left Coleridge plenty of time for mountaineering. Was this so much to ask of one's closest friend? If he had, and he had, commitments of his own, in Germany he had worked desperately hard, in London 'harder than I ever worked in my life'. He needed a rest and to do another man's work, however dull, is a rest-cure compared with doing one's own. For he knew that he was doing another man's work, and the work was largely William's; the few poems by him would be mentioned as those of a friend, but would, if he could finish the thing, include *Christabel* —and he 'tried & tried & nothing would come of it'.

But Christabel was a lady born and bred in the Quantocks, who declined so abruptly to leave her setting. Does William really want her? And—a little more stiff mountaineering will do her no harm—on 31 August he goes to find out, and finds Dorothy 'walking in the still clear moonshine in the garden'. They 'sate and chatted till ½ past three, W. in his dressing gown. Coleridge read us a part of Christabel'.

So quietly is it said, in a voice so little different from that which tells us she drank tea with the Simpsons, one may miss the extraordinariness of having a Coleridge drop off Helvellyn by moonlight into one's garden; still more easily forget that Jane Austen was now writing. Young women did not sit chatting till three, unchaperoned, with the men. They retired in a maidenly way to bed.

The next day it was William's turn to submit his poems to Coleridge, Dorothy walking with them by the lake. Despite the fact that the air had 'somewhat of an autumnal freshness', the men—Coleridge perhaps unwisely—bathed. After dinner, however, he found—as he only could—if not Dorothy's 'summer shed', a 'rock-seat' buried on their 'domestic slip of mountain'. They cleared away the brambles; 'Coleridge', Dorothy wrote, 'obliged to go to bed after tea'. Later she 'broiled him a mutton chop which he ate in bed' and, with William by now retired for the night, herself doubtless perched on the bed while Coleridge demolished this: 'I chatted with John and Coleridge till near twelve'.

In the morning the men went to fish at Stickle Tarn. Dorothy 'baked a pie etc for dinner'. It was the day of the fair and later she went to see it. 'My Brothers came home to dinner at 6 o'clock', a bohemian hour, and, combining two functions in one, 'drank Tea immediately after by candlelight. It was a lovely moonlight night. We talked much about a house on Helvellyn. The moonlight shone only upon the village it did not eclipse the village lights and the sound of dancing and merriment came along the still air. I walked with Coleridge and Wm up the Lane and by the Church, and then lingered with Coleridge in the garden. John and Wm were both gone to bed, and all the lights out'. Is it not, must her Newbiggin aunt think, a hopeless case?

To return to the Lady Christabel and the charge against the Wordsworths in the matter of this and *The Ancient Mariner*. On the strength, according to Coleridge, of dining with a parson and drinking so much wine it was all he could do 'to balance' himself 'on the hither Edge of Sobriety . . .', his 'verse making faculties returned'. He also said that no poem had 'cost him such labour pangs'. There was more than one reason why it should. On 14 September (as Dorothy made bread with a thumb still sore from a cut, and read Boswell, noting 'the pear trees a bright yellow, the apple trees green still') Sara late that night, too, gave birth, 'the child' being 'a very large one'. Despite this, she three days later 'dined & drank Tea *up* in the parlour'; and got her due for once: 'There's for you', Coleridge wrote. But then Derwent, the child, was taken violently ill and threatened to die. Between *Christabel* and the *Morning Post*, Coleridge perhaps almost wished it would, 'with my wife now sobbing and crying by the side of me', while 'the child hour after hour made a noise exactly like the creaking of a door which is being shut very slowly to prevent its creaking'. Not till 4 October did he reach Grasmere, 'very wet', Dorothy recorded. 'We talked till 12 o'clock—He had sate up all the night before writing Essays for the newspaper. His youngest child had been very ill. . . . Exceedingly delighted with the 2nd part of Christabel.' On a further reading, 'we had increasing pleasure'. The next day 'Coleridge . . . did not get off . . . After tea read The Pedlar. Determined not to print Christabel with the L B'.

What has happened? The poem as it stood was both too long and unfinished, 'was running up to 1300 lines', wrote Coleridge (by which he presumably meant promising to run, since only 675 exist), '—and was so much admired by Wordsworth that he thought it indelicate to print two Volumes with his name in which so much of another man's was included —and which was of more consequence . . . in direct opposition to the . . . purpose for which the *Lyrical Ballads* were published . . . We mean to publish the *Christabel*, therefore, with a long blank verse poem of Wordsworth's entitled *The Pedlar*'.

In later life, estranged from Wordsworth, Coleridge accused him of 'cold praise and effective discouragement of every attempt to roll on in a distinct current of my own'. The 'cold praise' may partly derive from this visit. On the day of the second reading 'Wm went to bed very ill after working after dinner', and was 'still in bed and very ill' when Dorothy and Coleridge got back at nine that night from Ambleside. But it hardly ranks as 'effective discouragement' that William the following March bought Coleridge out of a commission from Longman's—to the tune of thirty pounds, no small sum for the Wordsworth pocket—in order to let him finish *Christabel* and publish this with 'little Drawings engraved or cut in Wood'. 'I long to have the book in my hand,' William wrote in April to Poole, 'it will be such a beauty'.

Meanwhile Dorothy did not lie—why should she in her journal?— when she wrote, 'Exceedingly delighted with the 2nd part of Christabel', nor that they had the next morning 'increasing pleasure'. But that Coleridge was shattered by its rejection is not in doubt, and shattered far beyond Dorothy's comprehension. For if William had been critical and not all ecstasy, their function was to act for each other as critics. They were, as friends, brutally frank. And the truth must be faced: *Christabel* had not travelled well.

The fate of *The Ancient Mariner* is another matter. Coleridge had done much fresh work on this, improving it and removing the archaisms. It now went from the front to the back of the book, with a tactless note by William apologizing for its admitted defects.

But in a book by 'W. Wordsworth' the place of so long a poem by the 'friend' was hardly at the front. Rather does its inclusion at all seem odd— except as a reaffirmation of their old first pact and a gesture of William's indebtedness to Coleridge. This, it may still be argued, does not excuse his note and perhaps it was inexcusable. It may, however, seem less so taken with the motto under which he himself now chose to publish, *Quam nihil ad genium, Papiniane, tuum!* ('How absolutely *not* after your liking, O learned jurist!')

For William and Dorothy were not alone in failing to recognize the greatness of *The Ancient Mariner*. On the contrary, Lamb was its sole defender. Original work that breaks fresh ground is seldom understood. And if it is objected that the Wordsworths, if no one else, ought to have seen a great light, I would contend exactly the opposite. We all have tastes in reading that preclude others. This is not a crime nor even our fault, any more than it is our fault that we are not musicians or athletes. If this is the case of the ordinary man, still more is it that of the artist. The remarkable thing, surely, is not that Wordsworth now failed to appreciate an art so removed from his own, but that matters had ever been otherwise.

How had he ever got in tow with the author of *Kubla Khan*? What had 'Lucy' to do with pleasure domes? The answer must lie in parity—and disparity. Wordsworth's illnesses were, in fact, caused by stress; he lived racked by tension and self-doubt. And in Coleridge with his great critical powers, exuberant, volatile, found a better cure than Dr Beddoes. While Coleridge in Wordsworth found one who let pass none of his woollier flights, and who supplied his own curious need to worship.

The child of an old father he loved but who died when he was eight, Coleridge (dispatched to Christ's Hospital and left by his mother to spend the holidays there) had signally lacked the love from which self-confidence stems and vital to a sense of identity. If he were asked to justify an interest in the questions 'Where am I? What and for what am I?' he wrote, 'I would compare the human soul to a ship's crew cast on an unknown Island'. Coleridge lived on that unknown island wondering and marvelling, and felt it incumbent on him to know its laws, incumbent on him—and possible. How should the Wordsworths have realized how fragile was his confidence in himself? Were not his powers extraordinary, and his vitality likewise? How grasp it in a man without fear, himself a match for these mountains, who made their peaks his playground and came bounding down Helvellyn like a child? Was not a brilliant future only now opening before him? How could they have foreseen that by December he would be writing Wordsworth 'is a great, a true Poet—I am only a kind of Metaphysician'?

The Wordsworths were blind to the malady, but the malady lay in Coleridge. And had by two people been detected. 'Coleridge is on a visit to his God, Wordsworth', Lamb the shrewd had written the previous spring. To Poole Coleridge had written shortly before: 'You charge me with prostration in regard to Wordsworth . . .' By November, he was beginning himself to feel the ballast he had forfeited in Poole: 'We were well suited for each other—my animal Spirits corrected his inclination to melancholy; and there was something' in Poole 'so healthy and manly that . . . my

ideas & habits of thinking acquired day after day more of *substance &
reality*'.*

I have dealt at some length with this vexed issue because to kill off a
poet, and that poet Coleridge, is a heavy charge. Especially is it so in
Dorothy's case. What has become of 'that sympathy always ready and
always profound'? How, loving Coleridge as she did, could she have failed
to divine his true state? But how, herself placing William above all men,
could she foresee the dangers of Coleridge doing so? Moreover although
Coleridge 'has done nothing for the L.B.' (it was still hoped that he would
contribute some short poems) but instead is working hard for the *Morning
Post*, he continues to arrive, to have 'done nothing'. Despite this, they
'were very merry . . . In the evening Stoddart came . . . Wm read after
supper Ruth etc.—Coleridge Christabel'. It is difficult to see how, on the
strength of this, Dorothy could have detected the worm in the bud.

In the interval they have acquired far from welcome neighbours. The
Charles Lloyds are settling at Ambleside. 'We are by no means glad',
Dorothy wrote to Jane Marshall, 'because Charles Lloyd is . . . perpetually
forming new friendships, quarrelling with his old ones, and upon the
whole a dangerous acquaintance'. But his wife—he has wooed and wed
his Sophia—'is very highly spoken of'; and then there is no getting out of
it, since 'It is true that Christopher is desperately in love and engaged to
marry Miss Lloyd'. Dorothy has 'not seen this Miss Lloyd, Priscilla she is
called'; but she is now to winter at Ambleside. That Christopher was
capable of being 'desperately in love' is already at this stage slightly
startling. For long, as the youngest, Dorothy's pet, her pleas that he would
visit them fell and continued to fall upon deaf ears.

John was the one who now counted. And on what seems to have been
the first time they screwed themselves up to dine with the Lloyds, they
learnt that John's ship, the *Abergavenny* was in. The next day John left,
Dorothy and William going with him as far as his favourite fishing tarn.
'We were in view of the head of Ulswater, and stood till we could see him
no longer . . . as he *hurried* down the stony mountain.' So she wrote five
years later. At the time she wrote: 'Poor fellow, my heart was right sad.'
But she 'could not help thinking we should see him again because he was
only going to Penrith'. John, moreover, cannot be sad for the voyage
ahead is a challenge, the first on which he will captain the *Abergavenny*.
And the next day she glories in getting soaked to the skin: 'Rydale was
extremely wild and we had a fine walk. We sate quietly and comfortably
by the fire. I wrote—the last sheet of notes and preface. Went to bed at 12
o'clock.' This is her notion of perfect happiness.

That, Priscilla or no, they now saw as much as they did of the Lloyds
may on the face of it seem mysterious. The reason at first is, in fact, not far
to seek. William is once more—has been since 10 October—locked with

* My italics.

composition, and often in vain. And the Lloyds are inveterate card-players. 'We drank tea with them . . . and played a rubber at whist—stayed supper. Wm looked very well.' Dorothy has found a way of killing two birds with one stone—Priscilla and the pain in William's side. The Lloyds not unnaturally after this counted the Wordsworths as friends, and when Priscilla left stuck like leeches. But bad art is acutely embarrassing; and Lloyd, who wrote bad poetry, always, he said, felt depressed in William's presence—no doubt with reason. Dorothy, incensed perhaps by some such episode as Lloyd tactlessly calling late at night—just when she 'thought I heard William snoring, so I composed myself to sleep'—flashed out in a letter to Mary, in June 1802, that they 'are determined to cut them entirely'. This threat was never carried out. They continued to go to the Lloyds, if as little as possible, and only 'that it might be over'.

Apart from Molly and Aggy, Fletcher, the carrier (under whose door a few yards from her own, Dorothy would sometimes slip her letters late at night), Thomas Ashburner who delivered the coal, Peggy, his delicate wife, and their flock of children—in and out of Dorothy's house like birds—there existed only one family with whom they were intimate. The Simpsons were far from being as dull as the name, for some unknown reason, or 'a Clergyman with a very small income', suggests. 'The old man', as Dorothy calls him, at 'upwards of eighty', would seem to have had something in him of William. He had been in his youth very wild, and, destined for the Church, relying on the great with whom he mixed to procure him a living and rapid advancement, had ended the pastor of shepherds in what must be one of the smallest chapels in England. After forty-three years 'the old man' was bloody but unbowed:

> Retained a flashing eye, a burning palm,
> A stirring foot, a head which beat at nights
> Upon its pillow with a thousand schemes . . .

fished in 'the Tarns on the hill-tops', as Dorothy wrote, 'with my Brothers', and, with them and Coleridge, climbed Helvellyn. But Dorothy's vignette of the wife, whom she loved, would alone make the Simpsons worthwhile: 'She was an affecting picture of patient disappointment suffering under no particular affliction.'

But Dorothy, when she wrote to Jane, was already in the process of forming a far more sparkling friendship. She and William are off to stay with the Clarksons. 'Mr Clarkson is the man who took so much pains about the slave trade.' She might have added, but did not, that Mrs Clarkson is the brilliant, witty, cultivated woman who had taken so much pains with Mr Clarkson. It is, however, proper that she did not. Christened by Coleridge 'The Moral Steam Engine' or 'The Giant with one idea', Thomas Clarkson's idea was badly needed: slaves apart, one fifth of the crew employed on slave ships perished through the brutality of their officers. Ever since, up at Cambridge, he had written on 'Is it lawful to make slaves of others against their will?', Clarkson had out-steamed any steam engine, on one occasion combing over seven hundred ships, scattered in ports throughout England, for a man who had been in central Africa, who might already have sailed, whose name he did not know—and whom he found.

The failure, in 1794, of the Abolition Bill left him at thirty-four a broken man. And, taking up farming, he built the charming house, Eusemere, on Ullswater, which Dorothy grew to love. But the turning-point came with the marriage of this humourless reformer. Catherine Clarkson might have married a cause—she was capable of it—and one to which her husband would return. When he did she identified with him. In the meanwhile she had taught him to prefer poets to abolitionists; poets, admittedly, as distinct from poetry: when later in life he received a tribute in the form of an ode, the poet was forced to come up with a prose translation.

According to Henry Crabb Robinson, who had known the élite of Europe and would one day be devoted to Dorothy, her new friend 'was the most eloquent woman I have ever known, with the exception of Madame de Staël. She had a quick apprehension of every kind of beauty and made her own whatever she learned'. If to this one adds simple manners and a passion for the poetry of William Wordsworth, the link seems obvious.

Meanwhile such, at Town-End, had been the spate of visitors—not only Jane's husband (worthy of Jane) but, among others, 'my Brother's companion on his pedestrian tour', who was not alone in staying a week—that between these and transcribing poems Dorothy's Journal lapsed. And was only resumed in time to catch the autumn: '. . . all colours, all melting into each other'. 'Kites sailing in the sky above our heads—sheep bleating and in lines and . . . patterns scattered over the mountains . . .' She had narrowly missed catching it at all; was caught, on 15 October, by 'a very cold frosty air, and a spangled sky in returning' (at night from the Simpsons). And sure enough, on the 27th she woke to snow, and notes, 'The Coppices now nearly of one brown'. Winter is upon them. The Lloyds all have colds. Rainy morning follows rainy morning. William has piles. Dorothy reads *Amelia*. With the post of Friday 14 November, '2 letters from Coleridge—very ill. One from Sara H.', we move to Scene II of Act I of the tragedy.

The post on a Friday did not come in till the evening. The next morning only 'a terrible rain' prevented William 'from going to Coleridge's'. Dorothy for some reason could not go; but when, at five, William got off, she left him at Dunmail Raise 'very sad unwilling not to go on'. Not content with hearing from Coleridge and William that he was better, she took herself to Keswick to see for herself and 'found them all well', or seemingly so. Coleridge's main trouble (the result of a cold, 'improved', he wrote, to its recent 'glorious state by taking long walks . . . spite of the wind, & writing late at night') has been his eyes. These have been 'so blood-red' he might have made 'a very good Personification of Murder', so inflamed he 'might as well write blindfold'. But he has had leeches twice and a blister behind his ear, and thanks to this his eyes 'are now my own'. 'We are sadly grieved for your poor eyes', was in the future to become Dorothy's constant agonized cry. And the pain he suffered is not in doubt. It is possible that this was already opium getting its own back, and that Coleridge failed to understand it when he said that he only now acquired 'the accursed habit'. One cannot however dismiss his reiterating it when he had ceased to be an addict, when he must have understood his own medical history better, and made it his mission to be a warning to others.

That he had in the past taken laudanum in large doses is not in question. In 1796 in particular, the period of *The Watchman*, he had suffered acute pain ('A devil, a very devil has got possession of my left temple, eye, cheek, jaw, throat and shoulder. I cannot see you . . . I write in agony'); and 'tottering on the edge of madness', sleepless with Fricker, financial and *Watchman* worry, he had frankly admitted recourse to this, down to specifying the large amount—twenty-five drops four-hourly—he was taking. The legacy of ague and rheumatic fever was a fiend ever ready to pounce. And if he resorted to laudanum as we may to Anadin; if the doses he took were a great deal larger than those Dorothy took for toothache or diarrhoea who can blame him? I would still myself incline to the belief that, in a climate fatal to him, it was the far stronger brand of laudanum brewed in Kendal, the lethal Black Drop, that was his undoing.

It began with pain; and when and where it took hold seems unimportant. More curious is the psychosomatic aspect. Already in the days of *The Watchman*, 'the fiend with a hundred hands' had been diagnosed as nervous in origin, induced by overwork or 'excessive anxiety'. On 28 November, staying at Town-End, he must have woken Dorothy by his screams in the throes of 'a most frightful dream of a woman . . . catching hold of my right eye and attempting to pull it out—I caught hold of her arm fast—a horrid feel. Wordsworth cried out aloud at hearing me scream—heard his cry and thought it cruel he did not come / but did not awake till his cry was repeated a third time . . . When I awoke my right eyelid swelled'.

Now as in Bristol dunned and in debt, with a book commissioned by Longman, another on Lessing promised to Tom Wedgwood, 'those two Giants yclept Bread and Cheese' the declared enemy of all that he wished to do and wished not to do—with the terrifying necessity of now proving himself, he was not only crippled by bodily pain. The disease made sure of him—attacking his eyes 'to a degree that rendered reading and writing scarcely possible'.

He was not by this time being attacked only from within. Where Sara, happy with Poole and his old mother, could bear with the to-ing and fro-ing that went on at Alfoxden, matters at Keswick stood very differently. Mr Jackson, the carrier, who had risen in the world, built Greta

Hall and lived in the other half, might, such was his pleasure in Hartley, accept no rent; and Samuel might think it 'no small joy to her' to have a carrier's housekeeper as companion. But she did find it a small joy. And a still smaller one that when he went to the Wordsworths' it now meant a jaunt of several days. At night, cutting short a lonely evening, threading her way through the maze of corridors behind the big empty rooms, she must often have felt ready to jump at the shadow cast by her own candle. At best it was a lonely life, with Samuel out on the mountains and then spending the nights in his study working. This, however, she might have borne, had he only continued to spend the nights working in his study— worked as hard on the German book and for the *Morning Post* as he seemed to work at catching cold from wet. She was sorely tried and now had the Wordsworths come upon her with a guest of theirs, Miss Sara Hutchinson. Hartley was ill in his bowels, and no sooner had they left than this proved to be the yellow jaundice. Then just when Samuel seemed better he was ill again, with six great boils upon his neck. With these to be dressed and poulticed, and in too much pain to *work*, what should he do but *walk* to Grasmere; stay there from Friday to Tuesday, return to her for two nights—only again to head back to Town-End. Four days after he was home, Mr Wordsworth (having finished his work it seemed the day before) brought the poem and Miss Wordsworth and, in the bargain, Miss Hutchinson to Keswick for four more. Not that she minded Miss Hutchinson, a plain dumpy thing, who seemed as if she thought her hair a beauty since she wore it very long; but then she let Hartley pull it and Derwent play with it and was a deal more help than Miss W. was.

Nothing, in point of fact, is known of the first reaction of the two Saras to one another; or nothing more than that Miss Hutchinson would shortly be invited for a fortnight to Greta Hall, and stay there once again, it would seem, in March. But the likelihood would appear to be that the second Sara's presence was, at this stage, welcomed by everyone. And if Coleridge did in great part now, and in the winter ahead, drag himself to Grasmere on her account, Asra's 'entertainingness' was what an invalid needed and the harassed Sara signally failed to provide.

Especially, harrowing as Coleridge's plight became, was she what was needed by Dorothy. One catches the note almost as soon as she comes. Not only is 'Wm very well and highly poetical', and Asra writing to Hartley aged four and a half. When, after Coleridge's second visit within the week, 'Coleridge and Wm set forward towards Keswick', no sooner are they got rid of than 'Sara and I had a grand bread and cake baking'. It was no weather, however, for a sick man to walk twelve miles, and 'the wind in Coleridge's eyes made him turn back . . . We were very merry in the evening but grew sleepy soon though we did not go to bed till 12 o'clock'.

All the Coleridge family came to Grasmere for Christmas. Unhappily at this point the scene fades out, a portion of Dorothy's journal having been lost. Her second from last entry for 1800, however, tells its own ominous tale: 'Saturday. [20th] Coleridge came. Very ill rheumatic, feverish. Rain incessantly.'

To picture Dorothy in the nine months ahead, we can only—with the invaluable Jane replaced by Mary as Dorothy's chief correspondent—fall back on one letter of April 1801:

> My dearest Mary,
>   We left poor Coleridge on Monday evening: we had been with him a week and a day. You know that I wrote to Sara on the Friday Evening . . . giving her the joyful tidings that C was better, but alas! on Saturday we had a sad account of him. I was determined not to give you unnecessary uneasiness therefore I did not write. We left home at one o'clock on Sunday—and reached Keswick about six. We both trembled, and till we entered the door I hardly durst speak. He was sitting in the parlour, and looked dreadfully pale and weak. He was very, very unwell . . . ill all over, back, and stomach and limbs and so weak as that he changed colour whenever he exerted himself at all. Our company did him good . . . but he was never quite well for more than an hour together during the whole time we were there. . . . I do think he will never be quite well till he has tried a warm climate . . .

He and Hartley are to come to Town-End tomorrow, Hartley to stay and go to Grasmere school. Dorothy hopes that

> C. will grow well in a short time after he comes to us, but there is no security for his continuing so . . . Mrs C. is in excellent health. She is indeed a bad nurse for C., but she has several great merits. She is much very much to be pitied, for when one party is ill matched the other necessarily must be so too. She would have made a very good wife to many another man, but for Coleridge!! Her radical fault is want of sensibility and what can such a woman be to Coleridge? . . . She is to be sure a sad fiddle faddler. From about ½ past 10 on Sunday morning till two she did nothing but wash and dress her 2 children and herself . . . When I say I would not give you any uneasiness about Coleridge, do not fear that I shall not inform you at all times when he is *very* ill, but as his relapse was only a common one I did not like to give you pain . . .

This and the rest of the letter tells us all, or almost all, of Dorothy's life in the months when her journal is silent. One has only to read Coleridge's own letters (December 1800—June 1801) to realize how often she and William must have reached Keswick in just such fear and trembling. Though after the first five weeks of rheumatic fever—already upon him when he reached Grasmere for Christmas—followed by what was called a Hydrocele (an enormously swollen testicle), despite the fact that relapse followed relapse, he is till the end of May invariably hopeful: 'My health is better—I am indeed eager to believe, I am really *beginning to recover*.' Nor does he dilate upon his sufferings: 'I have written a long Letter & said nothing of myself [he has indeed written many such]. In simple verity, I am disgusted with that subject . . . What I suffer is mere *pain* almost incredible . . . at present the Disease has seized the whole Region of my Back, so that I scream mechanically at the least motion . . . not that my bodily pain affects me—God forbid! Were I a single man & independent I should be ashamed to think myself wretched merely because I suffered pain . . . It is not my bodily Pain', this is 'a trifle compared with the gloom of my Circumstances . . . the gloom & distresses of those around me for whom I ought to be labouring and cannot'.

Coleridge was neither an indolent nor weak man. He could claim with truth and might have said with pride, 'I have been *thinking* vigorously during my Illness'. Despite the fact that 'the sense of lassitude, if I only sate up in bed was worst of all . . . so treacherous were my animal spirits to me', he set himself to make a thorough study of Locke, and in temporary place of the *Lessing* promised Tom Wedgwood, set out his findings in four long philosophical letters. So hard, in fact, did he mentally drive himself that William insisted he desist from speculations that exhausted his small reserves of strength. Opium or no, all this—together with the letters, hopeful and even humorous—does something to explain the will which in the end enabled him to beat the enemy.

Among his letters early in this period is a rare one—to Dorothy, rare in being one of the few to survive, and in that it suddenly opens a door on their relationship. It should be explained that Rotha was his name for her, that 'Wm's stomach is in bad plight', and that—if this needs explaining —the Fichte is a farrago of nonsense on which he can rely to make her laugh:

Monday, February 9. 1801

My dearest Rotha

The Hack, Mr Calvert was so kind as to borrow for me, carried me home as pleasantly as the extreme Soreness of my whole frame admitted. I was indeed in the language of Shakespear, not a Man but a Bruise—I went to bed immediately & rose on Sunday quite restored. If I do not hear any thing to the contrary, I shall walk half way to Grasmere, on Friday morning . . . in the hopes of meeting Sara [H.] partly to prevent the necessity of William's walking so far, just as he will have begun to tranquillize, & partly to remove from Mrs Coleridge's mind all anxiety as to the time of her coming, which if it depended on William's mood of Body might (unless he went to the injury of his health) be a week, or a fortnight hence . . . all this however to be understood with the usual Deo Volente of Health and Weather. . . .

I had a very long conversation with Hartley about Life, Reality, Pictures, & Thinking, this evening. He sate on my knee for half an hour at least, & was exceedingly serious. I wish to God, you had been with us. Much as you would desire to believe me, I cannot expect that I could communicate to you all that Mrs C. & I felt from his answers. . . . He pointed out without difficulty that there might be five Hartleys, Real Hartley, Shadow Hartley, Picture Hartley, Looking Glass Hartley, and Echo Hartley. . . . One thing, he said, was very curious—I asked him what he did when he thought of any thing—he answered—I look at it, and then go to sleep. To sleep?—said I—you mean, that you *shut your eyes*. Yes, he replied—I shut my eyes, & put my hands so (covering his eyes) and go to sleep—then I WAKE again, and away I run.—That of shutting his eyes & covering them was a recipe I had given him some time ago / but the notion of that state of mind being Sleep is very striking, & he meant more, I suspect, than that People when asleep have their eyes shut, indeed I *know* it from the tone & *leap up* of Voice with which he uttered the word 'WAKE'. Tomorrow I am to exert my genius in making a paper-balloon / the idea of carrying up a bit of lighted Candle into the clouds makes him almost insane with Pleasure. As I have given you Hartley's Metaphysics I will now give you a literal Translation of page 49 of the celebrated Fichte's *Uber den Begriff der Wissenschaftslehre*—if any of *you* . . . have any propensity to *Doubts* it will cure them for ever / for the object of the author is to attain absolute certainty . . . 'Suppose, that A in the proposition A = A stands not for the I, but for something other or different, then you may deduce the condition under which it may be affirmed, that it is established, and *how* we are authorized to conclude, that if A is established, then it is established' [etc.etc.] Here's a numerous Establishment for you / nothing in Touchstone ever equalled this—it is not even surpassed by Creech's account of Space in his notes to Lucretius . . . Heaven bless you my dear friends! S.T.C.—

His notebooks for the same period contain perhaps the most tantalizing of all things pertaining to Dorothy: 'In the Essay on Criticism to examine whether or no a great Critic must needs be himself a great poet or painter —and to introduce a *highly* written character of Rotha . . .'

What would one not give to have had this assessment of Dorothy as critic—and from Coleridge. For to suppose her function confined to that of secretary, gardener, observer, Defender of the Faith, is to forget that for Coleridge she was part of 'the Concern'. And so rarely does she reveal herself in this role that we tend to forget it. Happily the Ambleside postmistress never forgot how often and gladly her husband would get out of bed, 'be it as late as it would', to hand back a manuscript, posted earlier, but which would not leave with the mail till one in the morning: 'And then they [William and Dorothy] would sit up in our parlour or in the kitchen discussing over it and reading and changing till they had made it quite to their mind, and then they would . . . knock at our bedroom door and say "Now, Mr Nicholson, please will you bolt the door after us? Here is our letter for the post. We'll not trouble you any more this night." And, oh, they were always so friendly to us and so loving to one another.'

To return to Dorothy's letter to Mary describing their visit to Coleridge. I have said that it tells us almost everything we need to know to picture her in the months when her journal is silent. And so, *in extenso*, I think it does. 'My dearest Mary', she continues, 'I look forward with joy to seeing you again. You *must* come in Autumn or before . . . William is better . . . he is taking a stomachic medicine . . . but his digestion is still very bad—he is always very ill when he tries to alter an old poem—but new composition does not hurt him so much.' It is seven o'clock and 'the thrushes are singing divinely in the orchard . . . Wm is lying upon the outside of the bed that has its back to the window. I have the little round green table beside him. We are going to tea and then for a walk. Wm will take the pen', while she gets the tea.

William writes:

We are very happy to have such good news of your health mind you take care of yourself and contrive to grow fat not as Dorothy does fat one day and lean another, but fat and jolly for half a year together. D. and I sat two hours in Johns firgrove this morning, 'twas a burning hot day but there we had a delicious cool breeze. How we wished for our dear dear friends you and Sara. You will recollect there is a gate just across the road . . . this gate was always a favorite station of ours; we love it far more now on Saras account. You know that it commands a beautiful prospect; Sara carved her cypher upon one of its bars and we call it her gate. We will find out another place for your cypher, but you must come and fix upon the place yourself. How we long to see you my dear Mary.

We had a melancholy visit at Coleridge's—Adieu—love to Tom—I now transcribe a short poem to be read after She dwelt among

> I travell'd among unknown men,
> In lands beyond the sea;
> Nor, England did I know till then
> What love I bore to thee.
>
> 'Tis past—that melancholy dream!
> Nor will I quit thy shore
> A second time; for still I seem
> To love thee more and more.
>
> Among thy mountains did I feel
> The gladness of desire
> And she I cherish'd turn'd her wheel
> Beside an English fire.

Thy mornings show'd thy nights conceal'd,
The bowers where Lucy play'd;
And thine is too the last green field
Which Lucy's eyes survey'd.

God forever bless thee, my dear Mary—Adieu.

Does Dorothy see what William writes? Almost certainly. And know its import in April 1801? I would say that she did, that she would be the first to know, that William would under no consideration have made even this sticky move without her full compliance: if she *had* quailed he has had this from her. William, not she, is the more apprehensive—since she will not lose him and, if she must share him, Mary is the person she would choose.

This, in fact, is largely why William has chosen her and remained, despite Dorothy, dubious. Dubious enough to sit up with Coleridge (during this last visit perhaps) the whole of one night thrashing the matter out. On 12 May 1808 Coleridge wrote in his notebook, 'When in bed—I then ill—continued talking with Wordsworth the whole night thru' till Dawn of the Day urging him to conclude in marrying [name heavily erased] a blessed marriage for him and for her it has been.' As to when this discussion took place must be pure speculation. Nor does Coleridge claim that he was successful. But one thing, to my mind, is clear from the tone of Dorothy's journal when Mary arrives the following autumn: that during this summer she faced the thing she most feared, faced it for William's sake and was able to do so, to meet Mary when she came as William's potential bride—because it did not entail the thing she feared. Because with the thrushes singing divinely in the orchard, William is, as we invariably find him, beside her as she writes. Because he could no more contemplate the thought of life without her than she that of being thrown upon the world. He had told her so quite explicitly and only recently, in a poem, ''Tis said that some have died for love', about the man on Helvellyn who had lost his wife, and now could not bear the glad song of a thrush, the sight of the eglantine heartlessly dancing in the wind, the very sight of the smoke from his own chimney:

Ah gentle Love if ever thought was thine
To store up kindred hours for me, thy face
Turn from me, gentle Love! Nor let me walk
Within the sound of Emma's voice, nor know
Such happiness as I have known today.

It is now nearly a year since he last set eyes on Mary, but he does not now ride post-haste to Gallow Hill, but confines himself to the use of the 'thee' and a veiled declaration of love. After tea he will go for a walk with Dorothy. And then, as the thrushes now tell her, she will know—has she not been told?—that his love for her is deep and unchangeable.

XV

Shadows into Substances

Coleridge, *Notebooks*

1801–1802

MEANWHILE, DESPITE DOROTHY'S hopes of the 'stomachic medicine', William's stomach continued 'in bad plight'. And by late May, sending 'a few baked trouts the first trouts we have had this season' to Coleridge ('poor John, dear John! we think of him whenever we see . . . a trout'), she writes: 'We have put aside all the manuscript poems . . . and I am not to give them up' to William 'even if he asks for them'.

With Coleridge an increasing anxiety and William far from well, Hartley's visit could hardly have been more timely. Dorothy does not write well of children but she delighted in them; 'Sally with me', is one of the Ashburner children, and when she had been alone last year, 'little Tommy came down with me, ate gooseberry pudding and drank tea with me'.

Of all the children born it is not surprising that Coleridge's should have been one of the most enchanting. The face, tragi-comic as any of Shakespeare's jesters', tells us, perhaps, as much as we need to know of the child called Moses by Southey and whom Wordsworth thought a genius. At the age of three and a half, on Coleridge's telling him that Southey had written and 'sent him his love in the letter', this infant Wittgenstein had 'thought and thought, and then burst into a fit of laughter'. Dorothy described him as the 'original sprite'. 'A spirit dancing on an aspen leaf . . . indefatigably joyous', he entranced and fascinated Coleridge: 'At this moment I hear his voice distinctly shouting to some foxgloves and fern he has transplanted, what he will do for them if they grow like good boys.' Only two months before he now came to Dorothy, and two days before his fifth birthday, after looking 'steadily and for some time' out of Coleridge's study window, he had asked: 'Will yon mountains *always* be?' 'The boy's delight is to get his father to talk metaphysics to him', said Southey, '—and few *men* understand him so perfectly'. In Coleridge he found a fellow-child—who took him seriously; as, more surprisingly, did Sara. Their love for their children Dorothy must for some time have seen was all that now held the Coleridges together.

What she perhaps did not yet know was the inside story of Sara Hutchinson's visits to Greta Hall. Nor would it be necessary for us to know this had Dorothy not loved Coleridge as deeply as she did and the outcome borne so heavily on her. The most that she is, at this stage, likely to have known is Sara's own reports of her visits to Keswick. It is doubtful if she knew what, I would suggest, was Sara's secret—that the arrow *had* flown in, not for Coleridge but for her at Sockburn. I have given my reasons for thinking it did not then do so for Coleridge. Admittedly he had written a poem called 'Love', clearly the fruit of Sockburn, but it was not called 'Love' at the time and, one perfect stanza apart, was a good deal more Gothic than amorous. In March 1800, on his way to Grasmere, he would appear to have broken his journey at Sockburn. But his note, 'Mr Coleridge. A little of Sara's hair in my pocket', only suggests that Sara's hair asked for this; seems only to conjure a Sara cornered with scissors conceding defeat, on condition that she herself do the lopping, and mockingly handing over 'a little of Miss Hutchinson's hair for Mr Coleridge'—rather than hopeless passion.

How did she ever come to be invited to Greta Hall, and stay on when she was long due back at Town-End? The invitation must have been issued by her hostess, but was almost certainly instigated by Coleridge, who wanted a 'sister' in Asra but was equally anxious that the two Saras should be friends. Only in this way could his own aim be accomplished— a fraternal marriage of true minds. The goal seemed not unattainable, since 'Mary and her sister [Asra]', as he wrote with truth to Sara, 'are far less remote from you than they' (the Wordsworths). In such a friendship, moreover, in Asra's example and influence, lay perhaps the sole chance for his marriage.

It is to Coleridge's credit that in his letters and notebooks he had so far uttered no word against Mrs C. Perhaps it was also still to the latter's credit, for Dorothy is surprisingly compassionate—as she would hardly have been had she glimpsed Sara, the virago. But more probably by deliberately fiddle-faddling and keeping out of the room as much as she could with visitors she disliked, Mrs C. in a double sense pulled the wool over Dorothy's eyes.

Initially, however, it would seem that Asra's stay at Greta Hall, since this was prolonged, went well. Asra's conscience was strong, and her relationship with Coleridge must depend on being friends with Mrs C. Mrs C., however, wished for no exemplar. While for Coleridge the contrast between the two far outweighed any similarity. Unhappy as he was, it was bound to end as it did, would seem to have done by March and at Keswick:

> . . . where those meek eyes first did seem
> To tell me, Love within you wrought!—
> O Greta, dear domestic stream.

It has been contended that love never wrought in Asra, only pity; that no one could love a man with boils on his neck. The feat seems not impossible if that man was Coleridge, if one had twice met him, as she had, in health and high spirits. If Coleridge had held one's hand a long time behind one's back, I suspect one would have gone down like a pack of cards. She herself admittedly is as silent as the grave. There does, however, exist proof that she loved him, that not only did she accept letters from him written in lover-like terms, but herself wrote back in a similar vein: 'If I have not heard from you very recently, & if the last letter had not happened to be full of explicit Love and Feeling, then I conjure up Shadows into Substances—& am miserable.' So Coleridge wrote in October 1803. That Mary (according to Wordsworth's grand-daughter) burnt all, as she thought, of Coleridge's letters to Sara after the latter's death, both shows that Sara kept these and that Mary found them incriminating.

Mrs Coleridge clearly smelt a rat by the spring of 1801. If Dorothy did it must have seemed immaterial, since not only was Coleridge by July no better, but as William wrote to Poole 'is himself afraid . . . the disease' being 'now manifestly the gout . . . he may be carried off by it with little or no warning. I would hope to God that there is no danger of this; but it is too manifest that the disease is a *dangerous* one'. William, in fact, with Dorothy at his side, is asking Poole if in the event 'of Coleridges death you could afford to lose £50 or more', in order now to send him to the Azores.

With the death of Coleridge as a thing to be talked of even, Dorothy must have been beside herself. And her joy and relief unbounded when in July he rose from his bed and, in one of his fits of convalescence, took himself off to Durham 'for the purpose of reading . . . Duns Scotus'. He had gone with a painful boil on his gullet which, poulticed, he now wrote gaily, made him 'smell so like a hot loaf, it would be perilous . . . to meet a hungry blind man'. Bishop Middleham, where Sara kept house for George, was convenient for Durham. And he was next heard of bathing at Scarborough. He had 'foolishly walked . . . from Durham' with the inevitable result, a knee swollen and 'pregnant with agony'. For this the doctor had recommended 'horse exercise'—in other words, riding with Sara to Gallow Hill, where Tom was now farming with Mary; and 'sea bathing'—in other words staying with Sara at Gallow Hill, twenty minutes from the waves at Scarborough. By 12 August—the doctor, presumably, having said that George could spare Sara no longer—he was back at Bishop Middleham, where he remained until 24 August.

'Oh, for one letter of perfect uncomplainingness!' Dorothy had written when sending the trout. Now at last she must have had more than one. Doubtless she also had reports of him from Mary during the time he spent at Gallow Hill, and perhaps Mary's version of, or some reference to, what is known as the lazy-bed incident. A lazy-bed is a chaise-longue, the one at Gallow Hill being apparently wide enough for three, to accommodate Coleridge between Mary and Sara, *and* with the candle burnt out in its socket—an event found deeply shocking today, in an age which hot for permissiveness and perversion grows daily more puritanic. Coleridge's account of this, as read to Dorothy, rather makes to my mind pathetic reading—pathetic in its craving and gratitude for affection:

> O that affectionate and blameless Maid
> Dear Mary! on her lap my head she lay'd—
> Her hand was on my Brow
> Even as my own is now;
> And on my Cheek I felt thy eye-lash play.
> Such joy I had, that I may truly say
> My Spirit was awe-stricken with the Excess
> And trance-like depth of its brief Happiness.

Brief indeed—a month of unclouded happiness and love; but a love which, so long as it brought any happiness to the two concerned, one patently so ill-married, it never occurred to Dorothy not to accept.

For the moment, however, it brought the reverse of happiness. On 26 August, returning to Keswick, Coleridge met with a stinging reception from his better half and Asra, it seems, received an anonymous letter. From now on despite real efforts at reconciliation, the tale (if it had not already long been so) would be pretty much as told to Tom Wedgwood a year later: 'Ill-tempered Speeches sent after me when I went out of the House, ill-tempered Speeches on my return, the least opposition or contradiction occasioning screams of passion . . .' Whether or not Dorothy learnt it now we do not know. Probably not, since by 6 September William was in Scotland for the wedding of Montagu and did not return until the end of the month. Coleridge specifically writes of Wordsworth, not the Wordsworths, being in Scotland. But clearly Dorothy did not remain at Town-End. For a month she vanishes until, in 1801, her journal reopens: *'Saturday 10 October* . . . Coleridge went to Keswick after we had built Sara's seat.'

The entries which follow must, I think, be read as distress signals, if they do at first signal no more than a bilious attack. On the 15th Coleridge is back, on the 16th 'poorly', on the 17th 'poorly after dinner'. For the 18th—an echo of Alfoxden—she enters, 'I have forgotten'. On the day he had come, after feeling unwell on Loughrigg, she was 'very sick and ill when I got home, went to bed in the sitting room—took laudanum'. On the day he left she was ill in bed all day. But Tom Hutchinson is staying and she pulls herself together; and then it is 'a grand stormy day', just the day for an outing and she is the better for it. But Coniston can only be done with a horse—perhaps she went on a 'double horse' with Tom. For on the 25th she 'rode to Legberthwaite with Tom [one trusts also with William!], expecting Mary'—and *is* on Helvellyn taken out of herself, 'glorious glorious sights. The sea at Cartmel. The Scotch mountains beyond . . . Mists above and below and close to us, with the Sun amongst them'. They 'got bread and cheese—paid 4/- . . . reached home at 9 o'clock. A soft grey evening—the light of the moon, but she did not shine on us'.

Can this be the arrival of the bride-to-be? Or have they made the long journey for nothing? We are left with the glorious glorious sights and the price of bread and cheese; and, what is more, for two days the entry, 'Omitted'. 'The Clarksons came.' Then twice we must make do with 'Rain all day.' For 6 November we have 'Coleridge came', which is better than nothing, all we get for 7 and 8 November. This may be due to the fact that a page here has been torn out, containing the entries between the 4th and 9th. Why, and by whom torn out? And what—if the 4th, 5th, 6th were recoverable from Wordsworth's *Memoirs*—became of the three days Coleridge spent at Grasmere, perhaps the last, with his health, he would ever spend there?

The fate of the torn-out page may be wholly accidental. But the brief, taut entries during the past month, culminating (as, on 10 November, these do) in an outburst as unique as it is desperate, are surely no accident. Dorothy's brevity has, however, another significance. Had she, in the fashion of her time, made of her journal a *journal intime*, the repository of emotional outpourings, it would not have served her purpose. Control is her business. The product may often be a far cry from art. She has never conceived of anything she writes being otherwise. But art is intensity controlled.

And so, with no money forthcoming for the Azores and Coleridge about to winter instead in London, they accompany him back on the 9th to Greta Hall. Mrs Coleridge, happily, is away: 'We enjoyed ourselves in the study and were *at home*.' Mr Jackson, the kindly landlord, thoughtfully laid on supper. 'Mary and I sate in C.'s room a while.'

So Mary has come, came perhaps on 25 October and is now for the first time sitting at Dorothy's side, but not at Town-End by the hearth which may shortly be her own, and has been Dorothy's with William. Now quietly she slips into place and bears Dorothy company in the big ramshackle room dear to her. Here Coleridge has camped, with mountains, books, an Aeolian harp through which a honeymoon breeze once blew so sweetly, soon in another poem to make such tragic music; with a desk, a day bed on which—sleeping little and rising to make notes —he often slept. Here how often, at the end of twelve anxious miles, Dorothy has entered pale and trembling.

And then it is over: '*Tuesday 10th* [November]. Poor C. left us, and we came home together.' Mary's feet were sore; but 'C. had a sweet day for his ride. Every sight and every sound reminded me of him dear dear fellow —of his many walks to us by day and by night—of all dear things. I was melancholy and could not talk, but at last I eased my heart by weeping —nervous blubbering says William. It is not so. O how many, many reasons have I to be anxious for him'.

Never before have we heard or again will hear William be sharp with her. His own nerves, too, are at breaking point.

And the next day she does what all women do when emotionally disturbed, tidies the house, 'put books in order'. And then she 'put aside dearest C.'s letters, and now at about 7 o'clock we are all sitting by a nice fire—W. with his book and a candle,' and yes, Mary, too, is seated by Dorothy's fireside, writing to Sara.

The crisis point reached had been passed. And although the following morning her first act is still symbolic, and a fairly desperate one at that—'put the rag Boxes into order'—with Mary there and courtship staring the three of them in the face, the entries are from now on free and flowing. It is almost as if she does William's wooing for him. And perhaps she does; perhaps that, but for her, none would get done explains her tranquil happiness, on this same day even a moving exaltation: 'Wm and I walked out before tea—The Crescent moon—we sate in the slate quarry—I sate there a long time alone. Wm reached home before me—I found them at Tea. There were a thousand stars in the Sky.'

She absents herself constantly, gladly, to such good effect that within days her work is done. And by the 16th can record that 'Molly has been very witty with Mary all day. She says "ye may say that ye will but there's nothing like a gay auld man for behaving weel to a young wife.* Ye may laugh but this wind blows no favour—and where there's no love there's no favour."'

Dorothy can enter this with amusement, without pain, with, in a long entry, much other matter; be caustic about a neighbour who, when Dorothy praised the view from her window, 'observed that it was beautiful *even* in winter! . . . Wm . . . upon the whole pretty well . . . is now, at 7 o'clock, reading Spenser. Mary is writing beside me. The little syke [small stream] murmurs. We are quiet and happy, but poor Peggy Ashburner is very ill and in pain . . . I am going to write to Coleridge and Sara. Poor C! I hope he was in London yesterday . . . On Sunday I lectured little John Dawson for telling lies. I told him I had heard that he charged Jenny Baty falsely with having beaten him. Says Molly: "she says it's not so that she never lifted hand till him, and she *should* speak truth you would think in her condition"—she is with child. Two Beggars today'.

If there is any doubt of Dorothy's transformation, we have only to compare 'Rain all day' with some 920 words for 24 November and among them her description of a birch tree: 'It was yielding to the gusty wind with all its tender twigs, the sun shone upon it and it glanced in the wind like a flying sunshiny shower. It was a tree in shape with stem and branches but it was like a Spirit of water.' Nor is it only a tree that interests her. On her return she goes in to see Peggy Ashburner, and hears

---

* William and Mary were, of course, the same age. But William, at the age of thirty-nine, as he recounted with amusement, would 'never see three score' again; such was the opinion of his fellow-passengers on a stage-coach.

how they had fought to save their farm, 'how they had all got up at 5 o'clock in the morning to spin and Thomas [Peggy's husband] carded'; of the pleasure she used to take in the sheep and cattle: '"O how pleased I used to be when they fetched them down, and when I had been a bit poorly I would gang out upon a hill and look over t'fields and see them, and it"' did '"me so much good you cannot think."'

She does not, like William and Mary, go to the Lloyds 'that it might be over'. Instead she stays at home, bakes and writes letters—to Coleridge and Sara Hutchinson. 'I passed a pleasant evening but the wind roared so and it was such a storm that I was afraid for them.' But this is the extent of her fears. 'They came in at nine o'clock no worse for their walk and cheerful, blooming and happy.'

And so, one feels, she is herself throughout Mary's stay, which lasted till 22 January, though broken by Mary's visits to friends and relations. And perhaps without Mary the news from London would have prevented her being so. Initially all seems well, but then it is not; Mrs Coleridge, at least, has a contrary tale. And, collecting the post, Dorothy and Mary anxiously 'opened C.'s letter at Wilcock's door we thought we saw that he wrote in good spirits so we came happily homewards'—to learn the truth. 'It was a sad melancholy letter', only the first of too many such, 'and prevented us all from sleeping'.

The next morning, rising by candlelight, 'we', meaning Dorothy, 'determined . . . to go to Keswick if possible'. And leaving William behind to re-write Chaucer, she set off on a 'double horse' with Mary, and kept on though 'upon the Rays it snowed very much and the whole prospect closed in upon us'. But then it cleared, and though 'now and then a hail shower attacked us . . . Mary is a famous Jockey'. From Keswick, having seen Mrs C. and the children—'Derwent pale, the image of his Father'— they 'wrote to C.' presumably in the hope that good news of the children he missed so much would cheer him. After baby-sitting till dusk for Mrs C., 'We rode very briskly. Snow upon the Rays . . . Sate latish. I wrote a little to C'.

She has, in fact, done and does this almost every day, more often than she writes a complete letter, as if by this means he were kept still a part of their life. Everywhere the thought of him is with her, walking in the now snow-bound landscape, with 'the hips very beautiful, and so good!! and dear Coleridge—I ate twenty for thee, when I was by myself'. The 'when I was by myself' is surprising in her. For had William and Mary witnessed the act, they could not have guessed the thought; but for her it is an utterly private moment, one of the few in which we see what she will not allow even William to see, or not at the time. And perhaps there is in this an element of solace, a momentary sense of being a bad third, which she need not have felt had Coleridge been with them: 'I came home first— they walked too slow for me.'

Not only are there letters which distress her from Coleridge himself, there are frequent letters from Sara Hutchinson, her mood reflecting his state: 'Sara in bad spirits about C.' On 21 December it was, perhaps, Mary's turn for bad spirits. Ploughing alone through deep snow to Ambleside while Dorothy 'at home clapped . . . the small linen. Wm sate beside me and read the Pedlar'—about which he has new hopes, but wants Dorothy's opinion—Mary found '4 letters, 2 from Coleridge, one from Sara and one from France'. Coleridge 'had been very ill in his bowels. We were made very unhappy'. But what of the letter from France? Did Mary know, as she carried this back, about Caroline and Annette? The answer can by now only be yes. And that William felt himself morally bound to inform Annette of his desire to marry and gain her agreement. Letters had evidently ceased for some time to get through. What would prove a temporary peace with Bonaparte was, however, at this moment being negotiated; and William had commissioned Coleridge in London to seek some means of contact with Annette. This, by February, he had achieved. In the interval, it would seem, a chance letter got through; one less disturbing to Mary perhaps than its envelope, in its tone perhaps even reassuring to her.

For the only troubled note throughout Mary's stay is contributed, and almost daily, by Coleridge. Dorothy and William, going for his letters, walk 'home almost without speaking'. Riding her own troubles with the tight rein she did, that there is in the journal no hint that she or William ever thought Coleridge might have exercised some restraint in the matter of making them, too, miserable, shows how selfless was their uncritical compassion for him. They feel, it seems, nothing but distress. Even when he is 'poorly but better—his letter made us uneasy about him'. She 'was glad I was not by myself when I received it'. None of these letters survive; but if one compares his others for this period with those written at Keswick, there is a difference. He no longer jokes about an illness London has failed to cure, and which, since it prevents him doing the job he has gone to do—on the *Morning Post*—is, indeed, no joking matter. But this is still not the root of the trouble. 'For what is life,' he cries to Southey, 'gangrened as it is for me in its very vitals—domestic Tranquility?'

On the strength, presumably, of their 'modern' attitude to Asra, it has been said that the Wordsworths encouraged Coleridge to separate from Mrs C. The opposite is true. Now, two days before this shriek of pain to Southey, for the second time in three weeks they again went to what, for Dorothy, was 'dear Coleridge's desert home', to ensure that the children and gangrened vitals were well. Years later Dorothy would still be expressing the hope that he would somehow shake down with Mrs C. For what else *was* there to be done on 22 January 1802—as Dorothy, William and Mary sat in the sun in a field ringed round by a river as at Sockburn; and 'Dear Mary!' Dorothy wrote, 'there we parted from her'? What was to be done with the 'heart-withering Conviction' Coleridge was this same day expressing in London, that he 'could not be happy without my children, & could not but be miserable with the mother of them'?

With Mary's departure the note of the journal again changes. Perhaps because William, alone with Dorothy, is once more back at work re-writing *The Pedlar*, and with the usual disastrous effects of re-writing. But if he is working this has little to do with Mary's going. For a year he has done little but play with Chaucer. The last three weeks of her stay he spent with Dorothy at Eusemere, Mary being for the bulk of this time elsewhere.

Their return from Eusemere via Grisedale proved something of a nightmare, not only heavy going in deep snow, struggling against the wind; with no sign of the road, they had lost their way and feared they might end the night upon the mountains. But 'thanks to William's skill' had got safely home. 'O how comfortable and happy we felt ourselves sitting by our own fire when we had got off our wet clothes and had dressed ourselves fresh and clean.' They talked about Como, read some of William's early *Descriptive Sketches*, 'looked about us, and felt that we were happy'.

It is worth, for a week, extracting the moments they spend by 'our own fire'. Three days after their return they again 'sate nicely together and talked by the fire' but this time 'till we were both tired, for Wm wrote out part of his poem and endeavoured to alter it, and so made himself ill. I copied out the rest . . .', in other words seized it off him and put a stop to late night tinkering.

They came home on the Saturday. By now it is Wednesday: 'William raked a few stones off the garden, his first garden labour this year', and later 'wasted his mind in the Magasines'. A critical note—or a sign of mounting emotional tension? 'I wrote to Coleridge and Mrs C . . . Then we sate by the fire and were happy only our tender thoughts became painful.'

That night 'Wm slept better'. He has not, then, been sleeping well. Despite this they are 'both in miserable spirits', and very doubtful about going out to tea. They go however and 'played at cards', but to no good effect. William comes home 'out of spirits and tired. After we went to bed I heard him continually, he called at ¼ past 3 to know the hour'. On Friday he is 'very unwell. Worn out with his bad night's rest. He went to bed', and she tries to read him to sleep. Matters are not improved by 'a heart-rending letter from Coleridge—we were as sad as we could be'; and they even meditate 'Wm's going to London'. Perversely, however, William's sleep is improved—since he is not pedaling *The Pedlar* all night long?

It is now exactly a week since they were lost in Grisedale. William keeps dinner waiting on work till four, 'slept very ill', and rose tired with a bad headache. Dorothy suffers from neither complaint, and now drags him out round the two lakes, Grasmere and Rydal—and on this day enters: 'I always love to walk that way because it is the way I first came to . . . Grasmere'. Then there had been 'a rich yellow light on the waters'. Today they 'amused ourselves . . . watching the Breezes some as if they came from the bottom of the lake spread in a circle . . . Others spread out like a peacock's tail'. She 'found a strawberry blossom . . . uprooted it rashly, and felt as if I had been committing an outrage. I planted it again. It will have but a stormy life . . . let it live if it can'. Awaiting them at Town-End, they found William Calvert who 'carried away the Encyclopaedias'. The room looks as if it had lost a tooth; and she rummages round for books to fill the gap. But 'One good thing is . . . a nice Elbow place for William, and he may sit for the picture of John Bunyan any day'.

There is nothing much, one increasingly feels, wrong with Dorothy. She is even oddly resistant to William's condition. The Bunyan is beautifully apt; and when, after this, 'William's head was bad', she 'petted him on the carpet and began a letter to Sara' in a single sentence without punctuation. Now when 'the papers came in', it is 'a good thing for my William', and no longer 'wasting' oneself 'in the Magasines'. Night after night she sits by his bed and tries to read him to sleep; and till half-past one in the morning takes its toll. His room is, in any case, over hers and every sound can be heard; and she does for two-thirds of a day take to her bed.

Coleridge, on the other hand, retains the power to destroy all her peace of mind. And her mood might well have been less resilient had his letters poured in at their former rate. Now when on 6 February 'William . . . came home with two very affecting letters from Coleridge—resolved to try another climate', she 'was stopped in my writing, and made ill . . . William a bad headach; he made up his bed on the floor, but could not sleep—I went to his bed and slept not. . . .'

Meanwhile, there has been, 'as Molly expressed it, a Cauld Clash', snow, and rain so cold the snow still lies. They nevertheless go in 'a cold "*Cauld Clash*"' for letters and stop to break the seal of Coleridge's. Dorothy 'had light enough just to see that he was not ill. I put it in my pocket but at the top of the White Moss I took it to my bosom, a safer place. . . .' C.'s letter when read, 'somewhat damped' them 'about France. William wrote to him'. Then 'very unwell, tired . . . he went to bed, and left me to write to M.H., Montagu and Calvert, and Mrs Coleridge. I had written in his letter to Coleridge. . . . Wm left me with a *little* peat fire—it grew less. I wrote on and was starved', meaning frozen. At two in the morning she put the letters under Fletcher's door and had 'never felt such a cold night . . . I collected together all the clothes I could find . . . and could not sleep for sheer cold'. Lying awake, does she think, perhaps, of Coleridge? The next day writing up her journal, she adds at the end of a long entry: 'N.B. the moon came out suddenly when we were at John's Grove, and a star or two beside'. She is quoting *The Ancient Mariner*.

She is anxious about Coleridge, but herself strangely happy—since, if the peat fire is low, William leaves her to write his love letters for him? Perhaps she does not record his writing to Mary. But certainly we do not hear of him doing so, whereas Dorothy writes to her constantly. It comes, in fact, as a shock to learn that Mary has been all this time not back at Gallow Hill, but at Penrith. Perhaps it is no weather for travelling—not even for a lover? Would he not have stirred his stumps to take leave of her, to see her once more before on 15 February she departs to go so far away? Clearly but for a letter from Coleridge's Frenchman he would not. And even then, on 14 February, he has only half a mind to it; but 'The fine day pushed him on to resolve'. Dorothy also pushed. Molly was sent for the horse and 'off he went in his blue Spenser and a pair of *new* pantaloons fresh from London'. Dorothy nibbled some cold mutton 'without laying cloth and then sate over the fire, reading Ben Jonson . . . and other things. Before sunset I put on my shawl and walked out'; and when she came in view of Rydal 'cast a long look upon the mountains beyond. They were very white but I concluded that Wm would have a very safe passage over Kirkstone, and I was quite easy about him'. Not quite easy, since she 'slept in Wm's bed and . . . slept badly, for my thoughts were full of William'.

With William away, Coleridge diminishes in importance. When a letter the next day reports he is better, this is merely 'very satisfactory', but it is not an answer to William's letter; and not, one feels, the intense joy it would normally have been. There is also a letter from Annette, also more snow; is also so 'terribly cold' she had 'to run all the way to the foot of the White Moss to get the least bit of warmth'—and for obvious reasons she again slept badly.

The next day, having persuaded herself not to expect William—'I believe because I was afraid of being disappointed'—he 'came in just at tea time, had only seen Mary H. for a couple of hours between Emont Bridge and Hartshorn Tree', in other words only caught her at all already *en route* for home. '. . . his mouth and breath were very cold when he kissed me. We spent a sweet evening. He was better—had altered the pedlar'. She, on her side, was full of stories for him: of the carman with four carts and a family of potters she had met toiling up the hill the evening he left: 'The carman was cheering his horses and talking to a little lass about 10 years of age. . . . She ran to the Wall and took up a large stone to support the wheel of one of his carts and ran on before with it . . . to be ready for him. . . . Her business seemed to be all pleasure—pleasure in her own motions', and 'There was a wildness in her whole figure, not the wildness of a Mountain lass, but a *Road* lass . . . who had wanted neither food nor clothes . . . .'

But few walks, or days, fail to provide Dorothy with such figures, whether a young 'woman with 2 little girls one in her arms the other about 4 . . . a pretty little thing but half starved. She had on a pair of slippers that had belonged to some gentleman's child . . . it was not easy to keep them on but, poor thing! young as she was she walked carefully in them. Alas too young for such cares and travels. The Mother when we accosted her told us that her husband had . . . gone off with another woman and how she "*pursued*" them. Then her fury kindled and her eyes rolled. . . . She changed again to tears. She was a Cockermouth woman 30 years of age— a child at Cockermouth when I was. I was moved and gave her a shilling—I believe 6d more than I ought to have given'.

Another time it will be 'an old man, who I saw was begging . . . but from . . . a wanting to try him . . . I let him pass. He said nothing and my heart smote me. I turned back and said You are begging? "Ay", says he. I gave him a halfpenny. William . . . joined in I suppose you were a sailor? "Ay", he replied, "I have been 57 years at sea . . ." Why have you not a pension? "I have no pension but I could have got into Grenwich hospital, but all my officers are dead" . . . His coat was blue, frock shaped . . . it had been joined up at the seams with pale blue to let it out and there were three Bell-shaped patches of darker blue behind where the buttons had been. His breeches were either of fustian or grey cloth . . . His bags were hung over each shoulder . . . One was brownish . . . the other was white with meal . . . and his blue waistcoat was whitened with the meal. In the coarse bag I guessed he put his scraps of meat etc. He walked with a slender stick . . . but his legs bowed outwards'.

She will not state that his breeches were fustian; they might have been grey cloth. But in all this she is working on many levels. Her eye, intellect, social conscience, feelings are all involved. She misses nothing; and countless as are her tales one cannot give them since one cannot summarize—only omit the essential, quintessential.

At Town-End itself she is seldom content with giving alms, even to one she does not fully trust: '. . . a poor woman came, *she said* to beg some rags for her husband's leg . . . but she has been used to go a-begging . . . her little Boy [the pretty boy Dorothy and William had met going '"to late" a lock of meal'] looks thin and pale. I observed this to her. Aye says she we have all been ill. Our house was unroofed in the storm nearly and *so* we lived in it for more than a week. The Child wears a ragged drab coat and a fur cap, poor little fellow, I think he seems scarcely . . . grown since the first time I saw him . . . This', Dorothy reflects, 'was but a *common* case.—The snow still lies upon the ground. Just at the closing in of the Day'—this same one—she 'heard a cart pass . . . and . . . the dismal sound of a crying infant. I went to the window and had light enough to see that a man was driving a cart which seemed not . . . full, and that a woman with an infant in her arms was following close behind and a dog close to her. It was a wild and melancholy sight'.

Often it is those who have known better days, often widows, 'broken soldiers', old sailors. But it may be a young one, 'faint and pale when he knocked . . .', with whom they sit talking for two hours. 'His name was Isaac Chapel . . . He had been on board a slave ship . . .' where a boy had been lodged with the pigs and half eaten, another put to watch in the sun till he dropped down dead. 'He had twice swum from a King's ship . . . and escaped, he said he would rather be in hell than be pressed [press-ganged]'. The poor man had not been in bed for three nights. 'He had called at a farm house to beg victuals. . . . The woman said she would give him nothing. "Won't you? Then I can't help it." He was excessively like my Brother John.'

XVI

My beloved is mine, and I am his

1802

THE LIFE OF her times may continue to be Dorothy's daily tale. It is far, however, from being her main matter, now against all reason nearer that of the Song of Songs. Her tone grows increasingly lyrical. With William on 4 March gone for three days to Keswick, where Coleridge was hourly expected home from London, we pass through a door suddenly flung wide:

> Since he has left me (at ½ past 11) it is now 2 I have been putting the Drawers into order, laid by his clothes which we had thrown here there and everywhere, filed 2 months' newspapers and got my dinner 2 boiled eggs and two apple tarts . . . Wm has a nice bright day . . . The Robins are singing sweetly. Now for my walk. I *will* be busy, I *will* look well and be well when he comes back to me. O the Darling! Here is one of his bitten apples! I can hardly find [it] in my heart to throw it into the fire. I must wash myself, then off—I walked round the two Lakes . . . Sate down where we always sit. I was full of thoughts about my darling.

This passage does more than admit us to Dorothy's state of mind. It tells us as much about the man who inspired it, the loving farewell he has taken of her that morning and the tenderness of his last instructions. And then he is back to her—a day ahead of time: 'How glad I was. After we had talked about an hour I gave him his dinner, a Beef Steak [no boiled eggs], we sate talking and happy.'

There had been no Coleridge at Keswick, but winter is over and gone. Gone *The Pedlar*, gone the pains of revision, and the toll this had started to take of Dorothy's bowels and strength. Now in its place is poetry—prolific as never before? Or as he feels it may never be again? Poetry inspired by Dorothy's tale of a beggar woman she saw when he and John were in Yorkshire two years ago. She 'sate with him at Intervals . . . took down his stanzas etc.'; 'etc.' meaning listened, approved, suggested. And that same day as they walked he warmed to the idea of and half cast a poem about the children of the 'woman tall beyond the measure of tall women', whom she had also seen two years back. But then, as we know, she had looked up her description for him, 'and an unlucky thing it was for he could not escape from those very words, and so he could not write the poem'.

But the next day, by nine in the morning,

he had finished the Beggar Boys, and while we were at Breakfast that is he [for she had breakfasted] with his Basin of Broth before him untouched . . . wrote the Poem to a Butterfly! He ate not a morsel, nor put on his stockings but sate with his shirt neck unbuttoned, and his waistcoat open while he did it. The thought first came upon him as we were talking about the pleasure we always feel at . . . at a Butterfly. I told him that I used to chase them a little but that I was afraid of brushing the dust off their wings, and did not catch them—He told me how they used to kill all the white ones when he went to school because they were frenchmen.

If on the next day, prompted by a letter from Caroline, it is in some sort Annette's turn ('The Emigrant Mother'), it is never Mary's; a hugely fertile period brings no single love poem, or none to her. It is still, moreover, necessary to read William to sleep: 'I read Spenser while he leaned upon my shoulder.' The next day they again 'made a pillow of my shoulder, I read to him and my Beloved slept'. Later she walked to Rydal, which had happily replaced the post office at Ambleside. 'A sweet Evening as it had been a sweet day', and she

walked quietly along the side of Rydale Lake with quiet thoughts—the hills and the lake were still . . . I looked before me and I saw a red light upon Silver How as if coming out of the vale below.
> There was a light of most strange birth,
> A light that came out of the earth
> And spread along the dark hill-side.
Thus I was going on when I saw the shape of my Beloved in the Road at a little distance—we turned back to see the light but it was fading . . . The owls hooted when we sate on the Wall at the foot of White Moss, the sky broke more and more . . . we sate on. When we came in sight of our own dear Grasmere, the Vale looked fair and quiet in the moonshine . . . We walked backwards and forwards . . . William kindled . . . We carried cloaks into the orchard and sate a while there, I left him and he nearly finished the poem. I was tired to death and went to bed before him—he came . . . and read the Poem to me in bed.

The next day—with William again off to see Coleridge, home at last, and bring him back on the following one to Grasmere—she went though unwell, and though 'William charged me not to', to the Lloyds. And 'sate ½ an hour afraid to pass a Cow. The Cow looked at me and I looked at the Cow and whenever I stirred the Cow gave over eating'. Her night walk

153

home, dark as it is, holds no such terrors for her. 'Once there was no moonlight to be seen but upon the Island house and the promontory of the Island where it stands . . . when I saw this lowly Building in the waters among the Dark and lofty hills, with that bright soft light upon it, it made me more than half a poet', she wrote. She does not dream that she is one, that she has that day written a poem that will never be bettered—about a cow.

In the morning, 'a very rainy' one, she went gathering moss 'to make the chimney gay against my darling's return. Poor C! I did not wish for, or expect him it rained so'. But about half-past four 'Coleridge came in. His eyes were a little swollen with the wind. I was much affected with the sight of him—he seemed half stupefied. William came in soon after. Coleridge went to bed late, and Wm and I sate up till 4 o'clock. A letter from Sara sent by Mary. They disputed about Ben Jonson. My spirits were agitated very much'.

That it could be Mary and Sara who disputed about Ben Jonson, when obviously William and Coleridge are meant, betrays her distress as still great when she entered this. As she sat up with William, it seems probable that he now broke to her Coleridge's enslavement to opium.

Coleridge stayed for two nights, and on the day he left he 'and William lay long in bed', perhaps talking, with Coleridge in the spare bed in William's room. His wish is that, after William's marriage, they should all go for two years to 'bluer skies & a more genial sun'. Presumably his wish includes Asra. But Coleridge's letters from London have, as Dorothy knows, not only worried S.H. but made her ill. Is she not herself harming Coleridge's health and marriage, for are not the two things synonymous? And perhaps it was more the fear of losing Asra than anything else that had brought Coleridge home with the real intention of making on his side an effort to salvage his marriage. To Sara, reinstated as 'My dear Love' in his letters, he would 'return in Love & chearfulness'.

By the time he reached Keswick, however, these plans were all awry. Ten days had been spent with Asra on the way, and had not been happy ones. In the entry he made in his notebook for this visit he wrote, '"Wept aloud". You made me uncomfortable.' If Asra had said that his letters had made her weep aloud, and reproached him for writing as he did, in the eyes of Mrs C. the return via Bishop Middleham put the kibosh on 'love and chearfulness'.

His visit now to Town-End can have been happy for no one. Certainly it upset Dorothy, and after he left William seems to have tried to comfort her: 'We had a sweet and tender conversation.' This, on the other hand, may have related to William's problem—marriage. For that it was one is not in doubt. Had Coleridge 'pushed him on to resolve'? We know only that after he left William was 'very unwell', and still the following morning 'very poorly'. But that same day an important decision was reached: 'We resolved to see Annette, and that Wm should go to Mary' in order, one assumes, to explain to poor Mary that he could not feel free without this, and to ask that the marriage be yet further delayed. Dorothy's addendum, 'Wm wrote to Coleridge not to expect us till Thursday or Friday', may in retrospect seem remarkable for its bathos. It was in fact tantamount to her entering: 'March 26th, *The Rainbow*; March 27th, *Ode: Intimations of Immortality*'.

One cannot, however, but contrast the tone of her entry here with that recording the night of Coleridge's coming. Now surely she has cause for agitation. Instead all is calm, tranquil as never before, happy, exquisite as never before: William works at 'the Cuckow' poem, Dorothy sews beside him: 'and at the closing in of day went to sit in the orchard. He came to me and walked backwards and forwards . . . He is now reading Ben Jonson I am going to read German it is about 10 o'clock, a quiet night. The fire flutters and the watch ticks I hear nothing else save the Breathing of my Beloved and he now and then pushes his book forward and turns over a leaf'.

On the following day Dorothy made her own odd resolve, odd chiefly in being unequivocally hers: 'I made a vow that we would not leave this country for G. Hill.' How could the need for any such vow have arisen? Gallow Hill, according to John, was 'a vile abominable place'; he could not bear to think of Mary there. William would never quit his native land. Dorothy's vow seems only explained by a feeling of insecurity, renewed with marriage suddenly looming large.

Meanwhile it is Wednesday; on Friday William had worked without success. Then, 'While I was getting into bed he wrote the Rainbow'. And the next day went back on wishful thinking?

Here is the birth of a great poem: '*Saturday 27th*. A divine morning. At Breakfast Wm wrote part of an ode. Mr Oliff sent the dung, and Wm went to work in the garden [!].'

Before forking the manure this is what he wrote:

There was a time when meadow, grove, and stream,
The earth, and every common sight,
     To me did seem
   Apparell'd in celestial light,
The glory and the freshness of a dream.
It is not now as it has been of yore;
    Turn wheresoe'er I may,
      By night or day
The things which I have seen I now can see no more.

Wordsworth wrote countless poems to Dorothy. How can the *Ode* not be counted among them? For this, so far from being the elation of a lover, is in Wordsworth a perennial mood—heightened. Dorothy lived in a 'Paradise Gained', he in a 'Paradise Lost' and mourned as early as in *Tintern Abbey*. His sensual response to life had suffered an early check in Annette. He after this wrote at Racedown of having 'Forgone the . . . clear

and open soul, so prized in careless youth'. And one cannot discount his
usage of 'forgone'; cannot but feel that he reinforced the loss of his
boyhood sensations with the sense that he had forgone the right to these.
Under the surface of Wordsworth's nervous tension would seem to lie
something like the cliff which, as a boy in a stolen boat, had inspired such
panic fear—and, later, poetry. For the incident itself must seem less
important than its importance for him twenty years on, or than the words
he then found to describe this; how 'growing still in stature', the cliff 'with
measured motion like a living thing / Strode after me'. In the *Ode*, now, he
portrays himself as against all reason an outcast:

> Now while the birds thus sing a joyous song
>
> .   .   .   .
>
> To me alone there came a thought of grief:
> A timely utterance gave that thought relief,
>   And I again am strong.

He has both his grief—and the cure, his indubitable power as a poet. But
everything 'speaks of something that is gone'.

> Whither is fled the visionary gleam?
> Where is it now, the glory and the dream?

These, in his eyes, were fled when he wrote *Tintern Abbey*; and restored to
him, as he then said, by Dorothy. She had met him on both counts—guilt
and the loss of childhood. But now he stands on the brink of a new
parting. It is not that the in dream is over but is as good as over, since
dreams will hardly support a wife and children.

That he felt in this way is surely the secret of Dorothy's happiness. But
his doubts and anguish are also hers. With the marriage plans no longer
vaguely embodied in the 'Frenchman', but in the Treaty of Amiens signed
that week, sufficiently so to explain her headache, as they left on the first
stage of William's journey to Mary, Greta Hall.

'C. was not tired with walking to meet us.' The atmosphere also seems
better, despite their having arrived 'wet to skin', a condition which has
never gone down well with Mrs C.; and despite the fact that Coleridge's
attempts to repair his marriage have been somewhat too ardent: 'there is
too much reason to suspect that Mrs C. is breeding again / an event,
which was to have been deprecated.' On the last day of their stay they all
went to tea at Greta Bank, the very unlakeland mansion, porticoed,
stately, which William Calvert had built along the lane from Windy
Brow—no Windy Brow. There, for it is still there, we may picture
Dorothy standing up in one of the large parlours, 'repeating' William's
verses to the assembled company. Since this, or reading aloud, was
frequently her office, it would seem that she did it well, without
stammering. Her recital on this occasion included, if it was not confined
to, four stanzas of the *Ode*. At this point the spotlight must switch to a
member of the audience. William had clearly shown the lines to Cole-

ridge. But now, it would seem, he was shattered afresh by their beauty. Whither had fled his own visionary gleam, was not, as was William's, a pointless question. And now William was going to be, if reluctantly, happily married. He was going to marry Asra's sister.

On getting back from Greta Bank, Coleridge retired to his study and began an ode on his own account. It was not the great *Dejection: An Ode* as we know it. It was called 'A Letter to——', to Sara Hutchinson. To elucidate his opening lines, he prefaced this with a quotation which, as premonitory, must give one pause:

> Late, late yestreen I saw the new Moon
> With the old moon in her arms;
> And I fear, I fear, my Master dear!
> We shall have a deadly storm.

The next day William and Dorothy left for Eusemere. And from there, on his thirty-second birthday, Dorothy went six miles with him on his way to Mary. He was leaving her in the best hands possible, with a woman temperamentally like herself, one who could be relied upon to talk and be stimulating but understand, too, when she wished to be alone. As the Quaker, Thomas Wilkinson, did not. She had walked through the snow to Yanwath to see the Clarksons' friend, whom she and William had met when last at Eusemere, and there received her letter, from William *and* Mary. 'It was a sharp windy night' and the well-intentioned Quaker accompanied her for part of her walk home, and 'all the way' questioned her 'like a catechiser': How was Miss Mary Hutchinson? Would she visit this year? And where had her brother gone, did she say? 'Every question was like the snapping of a little thread about my heart—I was so full of thoughts of my half-read letter and other things. I was glad when he left me.' 'Then' she 'had time to look at the moon', and think her own thoughts. Most of us would recognize such feelings, but who of us would do as she now did—'full of . . . my half-read letter and other things', observe that 'the moon travelled through the clouds tinging them yellow as she passed along, with two stars near her, one larger than the other. These stars grew or diminished as they passed from, or went into, the clouds'? 'At this time', she goes on, 'William as I found the next day was riding . . . between Middleham and Barnard Castle having parted from Mary.' Nor had she then known what soon she would—that riding past Raby Castle his thoughts had gone back to Racedown, to all she had been to him there and been since; that, dropping the reins on the pommel, he had written a poem for her in which it was she who was named his Love.

Not knowing this, she 'slept ill', and the next day 'was not well and obliged to go to bed in the afternoon'. After tea she 'walked along the Lake side . . . The air was become still . . . the hills darkening. The Bays shot into the low fading shores. Sheep resting all things quiet'. As she was returning the maid-servant came to meet her—'*William* was come. The surprise shot through me'. To Mary she wrote that 'he looked delightfully,

157

but it was a sort of flushing in the face for he was fatigued with his long ride—he got tea and very soon went to bed'.

No detail of their two-day walk home is left out in her journal, even the cattle are twice numbered exactly, perhaps, for once, simply because each detail is precious to her. It is now that they see the daffodils—'I wandered lonely as a cloud'—but it is she who writes of these not William, who plucked them from her journal in 1804. She does not say when he gave her the 'Glow-worm' poem, only that on the second day of their journey she wandered off alone along an exquisite path and 'repeated the Glow-worm as I walked along':

> Among all lovely things my Love had been;
> Had noted well the stars, all flowers that grew
> About her home; but she had never seen
> A Glow-worm, never one, and this I knew.

She had almost forgotten the incident, how, riding home with the glow-worm, 'when to the Dwelling of my Love I came' he had told her nothing about it but laid it in the orchard, and all the next day 'hoped, and hoped with fear;' and then 'At night the Glow-worm shone beneath the tree' . . . 'Oh! joy it was for her, and joy for me!' But William had not forgotten. And she hung now over a gate 'and thought I could have stayed for ever'.

But the point is she cannot. And she goes home to write to Mary, for the first time addressing her as 'my Sister'. How badly poor Mary needed this reassurance may be divined from Dorothy's letter to her:

> . . . My dear, dear Mary! I am deeply concerned to hear that you are so thin. Till I had seen William I had no idea how thin you were . . . For God's sake do not measure your exertions by your own self supposed ability, but put restrictions upon yourself . . . Study the flowers, the birds and all the common things that are about you. O Mary, my dear Sister! be quiet and happy . . . We are very anxious to know how you got home after you had parted with William, since he told me that you had owned that you felt weak, and have been very uneasy about you. We shall surely have a letter on Monday.

From here she proceeds to describe William's arrival at Eusemere and give a long account of their journey home:

> You ought to have been with us, we saw so many sweet things. Every foot of the road was new to me, and all that we saw was interesting, yet for ever changing. We sauntered and rested, loved all that we saw, each other, and thee, our dear Mary,—sauntered and rested, lounged and were lazy . . . William is now writing to Coleridge. We found a letter from him . . . poor fellow! I fear he has his own torments. He says if we wish to see him he will walk over next week . . . Dear Mary, we are glad

to be at home. No fireside is like this. Be chearful in the thought of coming to it . . .

If Dorothy's advice to Mary was, in the weeks ahead, needed anywhere, it was at Town-End. 'William was not well and I was in low spirits.' 'We went to bed . . . with prayers that Wm might sleep well.' 'I repeated verses to William while he was in bed . . . "This is the Spot" over and over again.' 'William slept not till 5 o'clock.' 'Again no sleep for Wm.' 'I was in bed all day—very ill.'

William's reluctant approach to marriage, clearly was partly inspired by fear of the effect on Dorothy. His loving concern for her was paramount. But that the signs of stress Dorothy was now showing derived in the main from William is equally clear. If many of his themes were suggested by her, the theme of one long poem she had not supplied—that of 'mighty poets in their misery dead'. In this, 'The Leech-Gatherer', were compounded William's feelings both about Coleridge's state and about his own: 'We Poets in our youth begin in gladness; / But thereof come in the end despondency and madness'.

'The Leech-Gatherer' (re-named *Resolution and Independence*) was 'finished' —that is, William thought it was—on 7 May. On the 8th, Dorothy wrote, they 'sowed the scarlet beans in the orchard. I read Henry 5th there. William lay on his back on the seat. "Wept, For names, sounds, paths, delights and duties lost" taken from a poem upon Cowley's wish to retire to the Plantations'. That she, too, had both Coleridge's plight and 'genial sun' in mind when she quoted this seems not in doubt. But if William in 'The Leech-Gatherer' had rejected retirement from poetry, the threat that he might be forced to 'retire' remained. And where in such a future would lie her 'path'? It was not for herself that she '"Wept"', however, but for Coleridge and William: 'I was oppressed and sick at heart for he tired himself to death', re-writing 'The Leech-Gatherer' on the 9th. On the 10th 'He will be tired out I am sure. My heart fails in me' was her pitiful cry.

But her journal was not all anguish, nor William's days confined to hacking his way into 'the Plantations'. Her entries are often long, and have a heightened beauty. Every moment of this time is precious, and in fewer than ever are she and William apart. Now when she gardens he helps her. When he has not slept and has a headache, they take the fur gown to the Hollins: 'We found a sweet seat and thither we will often go.' On another day they lie in a ditch, William

with his eyes shut and listening to the waterfalls and the Birds. There was no one waterfall above another—it was a sound of waters in the air —the voice of the air. William heard me breathing and rustling now and then but we both lay still, and unseen by one another. He thought that it would be as sweet thus to lie so in the grave, to hear the *peaceful* sounds of the earth and just to know that our dear friends were near.

There were times, too, with Coleridge that might belong to the *annus mirabilis*. It was, in fact, these and not the earlier period, that prompted William's description quoted on p. 69, 'Noisy he was and gamesome as a boy'. This, despite his arrival, on 20 April, with *Dejection: An Ode* in its early form in his pocket. The next day, Dorothy wrote, 'Coleridge came to us', as she and William were sauntering in the garden, 'and repeated the verses he wrote to Sara. I was affected with them and was on the whole, not being well, in miserable spirits. The sunshine—the green fields and the fair sky made me sadder; even the little happy sporting lambs seemed but sorrowful to me'; and small wonder. The wonder lies in Coleridge's power to rally; and rally them now during a five day visit: 'Coleridge and I pushed on before. We left William . . . feasting with silence—and . . . sate down upon a rocky seat . . . Above rose the Coniston Fells in their own shape and colour . . .' Then 'Coleridge went to search for something new'—and found 'a Bower, the sweetest . . . ever seen', festooned with ivy, surrounded by holly, hawthorn, mosses, flowers, with from it a view of the vale unknown to them.

But such now are the scenes laid on by Mrs C. if Coleridge goes to Grasmere or they to Keswick, that he is forced to ask them not to come. Thus was devised the plan of meeting to spend the day, one so hot that Dorothy and William were 'almost melted' climbing Dunmail Raise. A bird circling the crags 'looked in thinness and transparency, shape and motion like a moth'. And they fell back on a moss-covered rock in the river, there to laze away the day. 'Wm and C. repeated and read verses.' Dorothy topped up with 'a little Brandy and water and was in Heaven'.

But time is running out. William's main writing is done. Dorothy is the one who writes on—to preserve for herself forever what she now sees, holding to her journal as to life. And indeed, as the end draws near, the chatter of Molly and Aggy even will serve, it seems, to drown her thoughts. Though on 31 May she could enter: 'My tooth broke today. They will soon be gone. Let that pass I shall be beloved—I want no more.' And when two days later a beggar called and she talked with him and gave him some cold bacon, 'Said he "You're a fine woman!" I could not help smiling, I suppose he meant "you're a kind woman."' For has she not proof that same evening that she will be beloved, when, after walking with William on Butterlip How, they 'sate in deep silence at the window—I on a chair and William with his hand on my shoulder . . . deep in Silence and Love, a blessed hour'?

By now it is 15 June. 'William has not slept all night.' On the 19th William again 'has got no sleep'; Dorothy, too, has been 'ill in stomach from agitation of mind'—both on an entirely new score. That Lord Lonsdale is dead they know. They have hardly dared to hope, but now they have learnt that his heir will settle all debts. William goes away to confirm and look into this. Outside Dorothy's window the swallows are building. She watches them early and late. But there are other things to be done than watching swallows; all to be done with the house to be ready for Mary. All to paint, and all the paint to grind. And she can settle to nothing, and goes back to look at the swallows, leaving Molly to iron and glaze the curtains. Fortunately, 'Miss Simpson came to colour the rooms', which meant that she must herself start to whitewash the ceilings. And she did work till dinner; but afterwards went to bed and fell asleep leaving Miss S. still at it. And rose to find the swallows' nest fallen down. 'Poor little creatures they could not themselves be more distressed than I was. I had seen them sitting together side by side . . .' and one morning watched them 'for more than an hour . . . Every now and then there was a feeling motion in their wings, a sort of tremulousness and they sang a low song to one another'. Here a page has been torn out. When we find her again it is back at her bedroom window—the swallows have rebuilt—and 'Yes! there they are side by side . . . I have been out on purpose to see their faces'.

By 3 July a letter from Mary, combined with one from Annette, has the power to make her 'sleepless', 'sick and ill', unwell enough to lie in bed till four in the afternoon. William, too, needless to say 'sleeps ill', for by now it is the 7th and Dorothy doing the packing. In the afternoon they 'lay sweetly in the orchard'.

The next day is their last. Dorothy pays for the coal. William falls asleep as they are talking. Dorothy cannot sleep, but lies watching the swallows as they 'stole in and out of their nest and sate there *whiles* quite still, *whiles* they sung low for 2 minutes or more'. They do not know that tomorrow she will be gone.

But so it is, and in the very moment of leaving she has recourse to her journal in her anguish. 'Dear Mary William. The horse is come Friday morning, so I must give over. William is eating his Broth. I must prepare to go. The Swallows I must leave them, the well the garden the Roses, all. Dear creatures!! they sang last night after I was in bed—seemed to be singing to one another, just before they settled to rest for the night. Well, I must go. Farewell.'

XVII

The Wedding Ring

1802–1803

'WILLIAM, WHO IS sitting beside me reading Hamlet—we are both at the little green round table by the fireside, the watch ticking above our heads. Mary is with the sleeping Baby below stairs writing to Sara. William exhorts me to give over writing—so Farewell my dearest Coleridge. May God bless you! and your faithful and affectionate Dorothy Wordsworth.'

Apart from the sleeping baby the illusion is almost perfect. The watch might be ticking still in 1802. But the date is two years later. And Dorothy's agonized cry, 'I must give over . . . I must prepare to go', was not misplaced, her farewell to the swallows, 'the well . . . the Roses, all' more loaded with symbolism than she could know.

Both behind and ahead of her lies, in 1804, a stiffer haul than that over the Hambleton Hills to Mary. Never before that day had Dorothy, twice in one paragraph, been 'footsore, and could not walk quick'. 'Sweet Church and Churchyard', she noted in July 1802 of the church in which William would be married, and which he perhaps hoped she would pass without remarking, always a vain hope in Dorothy's case. Dorothy uses the word 'sweet' as the French use '*douce*', in a way we have lost the power to do. Our usage is sticky-sweet. Here, as so often, she somehow contrives to convey by it all that she does not say—'the tears of things'.

But for two and a half months more the church will not affect her. Instead William will be with *her*, in France. And even after France they will not immediately come north, but do as they had done between Keswick and Eusemere on the first lap of William's marriage journey, 'lingered and loitered and sate down together that we might be alone'. She had at the start of that day been not footsore but heartsore, having seen for herself how things now stood at Keswick. Coleridge had put them on their way, 'and we had a melancholy parting, after having sate together in silence by the Road-side'. But then, after leaving Eusemere, they had 'a chearful ride though cold' on the top of the coach and, caught by a heavy shower, 'buttoned' themselves 'up both together in the Guard's coat and . . . liked the hills and the Rain the better for bringing us so close to one another—I never rode more snugly'.

Five days after leaving Mary she was on the Dover coach crossing

Westminster Bridge and, in her journal, anticipating the sonnet—'Earth has not anything to show more fair'—William would write on recrossing this a month later. In the interval there would be four weeks seeing Annette in Calais (presumably chosen in part for its easy access, also its privacy; Annette led her perilous life in Paris). The beach, the sea and the sunsets are described by Dorothy—and Caroline, once, 'was delighted'. Annette fares one degree better, as a name mentioned twice. But Dorothy —Molly and beggars apart—has never in her journals aspired to depict persons or conversation. And if she now wrote to Mary on so delicate a topic, the lady was definitely for burning. For once one may fill the gap readily enough. To speak and read French as Dorothy did is one thing; to hear it gabbled in France quite another. Nor could the talk have touched on William's and Dorothy's ground. What Annette in her excitable way could talk of was politics and her own dangerous existence, no doubt embracing Caroline every ten minutes—very French, very un-Dorothy, quite unsuited to William; but, if gushing, brave, warm-hearted, moving. It must have been disconcerting to come face to face with the girl who had fascinated William in a woman *embonpoint* who, dressed in black as a 'widow', looked middle-aged and had a black moustache. Caroline, if with a look of William, was almost certainly spoilt and may well have seemed as a child painfully French, to Dorothy as empty-headed as William's sonnet—'It is a beauteous evening, calm and free'—suggests. For William the meeting was bound to be disturbing on every level. The Lonsdale money had still to materialize; until it did he could offer Annette nothing. Nor, in any proper sense, could he ever 'pay' Annette for the ten years during which she had reared his child. Could he, without Dorothy as a talisman against guilt, so courageously have braved Annette and the past? If his French was the more fluent, he was, according to Southey, in English even withdrawn and silent with strangers. And the probability is that he was so now—and thankfully fell back on the fact that Dorothy, as she said, 'was never famous for taciturnity'. Meanwhile if his political conscience had been stirred by France and Annette, the sonnets he was now driven to write were still in their form Dorothy's work, touched off by her reading of Milton's sonnets to him the previous spring.

On 30 August at Dover they 'looked upon France with many a melancholy and tender thought'. That evening saw them in London in Montagu's chambers which—with their host away—they had to themselves; and where they might linger and loiter three weeks more. Charles and Mary Lamb were near neighbours in Mitre Court, and Dorothy constantly climbed the stairs to their garret. She was not the only one. In contrast to Lamb's condition at Nether Stowey, here, young as he was, were to be found a set as remarkable, talk as good as anywhere in London. But Mary Lamb was the person who interested Dorothy most, and from now on the letters would flow between them. They had everything in common—except a love of nature? But the Lambs had only a week ago returned from staying with Coleridge, exploring the Lakes and even actually staying for two nights with the Clarksons at Town-End. And Charles was satisfied that 'there is such a thing as that which Tourists call the *romantic*, which' he 'very much suspected before'; 'glorious creatures, fine old fellows Skiddaw etc'. Mary has even herself tottered up Skiddaw —'a day that', as Charles says, 'will stand out . . . like a mountain in my life'. Dorothy cannot conceive the degradation they felt on returning; Charles 'had been dreaming he was a very great man'. Charles was extremely shrewd and Mary so ultra sane it seemed impossible to imagine her not so—to imagine the sight, familiar and moving to so many, of the pair weeping as they walked to Islington to the asylum, with Mary herself carrying her strait-jacket. She was sane enough to do so when she sensed the attack coming; sane enough for the seldom serious Lamb to confide to Dorothy that, at such times, 'I miss a prop. All my strength is gone, and I am like a fool bereft of her . . . I dare not think, lest I should think wrong; so used am I to look up to her in the least and the biggest perplexity'. Such fraternal interdependence and Mary's love for Coleridge could hardly fail as a bond with Dorothy, even had there not been Charles himself— shortly to forward William's 'strange thick hoofed shoes which have been much admired in London'.

They have not, however, been loitering and lingering for nothing. And, back from seeing her Canon uncle at Windsor, 'repaired immediately to Staple Inn where we were informed by Rd's Clerk that our dear John was arrived', and 'just as we entered the Temple Court . . . met Richard and John who were walking . . . by the light of the moon and the lamps. I could just see enough of John to know that he looked uncommonly well . . . His voyage has not been so good as we expected'. But she shall leave half this page for him, and John himself tell Mary about this.

For how long John had known of William's approaching marriage, and from whom one can only guess. But Mary had certainly written to him. Unpunctuated, with words left out, here is what he now wrote, on paper that does bear the mark of tears: 'I have been reading your Letter over and over again My dearest Mary till tears have come into my eyes and I know not how to express myself thou art [a] Kind and dear creature But what ever fate Befal me I shall love [thee] to the last and bear thy memory with me to the grave.'

Mary's sole wedding present was a gown brought back by John—for the woman he had lost to William. He did not address even William or Dorothy as 'thou'; only Mary was 'thou' to him in letters. He was now employing this to her for the last time. Nor would he ever, though pressed to do so, revisit the house where 'his Father's children had once again a home together'. Since self-contained John in his letters to Town-End never once mentioned his correspondence with Mary, Dorothy may not have known its frequency; certainly she did not know its tone. On the other hand it is possible that she did divine his feelings—he was not himself one to divulge these. And it may have been for this reason that she wrote—with relief?—that 'he looked uncommonly well'; and immediately afterwards scrutinizing him closely, 'saw that he was grown fat . . . looked very handsome', and 'God be thanked he is in excellent spirits'. It seems likely that something more than the sheer pleasure of seeing him prompted their staying on in London a further ten days. John, at all events, was not bitter against William—how should he be? William was Mary's choice.

It is hardly surprising, however, that he did not attend a wedding where the only guests were Mary's brothers. For different reasons Dorothy did not attend it. 'Although', she wrote from Gallow Hill to Jane, 'I have long loved Mary Hutchinson as a Sister . . . I half dread that concentration of all tender feelings, past, present, and future which will come upon me on the wedding morning'. Nor did Coleridge stand in as best man. On 4 October there appeared in the *Morning Post Dejection: An Ode*, in its final form impersonal, tragic, courageous. By what cruel accident did William's marriage, its date so long uncertain and postponed, finally fall on that of Coleridge's ill-fated marriage in 1795?

It was as well, and perhaps William's decision, that Dorothy did not attend the wedding. She had been taken ill on reaching Gallow Hill 'and continued to be during most of . . . our stay' (ten days). 'At a little after 8 o'clock' she watched them 'go down the avenue towards the Church. William had parted from me upstairs. I gave him the wedding ring—with how deep a blessing!' taking it from her own forefinger, 'where I had worn it the whole of the night before—he slipped it again onto my finger and blessed me fervently'. In their absence

> my dear little Sara prepared the breakfast. I kept myself as quiet as I could, but when I saw the two men running up the walk, coming to tell us it was over, I could stand it no longer and threw myself on the bed where I lay in stillness, neither hearing or seeing anything, till Sara came upstairs to me and said 'They are coming'. This forced me from the bed where I lay and I moved I knew not how straight forward, faster than my strength could carry me till I met my beloved William and fell upon his bosom. He and John Hutchinson led me to the house and there I stayed to welcome my dear Mary.

Dorothy, not the bride, in short, returned on William's arm. Nor did William do the least he could have done, take Mary on his other arm, since it apparently needed two strong men to haul Dorothy into the house. Now as on the no less strange honeymoon journey home, in the course of which William fell asleep with his head on Dorothy's breast and Dorothy upon Mary's, one's sympathy cannot but go out to the bride. And one can only hope Dorothy kept to herself 'the dear recollections' that in Wensleydale 'melted' her 'heart . . . away', recollections of the time when she and William 'were left to ourselves, and had turned our whole hearts to Grasmere as a home'; after, that is, they had shed George and Lily-Violet, left Sockburn and Mary for Town-End. Strung up as she was, one must fear that she did not. But why did they not as they habitually did, had done on their way to Mary, walk part of the way? If Dorothy in her agitation was tactless, how could she have been anything else, shut up in a chaise, with William writing a sonnet that may still bring a blush to the most hardened cheek:

> Dark and more dark the shades of evening fell;
> The wished for point* was reached—but at an hour
> When little could be gained from that rich dower
> Of prospect, whereof many thousands tell.

That Dorothy behaved as she did on Mary's wedding day, and devoted her longest journal entry ever to a journey for which one would readily understand her entering 'omitted', is the measure of her extremity.

Does she not, in fact, call Mary 'dear Mary' a shade too often? On 15 June she had entered in her journal 'a letter from M.H.'—and entered that William did not bother to read it. On the evening before their departure, William had come in 'about ½ past nine pressing me to go out; he had got letters [among them one from M.H.] which we were to read out of doors—I was rather unwilling, fearing I should not see to read the letters, but I saw well enough'. Rarely, if ever, has she been unwilling to comply with William's least wish; nor is there anything wrong with Dorothy's sight—quite good enough to sit on the wall making her shoes or sewing her shifts till long after half past nine.

She *was* devoted to Mary—and perhaps, as is happily claimed, it is true that never a cross word passed between them. But, if so, this seems barely human. Mary's quiet tongue was wry and could rap out sharply. It would hardly have done so now and to Dorothy. But if Mary had at last achieved a measure of what she wanted she had still, and for long, to bide her time. Not till 1812 would she receive—and weep with the happiness of it—a passionate love letter from her husband, and not a letter to her and Dorothy jointly. Meanwhile, in October 1802, the months ahead must surely have been a difficult patch for both women.

But briefly and first there was Coleridge to see, about to winter away acting as companion to sick Tom Wedgwood. On the 11th he joined them, but 'did not', wrote Dorothy 'come till after dinner'. Two days later they 'set forward with him towards Keswick and he prevailed us to go on. We consented, Mrs C. not being at home', consented, that is, to sleep in their clothes if need be—to act in the spirit of William's poem, 'No joyless forms shall regulate / Our living calendar', as it had always been their way to act. It was not Mrs C.'s way and her absence was a lure; but Coleridge's domestic news is good. He has waged a tremendous battle in their absence. Threatened with his going abroad for his health, even possible widowhood, 'Mrs C. has been made serious'; has promised an alteration in her manners, 'and to fight against her inveterate habits of

* An inn near Leeming Bar, Bedale.

puny thwarting and unintermitting dyspathy'. He, in return, has 'promised to be more attentive to her feelings of Pride, etc.etc. and to try to correct my habits of impetuous and bitter censure'. And the recipe is working. He is even hopeful that it will 'generate a greater inward Likeness'. If Dorothy was doubtful about this last, the rest is what she has long been hoping for. As for his other feats, Asra at Gallow Hill must have shown them his mountaineering 'journal', the notes he had made on the spot in the course of a solitary climbing expedition lasting nine days—on which the fame of Coleridge alone might rest. As he said, 'There is one sort of Gambling, to which I am much addicted; and that not of the least criminal kind for a man who has children . . . It is this. When I find it convenient to descend from a mountain, I am too . . . indolent to . . . wind about till I find a track or other symptom of safety; but . . . where it is first *possible* to descend there I go—relying upon fortune. . . .' He has also been thinking a great deal, and finds he has certain doubts about the Preface to William's last poems. These he is anxious for William to resolve. Since though it would be hard to say which of them, he or William, had conceived which idea in this, he has begun 'to suspect that somewhere or other there is a radical difference in' their 'opinions respecting poetry'.

If only he need not this winter have gone away! If Dorothy had 'blubbered' this time last year, how much more she would need him in the one ahead. As it is, her journal lapses four days after his going, only briefly to flicker into life when he returned to Keswick and Grasmere at Christmas. He stands for a past life continued into the present. And it is, one may feel, with this reassurance behind **her**—a restored confidence that 'the Concern' is still a going concern—that she takes up her pen in the moment and mood she does:

24th December 1802, Christmas Eve. William is now sitting by me, at ½ past 10 o'clock. I have been beside him ever since tea running the heel of a stocking, repeating some of his sonnets to him, listening to his own repeating, reading some of Milton's and the Allegro and Penseroso. It is a quiet keen frost. Mary is in the parlour below attending to the baking of cakes . . . Sara is in bed in the toothache, and so we are [?]—[My] beloved William is turning over the leaves of Charlotte Smith's sonnets, but he keeps his hand to his poor chest . . . Mary is well and I am well, and Molly is as blithe as last year at this time. Coleridge came this morning with Wedgwood. We all turned out of Wm's bedroom one by one to meet him. He looked well. We had to tell him of the Birth of his little Girl, born yesterday morning at 6 o'clock. W. went with them to Wytheburn in the Chaise, and M. and I met Wm on the Rays. It was not an unpleasant morning to the feelings—far from it. The sun shone now and then, and there was no wind, but all things looked chearless and distinct; no meltings of sky into mountains—the mountains like stonework wrought up with huge hammers. . . .

The simile is a grim and alien one.

Having begun, she does make a short summary of the week; but does not complete even this till Christmas Day: '. . . Saturday 25th December 1802. I am 31 years of age—It is a dull frosty day.'

On 20 January 1803 Coleridge once more departed. By the 14th this plan had still not been decided. But by the 17th, three days before he would leave, it must have been and, if so, known at Town-End. And on that day, despite Dorothy's recent resolution that she 'will take a nice Calais Book, and *will* for the future write regularly', there is no entry. We have come to the end of the Grasmere Journals.

Tom Wedgwood, she had written to John on Christmas Day, looked on the brink of the grave, a tragic sight, since 'he is a very good man'. Good, in Dorothy's eyes, because good to Coleridge. Her sympathy might have been modified had she seen him in his true light, as the worst possible influence. Opium-hooked, he had now asked Coleridge to bring some 'bhang' (hashish). The months ahead would be one long 'trip'.

Apart from this single letter to John, and a number to Richard—the usual fruitless business communications—her letters, too, now lapse till the following June. Why? Because Mary, long her chief correspondent, is living with her, and having Mary she feels no need for Jane. In the more important matter of the cessation of the journals, the reason usually given is the same: that having Mary to chatter to she is calmer and happier, and does not need the outlet of a journal. This simply cannot be made to wash. One need only compare her letter of April 1802 to Mary with her journal entry, both of these describing the 'daffodils' walk—to see that the letter contains no daffodils. To Mary she writes that they got very wet; that she had on 'Joanna's beautiful shawl . . . Alas the *Gloss* is gone from it! but indeed I do not see that is the worse'; that at the inn a visitor 'did more for me than Mrs Coleridge would do for her own Sister . . . made a smart lady of me', etc., etc. Nor does the fact that in November she had been ill; that, on the day Coleridge left (and removed his support?), she—like the flustered Sara at Stowey—poured boiling coffee over her foot and was then 'bad in' her 'bowels', suggest that she was calmer and happier.

What, then, is the real reason why she ceased to keep a journal? Is it the same reason that lies behind William's decision to marry, and his strange reluctant wooing? Did he marry as a desperate measure—because his relation with Dorothy was an incestuous one? All the ingredients for this would seem to be there: the early affinity, early separation; the meeting again after nine years, when Dorothy was fifteen, William seventeen; her willingness to go all lengths with him always—in the matter of Annette, his political stance, poetry; the undoubted fact that they were 'all in all to each other'. As such, must not lying together outdoors as they so often did, wrapped in one cloak, have constituted a strain for any man with no sexual outlet? Was she not 'impassioned Dorothy'? So De Quincey termed her; while William's features suggested 'animal appetites organically strong'. Does he not in poems habitually name Dorothy 'my Love'? And what of the poem quoted in full above (p. 80)

> It is a bed in shape as plain
> As from a hare or lion's lair
> It is the bed where we have lain
> In anguish and despair.

If this is not sufficiently explicit, how get away from the poem's concluding lines:

> Then tell me if the thing be clear
> The difference betwixt a tear
> Of water and of blood.

What of the isolation—and the cold at Goslar? Of the wedding day, the scene at the top of the stairs? The tone of the Grasmere Journals, surely, is hardly that of a sister. And did not Dorothy end by going mad?

The answer to this last question is no, she never 'went mad'. After gallstones and high blood pressure, her mind went as the result of arterial sclerosis, always finally doomed to damage the brain. As to the main issue here—was the relation of Dorothy and William incestuous?—there is far more evidence to prove that it was not, than can be mustered to suggest it was. The family today means little; the relation is accidental and frequently, on growing up, dispensed with. This was not so in an age without means of escape. Families, often immured throughout the winter, were wholly dependent on one another for love, understanding, diversion, as one has only to read Jane Austen to know. And were bound by ties we have ceased to understand.

In saying this I seek only to place Dorothy and William in an age far different from our own—pre-Victorian, pre-Freudian, far less inhibited. Their deprived early life sufficiently explains a love rare in its intensity. 'My love for my Brothers from the early loss of parents has grown into an affection "surpassing the love of women"'; so wrote Keats who loved Fanny Brawne. To assume—and it has been assumed—that this love was in William and Dorothy's case incestuous is to jump too many guns; the first being its utter openness, a love obvious to the Ambleside postmistress even, openly acknowledged in poem after poem. Peggy, the maid at Racedown, who followed to Alfoxden, would have gone with them 'to the world's end'. Still less than Peggy could Coleridge, a constant inmate of their house, who owned to a horror of incest, have failed to spot this. Would Mary—no fool—have married William had she done so? And would Dorothy in the anguished months before marriage have chosen the reading matter she did to soothe William to sleep: 'This is the spot over and over again'?

> This is the spot—how mildly does the sun
> Shine in between the fading leaves! the air

In the habitual silence of this wood
Is more than silent; and this bed of heath—
Where shall we find so sweet a resting-place?
Come, let me see thee sink into a dream
Of quiet thoughts, protracted till thine eye
Be calm as water when the winds are gone
And no one can tell whither. My sweet friend,
We two have had such happy hours together
That my heart melts in me to think of it.

'The bed of pain' was shared not with Dorothy but Annette; the 'tear
. . . of blood' both the blood of Caroline, and a tear of blood for the
bloodshed in which Revolution had ended. William moreover, it should
be remembered, had come to Dorothy caught, if ever man was, in the toils
of guilt; guilt on sexual as well as on other grounds—scarcely a state for
which incest would be a cure. Nor, deeply as she loved him, could
Dorothy's character and constitution have weathered the shock of this.
Trusting and guileless, she certainly could not have lived with him
married to Mary. She *had* slept with the wedding ring on her finger. And
William, when she surrendered this with her blessing, had replaced it on
her finger in a token gesture to show that theirs was a marriage of true
minds, to which Mary would be no impediment. The gesture today may
strike us as extraordinary—or as one of extraordinary delicacy. It is that
of a man whose 'violence of affection' Dorothy had early described to Jane
as shown 'in a thousand almost imperceptible attentions', in 'a tenderness
that never sleeps'.
   Potentially, I would admit that their love could have been incestuous.
And possibly William was aware of this; and Mary the remedy. Equally
possible is the fact that he simply needed to marry, as do most men. He
lived with a tension which only marriage might cure. For Dorothy there
was no remedy. But if the force of her love for William was in a sense
tragic (in that it stood in the way of marriage for her) it is doubtful if, even
loving less, having known William and Coleridge she could ever elsewhere
have found her match. Coleridge spoke of guilt as 'a thing impossible in
her'. In support of this her own words, 'Fraternal love has been the
building up of my being, the light of my path', bear the stamp of
transparent innocency.

'The only objection we have to our house', Dorothy had written to Jane in
the letter of 1800, 'is that it is rather too near the road, and from its
smallness and the manner in which it is built noises pass from one part of
the house to the other. . . .'
   In the June before the marriage she had exchanged bedrooms with
William. With her room hitherto directly below his, she had heard his
every movement and could not herself sleep till she heard him snoring.
His restless nights, clearly, were taking their toll of hers; and although

when 'he called to know the hour' he could hear her answer upstairs, noises overhead are far more distinctly heard than those below. In a cottage such as Town-End,. however, there was as she wrote to Jane no room in which 'a sick person could . . . be in quietness'. And if bed-curtains served to muffle the sounds or the silence that after marriage reached Dorothy, now above, these could hardly fail to have been more disturbing to her than anything heard in the days when she slept downstairs. Her position in honeymoon quarters so cramped was painful in the extreme. On any count it was a lonely business to lie alone while William retired to the nuptial chamber with Mary; and loneliness, not to be needed, separation from William, had always been the state she found hardest to face.

True, Sara H., too, was much of the time in the cottage and normally no one a better tonic for nerves. With Coleridge away she had actually been staying at Greta Hall, caring for Mrs C. before her confinement. But this was not a triumphant proof of the new 'Love and Concord' which Coleridge had established the previous summer—shattered once again by his own act. When, in November 1802, he had left to join Tom Wedgwood he had picked up the coach at Penrith—where Asra was. He had shown some restraint in staying one night only at Penrith, but one was enough to put paid to Love and Concord. He received a stinker from Mrs C., on, it would seem, the grounds of appearances as much as anything else; an old score, about which he now wrote back:

> . . . I love warm Rooms, comfortable fires, & food, books . . . but I do not care what *binding* the Books have, whether they are dusty or clean— & I *dislike* fine furniture, handsome cloathes, and all the ordinary symbols and appendages of artificial superiority—or what is called, *Gentility*. In the same spirit, I dislike, at least I seldom like, Gentlemen, gentlemanly manners, &c. I have no Pride as far as Pride means a desire to be *thought* highly of by others . . . I seem to exist . . . almost wholly within myself . . . & am connected with . . . *persons without* me, by no ambition . . . of having rank and consequence in their minds . . . with my especial friends, by an intense delight in fellow-feeling, by an intense perception of the Necessity of *Like* to *Like*.

Any lingering hope of 'Gentility' on the part of poor Mrs C. must have perished for ever with these words. But if she was unwise to unleash her jealousy, she was too astute not to know she had grounds for this. Asra's invitation to Keswick, extended at Samuel's wish, was a last minute token of reconciliation; her acceptance prompted by conscience not by guilt, by her earnest desire not to add fuel to such flames. All three nevertheless were playing with fire, a fire that by now burnt far too deeply in Coleridge to be put out.

'Long years of seriousness, of deep Passion', he would write in 1804, 'awful Incidents, seas traversed . . . & ever is that one Feeling at my

Heart—felt like a faint Pain . . . I talk loud or eager . . . read or meditate . . . & ever as it were within & behind I image *you*, and . . . talking of Government or War . . . there comes ever into my bodily eye some Tree, beneath which we have rested . . . where we sate beneath the rock, & those dear lips pressed my forehead. . . .'

Dorothy's feelings may, for once, have been tinged with a deeper compassion for Mrs C. when, at the end of December 1802, she took her turn as nurse at Greta Hall; this, while Coleridge was himself at Town-End—where Asra was, and she was not. Admittedly he was there for two more days on her return and then, having left, came back again; but for one night only—and only to bear Asra off to Keswick. All around her was mating and pairing. Mary was three months pregnant. In this coming spring the swallows would once again take up their abode outside her bedroom window. But how even in spring, least of all spring, could she take up her journal? Has nature then failed her? No, for with Silver How now before her she has forgotten—'that I have ever seen it so beautiful, every bit of grass among the purple rocks (which are all shades of purple) is green'. But she is only now remembering its beauty, only now recovering from a shock that has struck at the roots of her being, that could neither be exorcised nor kept within bounds by the keeping of a journal.

By April 1803 Coleridge was home but debarred, with the highly contagious brand of influenza of which people in London and Keswick were dying. Greta Hall, with all laid up, was 'a house of Squawling'. And just when Coleridge had thought himself on the mend, rheumatic fever set in, the worst attack yet. John, meanwhile, was about to sail for China; and Dorothy, dearly as she loved him, had refused to invest her share of the Lonsdale money in the voyage 'for this reason; that if I we[re to] lose it I should forfeit my independence'. She would have lent it had Richard been willing to stand security for her, but this he would not agree to do.

And now Catherine Clarkson too is leaving her, leaving a climate fatal to invalids. Dorothy went to say good-bye, William going with her as far as Kirkstone. The return journey, however, so often made with William, must this time be made and faced alone. 'You will rejoice', she wrote from Grasmere, 'with wonder, at my strength when I tell you that I reached home before five o'clock . . . without being the least heated or fatigued. I daresay Mr Clarkson was anxious . . ., for he would see the clouds upon the tops of the mountains . . . but . . . they only made my walk more interesting.' One does indeed wonder at her strength of mind and heart. But now there is Coleridge, to and fro as of old. And then she is literally 'surprised by joy', by a happiness so great as to be almost too great for the reader. Never again will she be quite the bore she is about the baby born on 18 June—although she will never when others come be able, like Sâra H., to say 'Why, it's just like all the rest!' Her ecstasy and wonder are such that William himself cautions her about dilating on Johnny in her letters. His words fall on deaf ears: 'Mary and I have never ceased to regret that you did not see our own darling child', whose wrists are already dimpling into bracelets, and whose nose '*will* be like his Father's'. But Catherine Clarkson will be consoled by receiving a lock of his hair. With William Hazlitt, the odd youth she had met at Alfoxden, now turned painter, painting the Coleridge household and painting William, she is wholly, blissfully wrapped up in this child which is 'ours', that is, also hers. The degree to which she went off the rails over Johnny is easily explained. In the first place he is William's child; secondly, this is as near as she will come to motherhood; thirdly, there is nothing so calming, as many women will know, as the diminutive pulse of an infant's breathing. This last factor must count high in Dorothy's case. Not only was it as if an abscess had burst; the stilling effect of a baby would always possess the power to soothe and calm her as could nothing else.

William sat for his portrait at Keswick. But Dorothy, it would seem, could not tear herself from the cradle to inspect this. 'At the gallows—deeply affected by his deserved fate—yet determined to die like a man', was a friend's comment. 'Hartley said, "it is very like; but Wordsworth is far handsomer . . ." But you and I, dear William', wrote Coleridge, 'pass for an ugly pair . . . which I fortell Dorothy will not admit.'

If Dorothy did not go to Keswick, Hazlitt came to Town-End—and De Quincey says proposed to Dorothy. This legend is unreliable as are all De Quincey's attempts to reconstruct the past of people he knows. Its basis must lie in Hazlitt, whose shyness and slovenly dress always led young girls to 'make game of him'. Especially had he a horror of 'smart and handsome young women', which makes Dorothy highly eligible. But Coleridge, actively disliking gentlemanly manners, found Hazlitt's '99 in a 100 . . . repulsive—: brow-hanging, shoe-contemplative, *strange*'. Though

attentive to, & patient with children . . . he is jealous, gloomy, & of an irritable Pride—& addicted to women as objects of sexual indulgence. With all this, there is much good in him . . . & tho' . . . from the bearskin at least of misanthropy, he is strangely confused & dark in his conversation & delivers himself of almost all . . . with a Forceps, yet he says more than almost any man, I ever knew . . . that is his own in a way of his own . . .

Such was Dorothy's almost certainly mythical suitor, whom undoubtedly she would have drawn out of his bearskin; but who, in her worst moments, could never have tempted her to leave William—even shared with Mary. Now that she has Johnny, in fact, she actually does not *want* to go off in an Irish Jaunting Car on a six weeks' tour of Scotland, as in the *annus mirabilis* alone with William and Coleridge—'the Concern'. Coleridge, too, was reluctant on another score:

. . . Dearest, dearest, dearest Friends—I will have 3 dearests that there may be one for each (and Godson John shall have one for himself) I begin to find that a Horse & Jaunting Car is *an anxiety*—& almost wish we could have adopted our first thought, & *walked*: with one pony & side-saddle for our Sister, Gift-of-God. . . .

Dorothy at the eleventh hour was taken physically ill, 'just when the Weather', wrote Coleridge on 12 August, 'had cleared up . . . one of her bilious Attacks brought on by the hurry & bustle of packing &c.'. She was thus the cause of their failing to meet Sir George and Lady Beaumont who, on a holiday in the Lakes, had taken rooms in Mr Jackson's half of Greta Hall. Sir George Beaumont was a rich and enlightened patron of the arts whose house, The Clock House at Dunmow in Essex, contained the nucleus of our National Gallery—which he was instrumental in founding. He was also a painter himself, though Molly Fisher's aesthetics would seem for once to have been nearer the mark than those of Coleridge or Wordsworth: 'To be sure the frame's varra bonny but for my part I can make nowt on't'. 'In point of quick enthusiastic feeling', Lady Beaumont, said Coleridge, 'is like Dorothy—only not Dorothy's powers'. She sounds, one is bound to confess, a bit of a joke, 'trembles and cannot keep the tears in her eyes', an intense female who told Coleridge that 'as she was reading your [Wordsworth's] . . . Point Rash Judgment, had you entered the room she believes she should have fallen at your feet'. She cannot, however, have been as silly as she sounds, married to the man whom Sir Walter Scott named 'the man in the world most void of affectation', as well as being 'by far the most sensible'. Both were kindness itelf and now —without seeing Wordsworth—presented him with a property, Apple-thwaite, at the foot of Skiddaw, in order that the two poets might live nearer. On 9 August the Wordsworths were to see it and meet the donors; this last they failed through Dorothy to do—perhaps as well, since Wordsworth ungraciously dismissed the gift as 'a few old houses with two fields attached'.

Sir George was far too guileless to see the dangers implicit in the very thing he admired in Coleridge: 'That Wordsworth, not Himself was his Theme, his friendship being above all Self-love.' He must have been stunned had he seen the treatment of this theme in the notebook Coleridge took with him to Scotland; Dorothy cut to the heart had she so much as dreamed that he could write as he now did in this.

What went wrong? Coleridge two months later ascribed the disaster in great part to himself, and chiefly to two things—to expecting one's friends to have no faults and to 'Envy', 'pain at the excellence of another': 'little ugly Touchlets of Pain & little Shrinkings Back at the Heart at the report that B. [Wordsworth] had written a new Poem / an excellent one!—& he [Coleridge] saw the faults of B. . . . & detested himself dwelling upon them'. This, written without self-abasement, was for Coleridge a moment of truth in a period when lucidity was rare. Meanwhile he had some reason to write as he did of Wordsworth on the third day only of the tour: 'Feckless in an inn, . . . with no want of Courage wants Kindness &

stateliness & gentlemanly dignity'. It is odd to find Coleridge requiring the gentleman. But Wordsworth's delicacy was reserved for those he loved. He disliked giving orders, and would all his life be crude and inept in such dealings.

Coleridge had other reasons for envy: 'What? Tho' the world praise me I have no dear Heart that loves my verses—I never hear them in snatches from a beloved Voice fitted to some sweet occasion of natural Prospect . . .' In other words, William did now hear this from his 'dear Heart'. What is more he had her with him to see with his eyes, and she him wholly to herself for the first time in the old way since the wedding. His love and attentiveness to her have, in the interval, been constant. But if Mary is tactful and 'with the baby below stairs', it is not the same as his leaving Mary, as soon as she could be left, to go for six weeks with Dorothy to the Highlands. It is Coleridge's turn to feel, if not a bad third, the desire to share what he sees with his beloved, to utter in his notebooks the cry, 'O Asra wherever I am, and am impressed, my heart akes for you. . . .'

But perhaps in a wet August the main source of trouble, as Coleridge had feared, the jaunting car. In this contraption the driver alone faced forward in solitary state, while the passengers, equally isolated, sat behind him back to back looking out to each side, without even the link of a common view. To Coleridge—sick in body and mind—Wordsworth's back could have seemed Wordsworth's back turned on him. While Dorothy's 'dear voices' could neither operate nor make themselves heard above the wheels. The relentless grating of these itself got on Coleridge's nerves, and 'the sitting in an open carriage in the rain is', he wrote with truth, 'death to me'. There was almost as much walking as driving to be had in fact, and though 'poor C.' was often too unwell to explore with William and Dorothy, there *was* talk, high spirits, even laughter. Here is Coleridge in Carlisle on the second day of the journey (also the day of the trial there and condemnation of the forger who had committed bigamy with one known to them all, Mary 'the Maid of Buttermere'): 'I alarmed the whole Court, Judges, Counsellors . . . Jurymen, Witnesses, and Spectators by hallooing to Wordsworth who was in a window on the other side of the Hall—*Dinner!*' And here is Dorothy on the seventh day: 'C. who is always good-natured enough to enter into conversation with anybody whom he meets in his way', does so with a fellow tourist at a waterall, who

observed that it was a 'majestic waterfall'. Coleridge was delighted with the accuracy of the epithet, particularly as he had been settling in his own mind the precise meaning of the words grand, majestic, sublime etc. and had discussed the subject with Wm at some length the day before. 'Yes, sir,' says Coleridge, 'it is a majestic waterfall.' 'Sublime and beautiful', replied his friend. Poor C. could make no answer, and . . . came to us and related the story laughing heartily.

Dorothy's *Recollections of a Tour made in Scotland* tells a very different tale from Coleridge's notebooks, nor is this due to the fact that they were recollections. And she specifically says she took no notes at the time—'I was always tired when I reached the inn at night and glad to lay my legs up and loll in indolence before the fire'. When a fire, or even an inn, was procurable. But filthy as were the inns and Highland huts in which they stayed, their primitive quality suited her taste exactly. And if there were times when it suited 'poor C.' less well—'poor C. could not sleep for the noise at the street door'—her references to him are throughout so tender one may wonder if she did know of his addiction.

The *Recollections*, being fuller, are in some ways more personal and allow us to see and hear more than in her Journals. She also now comes before us, if despite herself, as a 'writer'—in a book never intended for publication. Though those who would visit the Highlands today are well advised not to—to stay at home and see them through her eyes. For her, as for William, these offered a new brand of wildness, a land of solitude and desolation in which the human figure and voice at once stood out and were blent, one with their habitat—mountain and mist. Dorothy thought travel books the deadliest form of reading, but hers sticks in the mind with the quality of a work of imagination. Here she is returning, wet through and sick with cold, to a hut found by Coleridge in the morning, from the door of which he had 'hailed us with a shout of triumph';

> The good woman had provided, according to her promise, a better fire than we had found in the morning . . . C. had . . . a pan of coffee boiling for us, and having put our clothes in the way of drying, we all sate down, thankful for a shelter . . . We asked for sugar, butter, barley-bread, and milk, and with a smile and a stare . . . she replied, 'Ye'll get that' . . . We caroused our cups of coffee, laughing like children at the strange atmosphere in which we were: the smoke came in gusts, and spread along the walls and above our heads in the chimney, where the hens were roosting like light clouds in the sky; we laughed and laughed again, in spite of the smarting of our eyes, yet had a quieter pleasure in observing the beauty of the beams and rafters gleaming between the clouds of smoke. They had been crusted over and varnished by many winters, till, where the firelight fell upon them, they were as glossy as black rocks on a sunny day cased in ice . . .

It is tragic to think that Coleridge had that same day declined to enter a boat with William—who, he thought, looked up at him with a 'pig look' —and that night in the barn (shared with a fellow-traveller, an artist) slept as far from William as possible; tragic to think that the note he appended in 1812 to the entry he made in his notebook the following day could have been penned in full now in 1803: 'We slept in the Barn upon the Hay / My Friend (O me what a word to give permanence to the mistake of a life!) & the Artist . . .' What he would write within the week was a perfect case of the mote in one's own eye, one alas never to be plucked out: 'My words & actions imaged on his mind, distorted & snaky as the Boatman's Oar reflected in the Lake.'

With such sick undercurrents a break was inevitable. Two days later it came, to Dorothy merely in the guise of heavy rain 'and no hope that it would be over in less than three weeks. So poor C. being very unwell, determined to send his clothes to Edinburgh and make the best of his way thither' (via the Edinburgh coach from Stirling, and from Edinburgh home). They 'portioned out the contents of our purse before parting', and afterwards 'drove heavily along'. In this way they came to their first sea loch 'which might have appeared as beautiful as Loch Lomond . . . had we been in a more chearful mood'. Here they turned off into Glencoe. But 'our thoughts were full of Coleridge, and when we were enclosed in the narrow dale . . . I shivered at the thought of his being sickly and alone, travelling from place to place'. He was not in fact doing so.

Instead he had returned to the hut of the night before and, dry and warm while Dorothy shivered for him, sat writing in his notebook: 'Here I left W. and D. (*utinam nonq videssem!*)' *sic*—would to God that I had never seen them! From there, too, he wrote a letter to Mrs C., explaining that 'Wordsworth's hypochondriacal feelings' had 'kept him silent and self-centred'. Wordsworth, as he himself admitted, was subject to hypochondria. He did have 'hours that preyed on his flesh and blood'. The affliction was not an enjoyable one—and evoked no grain of sympathy from Coleridge. But what of the laughter 'carousing' their cups of coffee two nights ago; 'the meaning of . . . grand, majestic, sublime etc.', a subject 'discussed with Wm at some length'; of William doing all the driving and managing a horse whose nervous antics twice nearly killed them, at the same time taking in what he could of the scenery? Wordsworth's method with the delinquent Montagu had been 'to convey all the truth he knew without any attack'. Had an attack come from him now, had his silence even been stony, Dorothy's tone must have reflected this. As it was no attack came; though 'Wordsworth alone knows', Coleridge would write in February, 'to the full the extent of the Calamity' (opium). Tolerance, however, does entail restraint. And that Wordsworth's silence at times cost him an effort, is suggested by his breaking it only mildly in old age: 'Coleridge', he said, of the tour in his *Memoirs*, 'was in low spirits and somewhat too much in love with his own dejection'. Creditable efforts would, on both sides, be made, and even seem wholly to have mended the friendship. Dorothy's love would not falter, nor William's tolerance and loving hope—as Book VI of *The Prelude* amply demonstrates in its grasp of Coleridge's stormy course from the outset. In 1805 he would write:

> . . . it is a pang that calls
> For utterance, to think how small a change
> Of circumstances might to thee have spared
> A world of pain . . .

write also of Coleridge's lack of vital love:

> Of Thee, thy learning, gorgeous eloquence
>
> Compelled to be a life unto itself,

and add

> . . . But thou hast trod
>
> A march of glory, which doth put to shame
> These vain regrets; health suffers in Thee; else
> Such grief for Thee would be the weakest thought
> That ever harboured in the mind of man.

Meanwhile they travelled on, over and round the Highlands, back at the hut near Loch Katrine still 'bating our thoughts that Coleridge was not in his old place'—to the good plain fare, if one dull to our taste, of friendship with the Sheriff of Selkirkshire. Walter Scott, who was Dorothy's age, had not yet written a novel but would shortly be able to waive his Sheriff's salary on the strength of being the poet of *The Lay of the Last Minstrel*. He was still at work on the ballad, portions of which he recited to William and Dorothy—who froze with horror. The poem was a crib of Coleridge's still unpublished *Christabel*, which Scott frankly owned he knew by heart. How had he come to do so? In the same way that he had come to know them, through their acquaintance and Coleridge's friend, Stoddart. The Assizes were in session and, with the Sheriff in Court, William and Dorothy anxiously conferred. Ought they not to raise the matter with Scott? Must not the *Lay*, if published first, 'tarnish Christabel'? Scott, clearly, was quite unconscious of plagiarism. William had taken to Scott with a rapidity rare with him, 'and I think William might have done it', Dorothy wrote, 'but he had not the resolution'. In the end, however, she did 'not think it of much importance . . . Coleridge's poem . . . being so very much superior'. But that Scott now took Coleridge's seat in the jaunting car, if for three days only, marked the end of 'the Concern'. There could hardly be a fitter symbol.

XVIII

Fallings from us, vanishings
Wordsworth, *Ode: Intimations of Immortality*

1803–1805

NOT TILL 25 September did they return to Mary and Johnny—and the threat of invasion by the French. The Peace of Amiens had never been more than a tactical move on Bonaparte's side, and had given him fourteen useful months. Each village was raising its army, and William, within a week, had joined up with the Grasmere Volunteers. Dorothy thought he should have waited to be 'called' before subjecting himself to endless drilling. 'However if he . . . likes it, it will do him good', which was all she really cared about.

They had not by 9 October seen Coleridge since their return. But Dorothy was fully *au fait* with his news—with the 'miracles' that he had performed 'after we left him, which proves an uncommon strength somewhere'. It did indeed. On the morning after the parting Coleridge had noted with self-pity, 'am to make my own way alone to Edinburgh'—in 1812 to append the comment, '(O Esteesee! that thou hadst from thy 22nd year indeed made *thy own way & alone!*)'. This was precisely what in 1803 he did—instead of going home, making his own tour of Scotland. Nor did Dorothy exaggerate the performance: in eight days 263 miles (covered, as far as Perth, blistered and almost barefoot in shoes burnt drying them out before he left). He had only then been recalled by the death of 'the Passionate Pearl', the Southeys' first and long despaired-of child. Stricken and haunted, the Southeys had fled to Greta Hall; but 'here my spirits suffer', said 'cold' Southey, 'from the sight of little Sara [Coleridge's small daughter] who is about her size' (the Passionate Pearl's). In a month, however, with Edith again pregnant, Southey was taking his own cure for gloom—overwork. Coleridge was also 'taking a violent medicine in the hope', Dorothy wrote, 'of bringing his disease to a fit of the Gout'. In this he was all too successful, while 'The Horrors of my Sleep and Night screams' seemed to be 'counterfeiting the Tortures of Guilt'! By December there was nothing for it but flight; he will 'sail for Madeira by the first vessel that clears out from Liverpool for that place'.

This decision, he wrote, had the approval of 'W. Wordsworth . . . who has seen me in all my illnesses for four years'. Wordsworth looked on Coleridge as his dearest friend; nor was his love of the sort 'which alters when it alteration finds'. But he might have seen Coleridge less constantly now had he known the poison being poured out in letters behind his back. The well-known picture of Wordsworth, 'living wholly among *Devotees*— having . . . almost his very Eating & Drinking done for him by his Sister, or wife', derives from Coleridge, who now trembled 'lest a Film should rise, and thicken on his [W.'s] moral eye'.

Coleridge did come to Grasmere, and Dorothy went to Keswick, though not as often as she had done in the past. Colds and minor complaints took their toll at Town-End. This perhaps in her case was as well, since it allowed her time to get down to her *Recollections*, time which would soon be otherwise occupied. In the interval she had a visit from her 'suitor', at an odd hour and in odder circumstances. Early in December the household was knocked up at midnight by a more than usually incoherent Hazlitt. Whether he had, in fact, assaulted a local girl, or, led on and driven mad by a pretty one, merely, as has been said, spanked her bottom, the men of Keswick were out to give him a ducking. Coleridge who, with Southey, hid him at Greta Hall, later said the offence was a criminal one. Whatever the incident Lamb called 'the Scapes of the great god Pan', William now doled out money and clothes, and in March wrote to Hazlitt, signing himself 'Yours affectionately'.

On 20 December came one who, had he been Dorothy's suitor, might not have come on an errand so sad to her now—to say good-bye and, bringing Derwent, to stay for a few days only. Dorothy's misery at his going, though she could not be reconciled to it, was tempered by its clear necessity. For three weeks Coleridge was too ill to leave—'Day after day . . . detained by sickness, or bad weather, or both'. Mary meanwhile 'had a very bad cold' which 'made her unable', Dorothy wrote, 'to take an equal share with me in . . . the house, Molly was poorly, Coleridge continually wanting coffee, broth or something . . . the bed was moved into the sitting room night and morning'. With all this, 'so much uneasiness about him', two children 'and *so much to do*', she had little leisure for misery; and, without knowing it, had her reward in Coleridge's notebooks and letters—only now purged of viper thoughts. If a chapter was ending, and ending fittingly, this was in great part due to Dorothy. And for once, if she had '*so much to do*', he recognized the fact—with the conjunction, always fatal at Town-End, of 'the rooms . . . so small . . . & the Rain so incessant'. He even 'made Dorothy's bed in the bed' (presumably daily dismantled and replaced by his in the sitting room) 'and with her help made my own'.

Rain gave way to snow. And finally on 9 January 1804 he could write, 'In the Dark with my eyes shut / a loud Thaw wind. Derwent asleep in the other Bed, God love little dear Heart—& Dorothy in the Parlour, O dear Dorothy—& O dear Sara Hutchinson'. Asra did, it seems, put in an appearance, but only intermittently and briefly. Tom, who since Mary's marriage Asra had looked after, was moving to a farm, Park House near Eusemere. She was occupied with arrangements for this; they were 'crammed edge-full' at Town-End—and perhaps her heart already had its reasons.

Whatever the truth here, Coleridge, with his health 'barometrical', seized any chance to walk and look; to exclaim in his notebooks 'O remember it', and enter there: 'Ask Dorothy for a word'. Her judgement, harassed as she was, stood as high with him as ever, high enough for this to be recorded:

> Is more gained by repeating to a beloved House-mate . . . each night after supper the work of the Day? Or . . . the whole poem . . . whole Book . . . complete Part or Section in a prose work—Ask William and Dorothy.
>
> Dorothy thinks that it would be better to wait till something was finished . . . Ode or single Book or Chapter—

He also recorded something the results of which partly account for our knowing of Dorothy's existence: that on 'January 4th . . . Wordsworth read to me the second Part of his divine Self-biography' (*The Prelude*).

Not till the 14th did he get away to Kendal, and back with relief it would seem on the Black Drop; to write from the King's Arms there 'of my Kind Nurses, who tended me with Sister's and Mother's love', nurses, 'who, I well know, often wept for me in their sleep and watched for me even in their dreams'. Where Mary and Dorothy actually watched was, less romantically nodding, taking turns to sit up with him at night. They, however, fare best in a rambling letter that contains a passage all too often quoted out of context: Wordsworth 'deserves to be and *is*, a happy man . . . for . . . from the first Dawn of his Manhood he has purchased Independence and Leisure for great & good pursuits by austere Frugality and . . . Self-denial . . . happy . . . because . . . he regulates his Wishes, because he feels . . . we can do but one thing well, & that therefore we must make a choice—he has made that choice from his early youth'.

The increasingly ambivalent feelings exhibited by Coleridge, now fully opium-hooked, towards Wordsworth become tragically explicable. But 'Mr Wordsworth', he here goes on to write, 'does not excite that almost painfully profound admiration which I feel exclusively for T. Wedgwood', whose 'faults impress me with a Veneration . . . more almost than any other man's virtues: for under circumstances like his [consumption] . . . a Fault . . . is, I doubt not, in the eyes of God . . . a high Virtue. Who does not prize the Retreat of Moreau more than all the Straw-blaze of Bonaparte's victories?' The 'divine Self-biography', in other words, is a straw-blaze, Wordsworth demoted, his place taken by one with whom Coleridge soars aloft, his own 'Faults' shining like 'Virtues' in company with those of his fellow-junkie.

His state finds a further reflection in the gushing insincerity with which he now addressed Town-End itself: 'I conjoin you, my dearest Dorothy and Mary! as you love me' to copy '*all* William's MS poems . . . I feel, what a treasure, what an inspiring Deity, they will be to me when I am absent / I would not talk thus warmly if I did not know *how* much I am asking'. He could not know—the state of the manuscripts. Illegible, crossed-out, cross-written, often on odd leaves of paper that must somehow be sorted and pieced together, it was, William confessed, intricate weary work; 'I shall never, [I hope] get into such a scrape again'.

To this jigsaw puzzle, moreover, was fast being added fresh work, with William stockstill under an umbrella, fired to continue his 'divine Self-biography'. If he needed such encouragement or even flattery, one must bear in mind his long silences. It might surprise many people today to find Wordsworth writing of *The Prelude* 'as a thing unprecedented . . . that a man should talk so much about himself. I began because . . . unprepared to treat any more arduous subject and diffident of my own powers'. He *was* diffident—to the point of paralysis. And headstrong as he had been, with disastrous results, there is, as I have said, much to suggest that the illness brought on by rewriting derived from a chronic self-doubt —guilt, Annette.

What Dorothy thought of as 'The Poem to Coleridge' was, as is repeatedly said in this, in fact an apology to him—for not being equipped to write the poem Coleridge could not write himself. In *The Ancient Mariner* Coleridge was uncannily self-prophetic. He constantly said what he could not consciously know. It would not be strange if, in passing the buck, he had early wanted to strangle the Giant who made him feel 'a little man'.

Now, however, he wanted both all the unpublished poems and the poem booming out beneath the umbrella (since William composed aloud in 'a terr'ble girt deep voice' that had the locals 'flayt a'most to death'). The girt deep voice, however, was abruptly halted when for four days Dorothy was ill. William, beside himself, could write nothing. Standing over her as she wrote to Catherine Clarkson, he insisted that she describe her symptoms fully for the now infallible Dr Beddoes; and 'after', wrote Dorothy, 'reading over my letter is not half satisfied . . . he bids me add that I *always* begin with sickness and that any agitation of mind either of joy or sorrow will bring it on'. She was now under the stress of both, joy that William was writing and writing the poem begun with her at Goslar; sorrow that Coleridge was going, and 'great anxiety', since her fear is that the poems will not reach him in time, 'and his desire to have them made him almost miserable, while there was any doubt about it'.

By the time she wrote this the poems were dispatched. But Coleridge, the day after her, had himself been taken violently ill. This she knew. Had she also, on 20 February, known the cause the day before Coleridge did? —a letter from Asra, 'that put Despair into my Heart', he wrote, 'and not merely as a Lodger, I fear, but as a Tenant for Life'. Asra, in other words, had written to end a relationship that would be most easily severed now, to ensure that on this voyage in search of health, he make a clean break with feelings that had failed to make him happy and rendered her position untenable.

What made Coleridge unhappy had the power to make Dorothy And Asra could well have informed Town-End of her action, to arm the in the event of almost certain repercussions. We have, however, knowledge that she did so. And Dorothy, without this, was under considerable pressure—some eight thousand lines went to Coleridge and were duplicated to retain. If Mary shared the burden, she was not, as was Dorothy, equipped to help William sort the jigsaw, on top of which Dorothy had a critic's function. 'William is calling to me every instant to hear some lines he is writing', had been her excuse in November for ending a letter—'is writing' not 'something he has written'. Since marriage, in fact, he had done practically nothing. In the measure of his dependence on her still, freshly driven home during her illness, must have lain the deepest solace yet. And perhaps it was his relief and joy in her recovery that now led him to write something else—to complete the *Intimations of Immortality*, before returning to 'The Poem to Coleridge'.

Not till the third week in March could Dorothy relax, with all the poems and five books of *The Prelude* safely locked in 'an elegant thing', the little travelling desk Lady Beaumont had had made to contain these. The relief was immense. 'Thinking of his banishment, his loneliness', Dorothy wrote, 'the long distance he will be from all . . . he loves, it is one of my greatest consolations that he has those poems with him'.

By 4 April—with Coleridge in lodgings at Portsmouth—she had, and needed, other consolations. It had taken him an hour to summon up courage to open their letter, 'for the sight of Dorothy's Handwriting on the directions . . . moves me so deeply that my heart fails me'. After explaining how letters should be addressed to him, he went on, 'But of all things I most eagerly wish to have my beloved Dorothy's *Tour* / Southey goes to London . . . after his Wife's Confinement, if she do well. He could take it . . . O dear dear Friends! I love you, even to anguish . . .'

Dorothy had already written what she supposed her last letter: 'Our hearts are full of you . . . If you get this letter, write to us yet once again— and never, Dearest Friend! never miss an opportunity of writing.' 'We entreat you', William reinforced this in his postscript, 'to write . . . at all opportunities . . . We shall be so distressingly anxious'.

On 9 April Coleridge, clad in two flannel waistcoats, two other waist- coats on top of them under his coat, two pairs of flannel drawers under cloth pantaloons, and thick yarn stockings—equipped, in short, to enjoy the voyage on deck, sailed not for Madeira but for Malta. With the farewells floating out to sea left behind with the gulls, Dorothy, on 13 April, sat for the first time writing to Lady Beaumont to thank for a typical timely cask of ale. Her letter is filled with Coleridge, whom the Beaumonts have sent off furnished with everything from medicines to 'portable' soup. And then as she writes, a letter comes from him. She has half hoped but dared not hope that they might hear again. And now that she does, it is 'like another parting'.

In Dorothy's last letter to Coleridge before he sailed she tells him that William has written some more of the poem addressed to him, including 'some very affecting lines which I wish you could have taken with you'. The lines she was thinking of come in Book VI of *The Prelude* and would have been 'very affecting' to Coleridge. There were also lines, no less so, addressed to her, the first of the countless tributes which would come from William's pen between now and May 1805. With these the trauma of marriage was finally behind her. But so too would be William's greatest poetry. If Coleridge had wished to strangle the Giant he perhaps, in part, succeeded. Wordsworth was an essentially lyrical poet. Great poetry and profundity as *The Prelude* contains, any epic poem must at times descend to prose. And this may from now on, with other factors, have encouraged Wordsworth to accept from himself as poetry what was often prose.

But another main cause of this deterioration must have been Dorothy's changed function. In May she had a taste of the life to come. With Mary five months pregnant, lame and thin as a lath, it fell to Dorothy to help Asra; to foresake poetry for the elaborate fitting up of fourposter beds at Park House. From a fortnight of this she expressly arranged to be back for 'Whitsuntide cleaning, colouring and painting &c &c before the coming of our new Servant'. Aggy Fisher had died and Molly been 'promoted to the high office of her Brother's Housekeeper'. To Dorothy this was 'a great comfort' for 'we were afraid of breaking her heart by telling her that she was not fit for her place which indeed has been the truth for . . . months'. 'My Sister', she wrote to Lady Beaumont, 'not being very strong I was glad to take upon myself the charge of putting things in order'. But this has meant for Dorothy, since she returned on 18 May, 'no leisure, I had almost said no comfort, till today [29 May]'. During this time she has 'really been overwrought with positive labour'. And now Mary and Johnny are to go with William to Park House for three weeks, 'a long time', Dorothy writes, 'for me'. On 20 June she is 'writing from my solitary cottage on this the seventh day of my solitude', restlessly unable to settle to letters. William will return this week but 'the heartsomeness of the house' is gone without Johnny's turbulent cries.

There has, however, been indirect news of Coleridge—at Gibraltar. His family in his absence are never neglected. William, no fan of Mrs C.'s, spent three days at Keswick during Dorothy's stint at Park House. In June they all went to Greta Hall. William, Dorothy wrote, 'walked on before to warn them . . . Derwent was half mad with pleasure. They said he ran up and down . . . shouting "Mary's coming, Dorothy's coming" (he always', she explains to Lady Beaumont, explaining much, 'calls us by these names) . . . Hartley has so much thought and feeling in his face' no one 'with any tenderness of mind . . . could look at him with indifference'. But she cannot tear her eye from little Sara, slender, delicate, 'fair as a snowdrop' as she 'twirled about' with 'exquisite grace'; all this, with—at eighteen months—'her interesting countenance made her an object of pure delight'. She proves in addition 'at times a little vixen' when the Coleridges stay at Town-End in July—'she squalls', Johnny 'roars', and they are parted by force. The cottage was in August again 'edge-full' with Coleridges when Johnny acquired a sister three weeks early. She will be called Dorothy; 'Mrs Coleridge exclaims against the name, but my Brother will have it so'.

Within five weeks of the birth Dorothy and William were off alone to Ennerdale and Wastdale, thankful for news of Coleridge safe at Malta. In the light of the crossing to Hamburg, Dorothy had been happy in the thought that he would at least enjoy the voyage. Instead he had been violently ill (with, among other things 'a dangerous constipation which compelled the Captain to hang out signals of distress to the Commodore for a surgeon to come on board'). This they had learnt from a letter to Mrs C. Their own had been mainly filled with lamentations that he had had 'no letters from *any Body*'.

Meanwhile, after a houseful during the christening, they 'began to be quite sickened at our small dwelling'. But could not find another. This Dorothy thought was just as well, since 'Coleridge will certainly not settle in the North'; and he '*cannot* do it now, for Mr Jackson has sold Greta Hall . . . poor Mrs Coleridge will be turned adrift' and Dorothy cannot bear to think of Coleridge, who 'will be heart-struck at . . . no more returning to his old Books in their old Book-case looking to Skiddaw . . .' Mr Clarkson says Kent is cheap. 'But Oh! my dear Friend, it will be a hard thing when we leave these dear Mountains . . .' Perhaps for them the hardest thing in the world. But for Coleridge, there is no question in Dorothy's mind, they will do it: 'Where he settles we shall settle'.

Richard, staying in the district and now lured to Grasmere but only by Dorothy verbally on her knees, was no substitute for John back from a better voyage and covered with glory—glory made more glorious by a 500 guinea reward for his part in defeating the French in a battle at sea. He had now through Wilberforce, the friend of their Canon uncle, obtained the most coveted voyage of all—'the Bengal and China'. With a cargo valued at £200,000—as well as a new and lucrative form of freight, two hundred passengers—he had no doubt of making a very good voyage, 'if not a *very great* one'. The preparations entailed were perhaps a valid excuse for not coming north, but Dorothy's disappointment can only have been assuaged by John's belief that this voyage might be the last he would need to make. Assuaged, too, by the poem on which William was still working, perhaps less 'quick and slow as the fit comes', as he himself put it, than as the cottage allowed the fits to come. With the autumn exceptionally mild, it may have been Dorothy who now suggested building her 'summer shed': 'it is coated with hether and lined with moss . . .—it will be circular'—in other words a sound-proof nest for William. Until with 'all the glory and stillness of winter about us', and in January Grasmere Water frozen, there were better things for poets to do. And not only poets: 'We were all taking our pleasure on the ice. William and George Hutchinson pushed us along on their skates [presumably Mary and

Dorothy seated on chairs] . . . and we carried the children on our knees, John and even little Dorothy'. The next day, in their exaltation, they carried them over Kirkstone to surprise Asra at Park House; and with Tom, Joanna, George and Hartley—at eight an adult—to make 'a Christmas party round the fire'. Nor was Hartley's father forgotten in their festive mood; they were 'all exceedingly anxious about Coleridge'.

A month later William, writing a letter, reports still 'no tidings of poor Coleridge'. Meanwhile it is 'Woe to . . . Grasmere for ever and ever! A wretched Creature, wretched in name and nature, of the name of *Crump*, goaded on by his still more wretched wife . . . has at last begun to put his . . . threats in execution; and when you next enter the sweet paradise of Grasmere you will see staring you in the face . . . a temple of abomination, in which are to be enshrined Mr and Mrs Crump'. They have had, he adds, 'a Letter from my Brother the Captain . . . from Portsmouth, speaking very favorably of his hopes and in good spirits'. It is 7 February 1805, and John, as he writes, has been two days drowned.

On the 11th Asra, at Kendal, saw the news in the papers and rushed to Town-End, with her usual presence of mind stopping at Rydal to pick up a letter from Richard informing William of the tragedy. 'You will impart this to Dorothy in the best manner you can', he wrote, even dull as he was foreseeing the effect. But Dorothy was alone at the cottage when Asra arrived; she had thus, as William said 'the whole to sustain'. The shock was catastrophic and her anguish intolerable, as was that of the whole family. She and Mary, wrote William 'are both very ill. Dorothy especially, on whom this loss of her beloved Brother will long take deep hold'. He will do his best to console her, 'but heaven knows I want consolation myself'. 'John was very dear to me.' He can say 'nothing higher' of him 'than that he was worthy of his Sister now weeping beside me, and of the friendship of Coleridge'. Coleridge in these first hours of grief was himself not overlooked: William 'trembled for the moment' when he would hear of John's death: 'It will distress him to the heart, and his poor body cannot bear sorrow'.

Perhaps Dorothy did not feel the need which William properly did to establish that John was wholly blameless. Off Portland Bill the *Abergavenny*, hit by a sudden gale, had—with a pilot sent on board—struck a rock and finally, in the course of a fearful night of storm and violent seas, sunk off Weymouth. More agonizing to her must have been the rumour that John had made no attempt to save himself. Lamb, at the India House, now endeared himself to them for ever by obtaining copies of reports and taking endless trouble to contact survivors. On one count only did he reserve some doubt. And John's cry, 'O pilot, you have ruined me!', must echo tragically in one's ears. Though, as William said, John 'was an excellent swimmer, but what could it avail in such a sea encumbered with his cloaths . . . ?'

Harrowing as must have been the reports of John's last hours, the worst for Dorothy lay all around her. Everything in the house served to remind her of him, and by May the garden so cherished by her 'has neither been cleaned nor dug—and the shrubs are run wild. We could not turn our eyes to it but with pain'. But if Mary on 7 March took it upon herself to write for Dorothy to Catherine Clarkson—'Dorothy will write as soon as she dare trust herself to address you'—Dorothy had 'a task of [her] own to perform', that of enabling William to write again. And somehow, with William's own courage, this was achieved. Dorothy meanwhile forced herself to return to her *Recollections* and complete these by 31 May. That same month William's own work was done; three more books added and *The Prelude* finished—with a concluding expression of love for her who now, as at Racedown, represented for him 'a saving intercourse / With my true Self'. For Dorothy copying, stricken still, such lines could not fail to provide their own form of 'saving intercourse'.

She was mending painfully, in the way that Mary Lamb had foreseen, 'that you would see every object with and through your lost brother; and that that would at last become a . . . source of comfort . . . I . . . very well knew from my own experience in sorrow, but till you yourself began to feel this I did not dare tell you so'. Mary Lamb, in fact, had felt too acutely for them—with the inevitable results, as poor Lamb, camouflaging the cause as late hours, wrote to tell Dorothy in June.

But the Lambs were far from being the only friends to rally. On the same day that Asra had seen the paper, Southey at Keswick had done so and instantly written to say that, should his presence be of the slightest comfort, he would come at any time. William, replying on the 12th, had said that he would be thankful if Southey would come on the morrow, which he did. Outwardly Southey was in all things the opposite of the Wordsworths: elegant and a lover of elegance, of books in beautiful bindings, with, in his study hung with marbled paper, exquisite folios displayed on brackets—his learning was as vast as the library he amassed, mounting from 400 books to 14,000. But behind Southey-elegant lay Southey-homely: 'Oh dear! Oh dear! There is such a comfort in one's old coat and old shoes . . . with a little girl climbing up to my neck saying, "don't go to London, Papa—you must stay with Edith"', so that she might get in his bed in the morning and pester him to sing her his new song:

> Over the water, and over the water,
> Over we go, Papa and his daughter.
> Where do we go-a? Where do we go-a?
> Over the water, to pretty Lisboa.
> Over the water, together we go,
> To the land where the grapes and the oranges grow.

Only under his auspices, in fact, would Greta Hall (which Mary Lamb had found an 'unhomely' place) become in the true sense a home; a happy one alive with children, cats, fun and nonsense. To Hartley he wrote: 'Nephew Job—Buona Marietta hath had kittens, all taking after their father Thomas, who there is reason to believe was either uncle or grandsire to Bona herself, the prohibited degrees of consanguinity which you will find at the end of the Bible not being regarded by cats . . .' Bertha, his fat small daughter, was 'Henry the Eighth from her likeness to King Bluebeard'; while Greta Hall, housing Edith Southey, Mrs C., plus their widowed sister, Mrs Lovel (a pain in the neck) itself became 'the Aunt-Hill'.

Such was the man whom William had, at Keswick, already warmed to, but to whom Dorothy only now came round; who, she wrote, 'was so kind and tender I loved him all at once—he wept with us in our sorrow and for that cause I think I must always love him'.

XIX

Things fall apart; the centre cannot hold

W. B. Yeats, *The Second Coming*

1805–1807

ONE FRIEND ONLY was lacking, the one they most wanted; by May they were 'looking anxiously' for Coleridge. Since by 27 March, when they had last heard from him, he must have been already *en route* for home. Dorothy had hastened to copy the letter for Lady Beaumont: his health being good, he would leave Malta in March, though whether he braved the sea voyage or travelled overland would depend on circumstances at the time. He had not said it depended on Mr Chapman; and Dorothy's sole fear was that the news of John's fate must catch up with him in the course of the journey. But nor had Coleridge mentioned that, the day before writing to them, he too, like Molly, had been promoted—by the death of the Public Secretary. This was high office indeed. But Coleridge, set up by the sun, had not been idle. He had also arrived set up, wrote Mary Lamb, with 'letters of recommendation to Governor Ball and God knows who'. She was writing to Sara Stoddart in Malta with her brother, newly appointed Judge Advocate there. And wished to write her own letter of recommendation: 'Behave to him as you would to me, or to Charles, if we came sick or unhappy to you'.

Among Coleridge's letters of recommendation had been one from Sir George Beaumont to a man who knew Lady Hamilton, on the strength of which Coleridge (through Nelson's agent at Brontë) might live rent-free in a monastery in Catania! But as Mary Lamb warned Sara Stoddart, 'he will talk and talk and be universally admired'. And so he did and was—with the result that in place of a rent-free monastic cell he was paid to inhabit a suite in the Governor's palace. Firstly doing secretarial work for Sir Alexander Ball, he rose to supply the place of Mr Chapman—the absent Under Secretary—a government appointment. The post of Public Secretary to which he succeeded in January was second only to that of the Governor himself. This he agreed to fill till Chapman's return. But on 16 March 1805 a despairing Coleridge entered in his notebook, 'Mr Chapman not yet arrived! And I am to stay another two months at least!'

Meanwhile at Town-End the wait went on, and not only for Coleridge in person, but for Coleridge to release them from Town-End. The sale of Greta Hall had after all not gone through; but a summer as wet as was this one drove home the point—that he could no more return there than they, with a poet, hold out in the cottage. 'At last', Dorothy wrote in July, 'we have had a letter'—from Coleridge still on 1 May in Malta. He had heard of John's death, but did not say he had done so only the day before, and casually in the Balls' crowded drawing-room. 'Nearly strangled', he had excused himself 'and got home led by the Sergeant and followed to the door by Sir A.B.' The shock had been all that Dorothy feared. His main point now, in a letter written in haste to catch the Convoy with which he had hoped to sail, was that he was determined to leave by the end of the month, 'let it cost what it may'. Dorothy must have been moved to her depths had she seen what he wrote in his notebook, and not only on the night after hearing the news. His agony for them all was prolonged—for John, for William, for Mary, 'and then Deep [hearted] and wide [hearted] Dorothy, my Sister! my Sister! So like to myself in the forms of our hearts / to thee 'tis *Shudder* . . . I cannot express the feeling'.

And it would, perhaps, at Town-End have been hard to say which was the worse—a summer with day after day nothing but rain, or the glory of the autumn which followed it. Both mercifully brought a stream of visitors. In July Mrs C. was invited for a fortnight to the overcrowded cottage with little Sara, now understandably spoilt and only redeemed by the fact that 'she grows exceedingly like her father'. Among many others in August were Walter Scott and his wife, and Catherine Clarkson who, for Dorothy's sake, heroically braved the climate she had been forced to leave and stayed for two months at Robert Newton's inn. In constant pain, she copied Dorothy's long *Recollections* in order herself to possess 'this treasure'; and be, Dorothy wrote, 'the cause of mirth at our fireside'— still at Town-End no inconsiderable feat. Other visitors included Halifax relations who gave a shattered account 'of poor Dorothy, who has grown so thin and old that they should not have known her, lost many of her teeth, and her cheeks quite sunk that it has entirely altered her profile'. Even Richard for once, it seems, registered her state, and presented her with a pony and side-saddle. This munificence Dorothy warmly acknowledged, but was sorry to add that they were afraid they would have to change the pony 'as it stumbles very much' and fell with Mary.

If Dorothy had needed anything more than Johnny and the certainty— which could only come with time—that she had not lost William, to make Mary a Sister indeed, grief had brought them all closer still. With Mary (not William) now away from home, Dorothy was impatient for her return. And William's pains in the side disappear from her letters to be replaced by concern for Mary's health. Now, in November, she actually did not want to go off with William unless they could take Mary too. But Mary was tied to Dorothy still unweaned. And so she went for six days on a tour that would later become her *Excursion on the Banks of Ullswater*. It is doubtful if it would have mattered where they went. 'As the mists thickened', she wrote, 'our enjoyment increased.' And by the time they had reached the top of Kirkstone, though they could not see fifty yards ahead, they 'were as happy travellers as ever paced side by side on a holiday ramble'. To take to the road with William (if on a pony that stumbled and on which William occasionally rode, while Dorothy kept up 'betwixt a walk and a run') was a recipe that for both would never fail.

Nor, from now on, would she let her spirits flag with Mary gone for five weeks to Park House and William dividing his time between them both. And no doubt that he did so divide it contributed to her calm. Though one may too readily picture Dorothy as a nimble, eager figure accustomed— as she herself said—'to do everything at once and as quick as I can'; forgetting that she could 'sink into a dream / Of quiet thoughts' with eyes as 'calm as water when the winds are gone'.

It is nevertheless rare for the reader to catch her in this mood. And almost as if she senses and seizes the moment for what it is—a lull before the storm. Writing alone at Town-End,

> the evening is very still, and there are no indoor sounds but the ticking . . . watch . . . and a breathing or a beating of one single irregular Flame in my fire. No one who has not been an Inmate with Children in a *Cottage* can have a notion of the quietness that takes possession of it when they are gone to sleep . . . It is at all times a sweet hour to us; but I can fancy that I have never enjoyed it so much as now that I am quite alone.

William 'has not yet begun fairly with his great work', but she hopes will after his return. They will 'then in right earnest enjoy winter quiet and loneliness'. Meanwhile she is sure Lady Beaumont will like 'The Solitary Reaper'. Two of its lines she finds 'inexpressibly soothing':

> Oh listen! for the Vale profound
> Is overflowing with the sound—

and she constantly catches herself repeating these.

On Christmas Day William is with her, with Mary still at Park House. Johnny, aged two and a half, 'is all alive at the thought of two plumb puddings . . . rumbling in the Pot, and a Sirloin of Beef that is smoking at the Fire. Old Molly and John Fisher are in the kitchen, but when dinner is ready they are to come up stairs and partake with us, and "*Johnny and all*"'. After this, with the 'Grasmere Fidler . . . going his rounds' and the neighbours' children come to join in the fun, she has 'been summoned into the kitchen to dance with Johnny and have danced till I am out of Breath . . . he was too shy to dance with any Body but me'. Eighteen-month-old Dorothy 'is in ecstacy', while Johnny 'looks as grave as an old Man'.

With the music and the 'pleasant sound' of 'little pattering feet upon the stone floor' still going on, she retreats upstairs to sit writing and musing on this, her thirty-fourth birthday: 'Six Christmases have we spent at Grasmere, and though the freshness of life was passed away even when we came hither, I think these years have been the very happiest of my life . . .

Though my heart flutters and aches striving to call to my mind . . . the more thoughtless pleasures of former years, and though till within this late time I never experienced a real affliction . . .'

Affliction in a deadly form is now heading for her. For the moment her mood is elegiac. But she has known for three weeks that Coleridge is on his way. Her reaction when she learnt this via Stoddart from Mary Lamb had, however, been one only of panic. 'The terribly long journey', with his health, 'in this cold season', and Vienna, for which he was heading, in French hands, as was half Europe—she wished, she wrote, 'I had not known it till the dangers were past'. William and Southey have both reassured her. But 'the weather is dreadful for a sea voyage. I am too often haunted with dreadful images of Shipwreck and the Sea when I am in bed . . .' 'Oh my dear Friend', she cries to Lady Beaumont, 'What a fearful thing a windy night now is at our house!'

In April, such was William's own nervous state, they packed him off to London for a month. In his absence there is a letter from a Mr De Quincey, to which Mary and Dorothy, forwarding this, seize the chance to add late at night a few lines. Dorothy takes the pen while Mary is undressing: 'The wind is howling away the rain beats. Oh my dear William that thou wast humming thy own songs in time to it . . . or resting thy hands upon my knees as thou art used to do in musing between while work pauses. . . .'

But in May he is back to her; and in the following month a new member added to the family. He will be christened William. But no, he will be Thomas, since Southey cannot have *two* William Wordsworths. And still the wait goes on—until 15 August, when Dorothy, with William and Mary away, is the first to hear: Coleridge has been at least ten days off Portsmouth completing the regulation quarantine. A Mr Russell is with him and has written to Exeter friends, they to the Coleridges at Ottery. And by this means Mrs C. has heard; 'for Coleridge', Dorothy wrote, 'has not written himself'. But she has 'no doubt (as Mrs C. thinks also) that he is afraid to inquire after us lest he should hear of some new Sorrow'. Meanwhile, her joy is almost too great to sustain. She has never so wanted William and Mary, 'as for these last three hours since Mrs Coleridge's note came'.

Ahead would lie over two months more of hourly expectation, silence from Coleridge, waiting, bewilderment. The agony was heightened by the fact that they could not wait, had already waited overlong to take up the farmhouse being lent them by the Beaumonts for the winter on their estate, Coleorton, in Leicestershire. They had kept the Beaumonts dangling to hand this over to them in case Coleridge should want them instead at Keswick. But no word came from him in response to this offer.

At last by October there was nothing for it: 'Judge of our distress', wrote Dorothy, 'at being obliged to set off without having seen him.' Within hours her distress would be greater still. At Kendal they picked up Asra, who, feeling the cold at exposed Park House, was to winter with them. And Coleridge—she had collected a letter written in Penrith half an hour earlier—was at Keswick. He could not, he said, come to Kendal to see them, only to part. 'Notwithstanding this', Dorothy wrote, 'we resolved to see him and wait one day at Kendal for that purpose'. A special messenger was dispatched to Greta Hall,

> but before seven o'clock he himself arrived at an inn, and sent for William. We all went thither to him and never never did I feel such a shock ... We all felt exactly in the same way—as if ... he were a person of whom we had formed an image ... without having any personal knowledge of him ... We (that is Mary and I) stayed with him from Sunday evening till Tuesday morning at nine o'clock; but Sara H. and Wm did not part from him till the following morning. Alas! what can I say? ... He is utterly changed; and yet sometimes, when he was animated in conversation concerning things removed from him, I saw something of his former self ... a shadow, a gleam ... but how faint and transitory!

His fatness is 'more like the flesh of a person in a dropsy ... his eyes are lost in it'. As for his talk, 'he scarcely ever spoke of anything that concerned him or us ... anything ... we were yearning after'. All they could gather was 'that he must part from [Mrs C.] or die and leave his children destitute, and that to part he was resolved'. They 'would have gone back to Grasmere, or taken a house near Hawkshead ... but this he was against, and ... it would have been ... useless, for he' promised 'to come to us here [Coleorton] in a month; and, if he do part, the further the better'.

If Dorothy's shock was great, it is almost unbearable to think of Mrs C. and the three children joyfully awaiting their wonderful father's return. When Mrs C. told Derwent she was taking an extra pillow from his bed for Coleridge, Derwent, aged six, exclaimed ' "Oh by all means. I would gladly lie on straw for my father" ', to a light-hearted Mrs C.'s 'delight and amusement'.

To unravel truth from fable in the saga behind Coleridge's transformation is outside the scope of this book. The climate could not, after six months, compete with banishment and the failure of letters to get through. The quest for health had been abandoned for opium laced with brandy, the longing to return home replaced by a growing reluctance to pitch his tent on the 'Aunt-Hill'. And when finally released, he had set off, not for home, but for a second holiday in Sicily. His actual return had been all that Dorothy feared, a nightmare of illness and narrow escapes from the French, with the voyage back as bad as the voyage out. Whether or not the Dutch captain, left holding the enema tube, had helped himself to some very outsize pearls that Coleridge claimed he was bringing home, his Maltese earnings had melted on the journey. But perhaps most fatal had been Asra's concession: she would not refuse ever again to meet him. Hope burgeoned in the desert like a vine; to become, after the Kendal meeting, a thread which in late December led inevitably to Coleorton.

Apart from the sheer relief of being, if in a farmhouse, released from the racket of cheek-by-jowl Town-End, the comparatively flat rolling country-side held one beauty new to Dorothy. These were the sunsets, at Grasmere shut out by the mountains. Pacing with William under the ancient trees of the old Hall, they lingered late until the moon rose, lighting up the new Hall, a turreted pile the Beaumonts were now building—for the land-scape gardening of which William had somewhat mysteriously been roped in as a Capability Brown.

Meanwhile, as long as the children had what might be whooping-cough, Coleridge could not risk this for Hartley and Derwent. But at last he arrived in time for Christmas. 'I think I was never more happy in my life', Dorothy wrote, 'than when we had him an hour by the fireside. For his looks were much more like his own self, and though we only talked of common things . . . we perceived that he was contented in his mind. . . .' She might have read his content in another light had she seen what lay written in his notebook, and written there after the Kendal meeting: 'I know you love me!—My reason knows it, my heart feels it / yet still let your eyes, your hands tell me / still say, often & often say, "My beloved! I love you" / indeed I love you / for why should not . . . all my outward Being share in the Joy—the fuller my inner Being is of the sense, the more my outward organs yearn, & crave for it—O bring my whole nature into balance and harmony.'

There were other things Dorothy did not know—the near certainty that Coleridge had barely glanced at the feverishly copied contents of the little travelling bureau furnished by Lady Beaumont. But nine whole Books of the poem to him Coleridge could not have seen. And only John, as he said, was now missing from the circle of all those he most loved, who in the evenings after Christmas sat round to hear William read a testament of love for him. In the group round the fireside one figure must have listened with her eyes constantly flitting to Coleridge's face. Such a declaration not only of love but deep indebtedness, rich in its recognition of Coleridge's powers, surely could not fail in its effect; especially when William was now handing over the poem for Coleridge to improve and criticize.

There can have been no more fatal reading. Moved as Coleridge was—even moved, as Dorothy hoped he might be, once more to take up his poet's pen—the real result was utterly to crush him, to 'awaken' as he wrote, 'a throng of pains':

> Sense of past Youth, and Manhood come in vain,
> And Genius given, and knowledge won in vain . . .

This poem in reply to William's was an all but incredible proof of Coleridge's own powers as a poet still, and of his resolution. And mentally ill though he was by now, it seems possible that without Asra he might have pulled up, if not through. As it was, doubly hooked—drug-wise and sexually—a new and explosive fantasy arose.

Sublimate as he might, Asra could not be his 'sister', for the simple reason that she was not. Were, he now wrote, 'Accidents of temporary desire' to take over, he would feel as if he 'had roamed like a Hog . . . in the rankest Stews of a city battening on the loathesome offals of Harlotry—but where love' is like 'a Volcano beneath a sea always burning . . . how can the water but heave and roll in billows'!

No wonder that he found cause to write, 'But a minute and a half with *me*—and all that time evidently *restless* and going'. Not only did Asra refuse to be pawed, the explanation was that she loved another, one 'better, greater, more *manly* & altogether more attractive to any the purest woman'. So attractive that Coleridge's 'minute and a half' is contrasted with 'An hour and more with [W.W.] & *in bed*—O agony!' Agony indeed —not least for those who, in their wildest imaginings, could never have dreamed up this one.

Nor were matters improved when Asra, finding herself now hopelessly out of her depth, applied for help to William; and occasioned a word of advice from 'the other man'. 'Dost thou command me', wrote Coleridge, 'to endure Asra's neglect and look on my Asra's averted eyes? And to know that she is false & cruel who was always so dear to me and always will be . . . Ah, let him perish who can make use of reasoning in love . . . What is and is not becoming, let those judge *whose minds are sound*' [my italics].

In spite of all this, 'Coleridge is still, by the middle of February, determined to make his home with us', Dorothy wrote. The only question in her mind is '*Where*? There is no house vacant in the North—and besides there would be something . . . indelicate . . . in going so near to Mrs Coleridge immediately after the separation'. When Dorothy, before seeing Coleridge had heard of his wish to separate, she had been wholly against it. 'Suppose him', she wrote in a letter going over the ground at length, 'once reconciled to that one great want, an utter lack of sympathy, I believe he may live in peace and quiet. Mrs C. has many excellent properties . . . and I am truly sorry for her'.

After seeing him she had second thoughts, and even briefly third ones—inspired by Coleridge himself, then at Keswick. 'Mrs C.', she wrote, 'had been outrageous'. But Coleridge himself is outrageous at Coleorton (though the word cannot, of course, be applied today to one who, by now, was simply a medical case). Dorothy did not have access to the notebooks. But she could not be blind to Asra's predicament, still less could she be blind to William's pain. Coleridge himself did no work. But nor did the 'Poem to C.' stir him to give back criticism even. After annotating the sixth book, that in which he himself chiefly figured and was celebrated, he not unnaturally dropped a task which could only reinforce his sense of failure. Still less, it follows, did he take any interest in the poems which William—lacking Coleridge's criticism and the confidence he alone could inspire—now decided to print in place of the long poem.

If Coleridge's determination to live with them was odd, Dorothy's attitude seems odder still. On 17 February Coleridge has just called her 'upstairs to read a letter from Mrs C. who, poor woman! is almost frantic, being now convinced that C. is determined not to live with her again'. Dorothy has been agitated by this letter and the matter of how and where Coleridge and they could live together:

> Coleridge had an idea that S[outhey] intended leaving Keswick, in which case he wished to have the house and we consented to take it though *very very* reluctantly—Mary and I having many objections . . . to taking Mrs C.'s place there. But in consideration of Coleridge's circumstances, the convenience of having his books already there and for the sake of . . . Hartley we had consented. But as Mrs C.'s letter informs C. that Southey has no thought of leaving . . . we are right glad in our hearts to be released.

She even has an excuse for the fact that Coleridge cannot get down to writing so much as a letter: it is that so long as the separation is not established as final, he cannot feel secure and must be hamstrung.

Coleridge remained till April. Perhaps for Asra's sake, a great many Coleorton letters vanished. Either Catherine Clarkson was in this as discreet as Mary, or Dorothy and William—hurt but hoping—took care to write no word that might travel back. Not till December did Dorothy, still without doling out blame, admit what was simply the cause of unutterable sadness: 'We had long experience at Coleorton that it was not in our power to make him happy.'

Meanwhile, her work and happiness lay where it had always lain—together, in restoring William's spirits, copying and helping prepare his poems for publication. This, had she known it, was the end of the road; and, cruel as was what lay in store, a fitting end. That the bulk of *Poems in Two Volumes* consisted of those written in the last late winter and spring before marriage made them in a special sense hers—theirs. Lodged in among these was a recent poem that, if it owed nothing to Dorothy, might tragically speak for her no less than William:

> *A Complaint*
> There is a change—and I am poor;
> Your love hath been, nor long ago,
> A fountain at my fond heart's door,
> Whose only business was to flow;
> And flow it did; not taking heed
> Of its own bounty, or my need.
>
> What happy moments did I count!
> Blest was I then all bliss above!

Now, for that consecrated fount
Of murmuring, sparkling, living love,
What have I? shall I dare to tell?
A comfortless and hidden well.

A well of love—it may be deep—
I trust it is,—and never dry:
What matter? if the waters sleep
In silence and obscurity.
—Such change, and at the very door
Of my fond heart, hath made me poor.

XX

Each man kills the thing he loves

1807–1812

> But thou, my Sister, doomed to be
> The last leaf on a blasted tree;
> If not in vain we breathed the breath
> Together of a purer faith . . .
> If on one thought our minds have fed,
> And we have in one meaning read . . .
> Together we have learned to prize
> Forbearance and self-sacrifice. . . .

These are grim and final tidings indeed, written after leaving Coleorton. If enshrined in a gothic tale—*The White Doe of Rylstone*—and addressed by Francis to Emily, the affinity William has in mind is clear, as, painfully so, are the multiple echoes.

> The one red leaf, the last of its clan
> That dances as often as dance it can

—so Coleridge had written at Alfoxden, himself deriving the image from Dorothy's journal. The Grasmere fiddler will go his rounds, the leaf in 1819 be dancing still—and with an agility that would repel Coleridge's exquisite daughter, the fastidious and brilliant 'Celestial Blue'. Though it was praised by Wordsworth 'in his beloved sister', wrote Mrs C., 'Good man he forgot . . . he was addressing one . . . so encreased in size' she 'could no more go down a dance . . . than fly over the Derwent'. But by 1807 the ball in its first essential sense was over; while for the leaf that would always cling to the tree, the dance now ahead would all too closely resemble that of the fairy-tale, the painful relentless dance of the Red Shoes.

Wordsworth was to deplore in Coleridge the habit of giving substance to thoughts unworthy of him by writing them down. Though he himself, one may feel, in dwelling on his fear that the gleam had gone encouraged his own decline. But few poets exist without this fear, and in Wordsworth its multiple origins were, perhaps, more deep-seated than most. There were later factors, however, and, by 1807, chief among these Coleridge himself. 'I have poured myself', Coleridge would write, 'into a hundred other men's streams', by which he meant Wordsworth's. And so he had—and in return received unstinted love. Nor would that love yet founder, though the wound he had inflicted on the poet of 'the Poem to C.' was poetically mortal. Humanly the wound went no less deep. Henceforward on Coleridge's side it was all take, no give. And if Wordsworth's liberal stance gradually stiffened, it was as that of a man stricken and disillusioned. Meanwhile he wrote with ghastly foresight,

> Hope nothing, I repeat, for we
> Are doomed to perish utterly.

In 'we' was included Dorothy-Emily.

Their return in July to Grasmere itself struck an ominous note. 'Many persons are dead', Dorothy wrote, 'old Mr Sympson, his son . . . , old Jenny Dockwray', from whom, in 1800, Dorothy got lilies and periwinkles. 'All the trees in Bainriggs are cut down, and even worse, the giant sycamore near the parsonage house.' Their own days at Town-End, too, were by now numbered, though this they could only see as a blessed release. In the autumn they will move to the sole house available—the Crump temple of abomination. But then, though the temple had not actually crumpled again—as, to the mirth of the vale, it had done last year—it could not now be ready till late December. The only means of getting through in a cottage where, as Coleridge said, they had not room for a cat was constant dispersal. And William, Mary and Asra were poised for flight as, on 4 November 1807, in what was at Town-End increasingly 'a sweet hour', Dorothy sat writing to Catherine Clarkson. They had heard about a month ago from Mrs C. at Bristol, 'in hourly' (predictably weekly) 'expectation of Coleridge', who was to escort her part way home from a curious and abortive mission—to obtain from his elder brother George the latter's blessing on their separation. George had thought the suggestion as odd as it was, and refused. Mrs C. meanwhile hung on in Bristol—Dorothy at Town-End: 'Coleridge has never written to us, and we have given over writing to him, for what is the use of it? We believe he has not opened one of our letters. Poor soul! he is sadly to be pitied.'

   She had scarcely closed the letter up, when she 'heard a tumult in the house and Mary shouted' (Mary could then shout). But 'guess', wrote Dorothy, 'my surprise and joy at seeing Hartley skipping about the room. His Mother and Derwent and Sara were at the door in a chaise, and a Mr de Quincey a young Oxonian . . . he found out Coleridge and is come for a week purposely to see William'. They had left Coleridge intending to depart at once for London, where he was to deliver a course of lectures. 'He talks of coming into the North in March.' But 'Poor dear Coleridge', Dorothy wrote, 'I am almost afraid to wish him here, fearing that we may be of [no] service to him'.

Somehow the whole party was put up for the night, overflowing into the Ashburners'. In front of De Quincey Mrs C. talked airily of only not accompanying Coleridge to London on account, with the children, of expense. What De Quincey—immortalizing Dorothy on this occasion— could not know was the grounds of her agitation, the painful conference being held behind the scenes. Mrs C. 'entreated us to say nothing', Dorothy wrote

> . . . that should make him suspect any-thing amiss between her [and C.,] spoke of the disgrace of a separation . . . To this M. and I answered that . . . we could see no disgrace . . . that there would be a buzz, and all would be over . . . 'Well', she replied, 'he may stay away if he likes I care nothing . . . if he will not talk of it'; and then she began again about disgrace . . . so people will go on saying that he forsakes his wife and children . . . and he will always have something to make him uneasy.

By the time she is writing this De Quincey has gone his way, having after four years achieved his end. He had first written to Wordsworth as a boy of seventeen, who the year before had run away from school and hidden himself from his rich mother and guardians in Greek Street, Soho. There he had slummed it, if with a rent-free bed—the bare cold floor-boards over a pawnbroker's shop; and had made friends with a younger and poorer waif, a pathetic little prostitute whom he loved and planned to save. Whether due to design, or to some hideous fate, she one day failed to keep their rendezvous at the corner of Great Tichfield Street and—known to him only as Anne—vanished into the ranks of London's poor. De Quincey had since returned to the fold and gone up to Oxford, from where he had twice approached within sight of Grasmere—to lose his nerve and flee like a guilty thing. Dorothy marvelled that, modest and shy as he was, he should ever have summoned up courage to write to William. He was not too shy, however, to appear remarkable. Nor was his learning lost on Southey, who only wished 'he was not so very little' and would not—in his terror—leave his great-coat behind him in the road.

They will not, it transpires now, be able to move till the spring or even summer. But there *have* been two letters from Coleridge, in London. 'He says nothing', Dorothy writes, 'of his private feelings, but that his thoughts have been with us continually'. His 'best news' is that he has written almost as much again as they have already seen of *Christabel*, and, as well, has rewritten his tragedy. Dorothy, in the meantime, will be very anxious for him with 'the bustle and fatigue he will . . . go through in London'. Her anxiety might have been mitigated had she known that his 'best news' was almost certainly 'a hum'—no additions to *Christabel*, at least, have been traced. As to his private feelings, his thoughts had indeed been with them continually—but were hardly fit for publication. 'Poor Soul', she had written, 'he is sadly to be pitied'. Would she in November have pitied him had she known the nature of his thoughts, still in September?

O agony! O the vision of that Saturday morning—of the Bed / —O cruel! is he not beloved, adored by two—and two such Beings, and must I not be beloved *near* him except as a Satellite . . . but does he, O no! no! no! he does not—. . . it is not . . . his nature to love *any* being as I love you . . . I alone love you so devotedly, & therefore, therefore love me, Sara! Sara! love me!

Perhaps she would still have pitied since no one better than she knew how painful can be the need for love, or sympathized more with Coleridge's own need. But the probability is she would not, and in this she would have been wrong. Of course Coleridge was jealous—of one beloved by three not two women. For Asra had grown deeply attached to William —because he loved not as Coleridge did, but showed his love in 'a thousand almost imperceptible attentions'; and was, as Crabb Robinson testified, consistently charming, tender, courteous to, and considerate of the women he idolized. Coleridge, however, was blinded not only by jealousy; to this flame was added the fuel of inside knowledge—that William had married Asra's sister not on the strength of a passion comparable with Coleridge's for Asra.

Had Dorothy known how things stood, she would scarcely have refused the Clarksons' wish to share Allan Bank, a mansion only taken on as a home for Coleridge also, with Hartley and Derwent. She does not now believe Coleridge will come; but to make him feel rootless might 'serve as a handle for despair' when they 'would fain give him all possible assistance'.

By February 1808 more material assistance was called for. Those who had booked for his lectures found locked doors; while the lecturer, to Southey, gave out that he was dying. William hastened to London 'to see him, and if he be strong enough', Dorothy wrote, '. . . prevail upon him to return'. In London, for over a fortnight, William hung around refusing all engagements—and refused admittance to Coleridge till four in the afternoon. Happily the lecturer, however, was not dying, and his critical faculties in excellent trim, since William thought of publishing *The White Doe of Rylstone*. But Coleridge had reservations about the poem. And if Coleridge had reservations William would not publish. *Poems in Two Volumes* had failed to sell; and it was with his confidence at rock-bottom that, breakfasting at Lamb's, he met Crabb Robinson, the cosmopolitan friend of Catherine Clarkson. To him Wordsworth proceeded to speak 'freely and praisingly of his own poems', despite which the civilized Robinson 'never felt this unbecoming but the contrary'. That Wordsworth could get away with this has been explained by the fact that he spoke of his poems as of those of another person, with a passion that itself exerted a spell. But if Lamb laughed and loved, if Crabb Robinson swallowed the pill, the defensive streak being shown by William in London was for Dorothy a dangerous one. Combined with her role of housekeeper-mainstay, it was to play its part in sounding the knell of the 'perfect electrometer'.

Already by the end of March she was sending Coleridge a note to give to William if he was still in town. He *must* overcome his scruples about the *Doe*: 'As to the Outcry . . . I would defy it—what matter if you get your 100 guineas in to your pocket? . . . New House! new furniture! such a large family! two servants . . .! We *cannot* go on so . . .' They will have to dismiss one servant and 'work the flesh *off our poor bones*. Do, dearest William! do pluck up your Courage . . . and we shall be . . . at our ease for one year at least.'

Coleridge, properly, was horrified by this letter; and not only because it showed in Dorothy 'a decaying of genial Hope and light-heartedness', but because he could 'not bear to think that her judgement should be in danger of *warping* from money motives'. Rather than that he would undertake alterations and arrange publication somehow.

Meanwhile, old Molly, with 'her legs . . . much swoll'n . . . grows daily weaker'. She talks cheerfully of death, and Dorothy can only wish her sufferings over. And then, with William still away, tragedy strikes at Grasmere in an altogether grimmer form. Isolated in Easedale a family of five children, one at breast, were discovered destitute, their parents' mangled bodies being found only days later deep in the snow at the foot of a precipice. The eldest, little Sally Green, had been employed by the Wordsworths, and Mary now sat on the committee formed to find homes and raise funds. Dorothy at times stood in for her and had to endure the rudeness of a certain Mrs North of Rydal Mount. But Dorothy's main work was, at William's request, to write *The Tragedy of George and Sara Green*—a masterpiece of narrative which she refused, though pressed, to publish on the grounds that such limelight must be bad for the children.

Asra, meanwhile, had been unwell with a pain in her chest and a cough —and then vomited blood. This was Peggy again. William, sent for, returned in haste—to Johnny, that same night taken violently ill. The symptoms, to Southey's horror, looked like water on the brain, the malady which had claimed the Passionate Pearl; and Johnny was given up for lost. But then the disease proved merely some local epidemic; and Johnny, 'sleeping . . . beautiful as an angel' contrives in Dorothy's eyes to combine 'a countenance quite divine' with looking more than ever like his father.

Asra, however, was a far more serious matter. 'She has made up her mind to live with us', Dorothy wrote, and will be 'treated as an Invalid till she is perfectly strong—and perhaps alas! that may not be for years'. Shaken as Coleridge was by the news about Asra, he did not lose sight of Dorothy's predicament as she now wrote to him yet again: '*We are very anxious* that "the White Doe" should be published *as soon as possible* . . . Our main reason (I speak in the name of the Females) . . . is that William may get it out of his head; but further we think that it is of the *utmost importance*, that it should come out before the Buz of your Lectures is settled.' So she sat writing on 1 May, as her 'suitor', William Hazlitt—whom, turned violently Bonapartist, William had, in London, declined to meet—stood 'brow-hanging, shoe-contemplative, strange', at the altar with Sara Stoddart, who was plain, well past her prime and bobbed her hair. Mary Lamb was bridesmaid and Lamb there laughing his head off—'anything awful always makes me laugh'.

Coleridge did not laugh on receiving Dorothy's letter. 'God forbid your sister', he wrote to William, 'should ever cease to use her own eyes and heart, and only her own'. He was already too late—with Town-End to pack up, Mary pregnant and with her right arm in a sling, Asra to nurse, three children aged five, four and two, and the move to be accomplished somehow.

It is hard to see Allan Bank, with its gables and Strawberry Hill windows, as the abomination the Wordsworths thought it—but such it was indeed to prove. Its exterior—that of a roomy family house—is deceptive. Inside the grandeur and scale are today daunting. Shattering when one thinks of Dorothy announcing 'we are determined to do everything ourselves'; on top of all to *make* the carpets. And the more so when one realizes that her 'we' meant 'the only two able-bodied people in the house', herself and sailor Henry Hutchinson. The latter, recently press-ganged, had only—about to sail—been extricated by Sir George Beaumont. In the nick of time also for Dorothy, since William (as with the Town-End move) 'is not expected . . . to do anything'. He was, in any case, useless at the job; whereas Henry, another John, could carpenter, cook, wash up—and sew. 'In another fortnight', she hopes on 5 June, 'all will be over . . . for Henry and I work body and soul, and with less we should never be done'—she never will be. For the moment, however, they begin to enjoy 'the comfort of having each a [comfortless] room of our own'—for one does not wonder that Southey thought their sticks of cottage furniture made a poor showing in such a setting. Nor today can we see its redeeming feature in Dorothy's eyes—the views she saw undefiled by abominations as, on 5 June, she sat 'in this my little Castle' writing: 'We have been miserably anxious about dearest Coleridge, having had bad accounts . . . from two quarters. But a letter from Lady Beaumont today tells us he is better. We expect one from himself to-night.'

It seems unlikely that Dorothy received any letter from Coleridge either that evening or before August, for reasons that were partly her own doing. Coleridge, authorized by William as he thought, had gone to considerable trouble to clean up the *Doe* and procure him his hundred guineas from Longman. Without informing Coleridge, William cancelled publication, denying Coleridge's right to act in this, and adding that the poem was not to be intrusted to him. These instructions were passed on verbatim to Coleridge who, naturally bewildered and bitterly hurt, replied to Longman quoting 'Miss Wordsworth', who 'always writes in her Brother's name'. But Coleridge around 11 May had laid into the opium and, on his own boast, lashed out right and left—at William in accusations he could only ascribe to one 'in a lamentably insane state of mind'; certainly in no state to fit the poem for the printers or, indeed, to have it in his hands. Coleridge's diatribe of May has not survived; but its gist may be made out from the reply William and Dorothy drafted. In this his charges are met at immense length one by one, with almost incredible balance and tolerance.

Taking the pen from Dorothy, William dealt first with Coleridge's jealousy of Stoddart: 'You stood in my mind at such an immeasurable distance from Stoddart, that I could no more think of anything he could say or do as a reflection upon your reputation than I should dream that the sun would be darkened . . . by a braken fire on one of our mountains'. From here he went on to deal with each wild accusation.

I now come to one sentence in which you speak of Sara's Letters being written under Mary's eyes and mine: these . . . were almost the only [words] . . . which rouzed me. Sara's Letters, either those she writes or receives do not any of them pass under my eye or Mary's . . . She is 34 years of age and what have I to do with overlooking her letters . . . I come now to the keystone of our offences viz. our cruelty . . . in infusing into Sara's mind the notion that your attachment to her has been the curse of all your happiness. So far from our having done this the very reverse is the truth . . . (for my part I have meddled little with the affair) . . . but they [D. and M.] always laboured to convincing her . . . that in fact . . . she might congratulate herself; had this passion fixed upon a [woman?] of a different kind what might you not have suffered?

What suffering might not all concerned have been spared had William and Dorothy seen the red light now. Instead she had merely sadly abandoned hope of his coming when on 1 September he arrived, in good form, with Hartley and Derwent. It was not the best moment, with Mary due to lie in, and William promptly carried him off to Keswick where Southey reported, 'Coleridge is come half as big as a house'. On the 6th Catherine was born; the next day the men were back bringing Sariola, as Coleridge called his daughter. Dorothy's happiness may, and must, be taken as read, with Coleridge hard at work and 'feeling', he wrote, 'a pleasure and eagerness in it I had not known for years'; *and* drinking lemonade not laudanum. He had 'left it off all at once', and is pathetically hopeful that lemonade with cream of tartar will work. How could it fail—now that he had a parlour shared with Asra, when in September he could write in his notebook: 'I fear to speak, I fear to hear you speak—so deeply do I now enjoy your presence, so totally possess you in myself, myself in you . . . We both, and this sweet Room, its books, its furniture, and the Shadows . . . slumbering with the low quiet Fire are all *our* Thought . . . The still substance of one deep Feeling, Love & Joy. . . .'

It is not surprising that no word came from Dorothy now, or (apart from one letter to Richard) till December. Not surprising, but none the less horrifying when one grasps what lay behind this silence. It is Asra who draws aside the all too palpable curtain, Asra who does have time to write letters, to remain her entertaining highly intelligent self, since her health demands that she should have this—time nevertheless bought at the expense of Dorothy's, *her* time, light-heartedness and powers of judgement. Asra's news, already in October, is devastating: 'We have at last got the chimney Doctor who has begun . . . in the kitchen'; but she fears 'it will be an age before they are all cured'. In the meanwhile one cannot conceive the '*misery* of this House in these storms—not a chimney will draw the smoke! and one day we could not have a fire except in the Study; and then you could not *see* each other'. Added to this, in 'a most ungenial Autumn', they 'have not been able to stir out . . . The Waterfalls are in all their glory if one could [Dorothy could!] but see them . . . Mrs C. was here . . . to settle the boys at Ambleside School; and carry back little Sara', who was never to forget 'the horrible smoke, the dirt, the irregular Scotchy ways'.

But how be regular with workmen everywhere, when they must cook and boil all water in William's study? How compete with smarting eyes and tempers growing short—and the children drawing on the walls? Of course, beloved as they were, they were chidden and cuffed—in a gimcrack house on a hill, 'exposed to all hails and blasts' where the cold 'cut' Dorothy 'through and through' as these swept down the long passages and set the doors 'clashing'. And, after a second '*Scientific* Doctor' from Kendal, only one chimney cured—in Coleridge's parlour. By November, with Asra confined to bed and unable to see the ceiling, we catch a glimpse through the smoke of 'poor Dorothy . . . kept trotting the day through, for the Servants' work [hers now] is never done—a fine day comes . . . then they clean up; and the next undoes all that they have done'. With Mr De Quincey now added, she writes, and the Coleridge boys at week-ends, 'we are a nice round family'—of fifteen. And, at times, 'a pretty noisy one—even now' she hears 'C. making racket enough for twenty' with Dora, as young Dorothy became; 'she cannot be too naughty for his taste; he calls her "beautiful Cat of the Mountain"' and with him 'she is . . . like a cat' and when he appears 'puts on all her airs'.

By 8 December Dorothy was alive to tell the tale, a less lively one, it follows, than that of Asra. For she and Mary 'have seldom an hour's leisure'; their days are all spent 'scouring (and many of our evenings also)'. Once, such was the smoke of the only fire, they 'were obliged to go to bed with the Baby in the . . . day to keep it warm, and I, with a candle in my hand, stumbled over a chair, unable to see it'. Unwittingly she tells a second tale. 'Dear Coleridge' though 'often obliged to lie in bed more than half the day . . . seldom fails to be . . . comfortable at night. Sara and he are sitting together in his parlour. William and Mary (alas! all involved in smoke) in William's study, where she is writing (he dictating)'. Where and with whom now is Dorothy? Not at the beloved little green round table with William, 'the watch ticking above our heads'. 'Mr de Quincey, whom you would love as dearly, as I . . . do, is beside me, quietly turning over the leaves of a Greek book.'

February saw the departure of both Coleridge and De Quincey, Coleridge intending to go only to Kendal, to make arrangements for *The Friend*, 'a weekly Essay', scheduled to begin on 1 April. Adequate supplies of government stamped paper, then required by law, must be ensured, and matters tied up with a printer. None of this, it turned out, could be managed at Kendal, which meant trying Appleby or Penrith. Dorothy thought it could all have been done by post; and was fearful lest, 'at this critical moment', anything 'disarrange his mind or body'. She was right to be fearful, but also ignorant of how hard was the fight Coleridge was putting up; as ignorant as she was of the question which agonized him: how much was Asra's love pity? Nor was 'the other man' out of the picture—Asra compared his sloth with William's vigour. Things were happier far than at Coleorton. But not only must withdrawal symptoms be fought—Asra and he had both to fight the fact that, as he wrote, 'I love you as a man loves a woman'.

William and Dorothy could not know the hell of withdrawal from drugs, or know that it could not be done by will alone. They knew 'what was known to the whole town of Penrith—sneered and laughed at . . .' to their 'great mortification'; that, after mumps at the Aunt-Hill, he went on a three-week bender, that there was no *Friend* and no letters.

De Quincey meanwhile, their guest of some months, had gladly agreed while in London to hasten the publication of William's pamphlet. By the Convention of Cintra (a treaty with Bonaparte's France, defeated at the Battle of Vimeiro) the English, William felt, had betrayed the common people, fighting in Portugal and Spain for liberty—a cause which still held its old place in his heart. And the poet was a brilliant pamphleteer. He was also, as a bewildered De Quincey was learning, in both roles a relentless perfectionist. Emendations fell through the letter-box daily. 'Oh how I shall rejoice', Dorothy wrote, 'for your sake . . . when the pamphlet is fairly published.' But then William discovered it might be treasonable, to the amusement of the 'Females' who, wrote Asra, 'have not the least fear of Newgate—if there was but a Garden . . . we think we should do very nicely'.

Dorothy not only pitied the tiny man in London; she had, with Coleridge closeted with Asra and William dictating to Mary, grown inside a month to love him dearly. Johnny, unknown to the family being cruelly beaten at school, slept in his room and was 'passionately fond of him'. De Quincey's own deepest devotion was reserved for Catherine, called by William his 'little Chinese Maiden', practically bald as she long remained, and a comic before she could utter, who could 'always set everyone in a roar'. Children were Dorothy's poems now. She was nevertheless happy to escape from the soot into the past, to sit alone musing in the moss-hut at Town-End. For De Quincey was to inhabit the dream cottage, to be made under Dorothy's supervision 'very smart', wrote Asra, 'the rooms new-papered', the 'furniture all new (mahogany)'. Though with 'Poor old Molly . . . at rest in the quiet grave', Dorothy, going to and fro to Town-End, 'had many a pensive thought' of 'her chearful happy ways'. 'It goes through my heart', she wrote, 'to see her empty chair, and a hundred little things that she prized . . . just as she left them, only dull and dusty'. If Dorothy gave fresh proof of her resilience in helping to banish much treasured dust at Town-End, for De Quincey she could do it. For the rest she would never allow herself to dwell on old, unhappy, far-off things.

But then the, if not yet old, unhappy far-off thing himself turned up, looking as good as new. Two copies of *The Friend* were out, and a third printing. He rises, he says, at six in the morning, and the next day 'came all alive to my door', Dorothy wrote, 'to ask if he could do anything for me'. The Quaker Thomas Wilkinson has wrought this miracle, and has been the father of *The Friend*. 'C. was happy', Dorothy wrote, 'in Thomas's quiet and simple way of life'—which included no spirits. One can only wish he had stayed for ever at Yanwath, for everyone's sake, for William's as much as his own, as the latter grimly applied himself to his daily stint— fifty laboured lines of *The Excursion*.

Had Coleridge—opium apart, a dyed-in-the-wool bohemian—returned to the old Town-End, all might have been well. Or at least considerably easier for everyone. There one might rise at noon with no moral stigma attached, talk all night, eat when a poem was done, William go for months at a time without writing. In a household of fifteen all this was changed, with regular hours for poems as well as food. With their long knowledge of Coleridge's history, moreover, he could hardly have failed to encounter at meals over-anxious eyes or William's averted gaze; 'when', Dorothy wrote, 'there have been weeks and weeks when he has not composed a line. The fact is that he either does a great deal or nothing . . . He has written a whole Friend . . . in two days. They are never re-transcribed' but 'dictated to Miss Hutchinson'.

The truth is he did gallantly—with all the odds against him: the Grasmere post was a disaster, the stamped paper failed to arrive, subscriptions to get through and then there was no money to buy the paper. Despite this, there were twenty-six numbers of *The Friend*. But that one could be polished off in two days was no cure when it meant Asra's midnight oil. Asra goading, evading; Mary fully alive to the explanation when Coleridge wrote in his notebook, 'You never sate . . . near me ten minutes in your life without . . . a restlessness and a thought of *going*'; Mary at William to act—in ways he declined to do; all, for a second winter, 'involved in smoke'; Mary pregnant; Dorothy, yet again, seen through a glass darkly, scouring—the strain on everyone was intolerable. And early in March Asra left for a holiday in Wales, where Tom and Joanna were now farming. 'We are all', Dorothy wrote, 'glad she is gone'. Admittedly she had kept *The Friend* on its legs, but Coleridge 'harassed and agitated her mind continually, and we saw that he was doing her health perpetual injury'.

The 'servants' at Allan Bank were untrained country girls who decamped altogether in summer to hay-make and harvest. One of these was Sally Green, only reluctantly re-employed after the tragedy. She was good-hearted and useless; and in April Dorothy, entering the kitchen, found Johnny and Dora making carrot bullets for their guns, and Sally's charge, Catherine, vomiting carrot. Neither Sally nor the carrots can today be held responsible for the seizure which took place under Dorothy's eyes, and left Catherine partially paralysed. She recovered slowly at first, but then more rapidly, though when she could walk again she remained lame. Sea-bathing was tried and proved useless, and after she could walk Mary gave her two fraught hours' massage daily.

Meanwhile the shock was fearful and full-time nursing required, with yet another baby due in May. 'Coleridge talks of going to Keswick for a short while'—Dorothy hopes over Mary's confinement, as 'there is his parlour to clean, fire to light—sometimes gruel—toast and water—eggs —his bed always made at an unreasonable time, and many . . . little things which tell in a house'. However understandable, it is grim that these, perforce, are the things that for Dorothy now count.

But for her there are things infinitely grimmer:

> As to Coleridge, if I thought I should distress you [Catherine Clarkson], I would say nothing about him . . . We have no hope of him—none that he will ever do anything more than he has already . . . his whole time and thoughts . . . are employed in deceiving himself, and seeking to deceive others. He will tell me that . . . he has written half a Friend; when I *know* that he has not written a single line . . . he lies in bed, always till after 12 o'clock, sometimes much later; and never walks out. Even the finest spring day does not tempt him.

He leaves his own parlour only for meals 'and then goes the moment his food is swallowed. Sometimes he does not speak a word.'

Dorothy is describing one for whom, always 'dearest C.' she now has no grain of pity or understanding. The iron has at last entered her soul— and is that Coleridge lies, lies constantly. That he can do so *to her* was, perhaps, the one blow she was temperamentally unfitted to sustain. 'Do not think', she cries, 'that it is his love for Sara which has stopped him in his work—do not believe it: his love for her is no more than a fanciful dream . . . No! He likes to have her about him as his own, as one devoted to him, but when she stood in the way of other gratifications it was all over.'

Dorothy in her pain is wrong—as she is innocent in her use of the word 'gratifications', by which she means laudanum and lying in bed. Her cry—'do not believe it!'—is a cry on her own account. Coleridge has forgotten his love for her, has demoted her so completely that he can lie to her. Wounded to the depths of her being, it is her turn now to demote his love for Sara to 'a fanciful dream'.

The tableau at meals is, however, a tragic one. Coleridge is silent because it is he, he thinks, who has been deceived by those with whom he sits. Asra's departure had been no impromptu move, but was at the last, it would seem, concealed from him—both perhaps in the interests of *The Friend* and for Asra's sake, who doubtless wished to be spared final scenes. When she left it was with an escort, her cousin, John Monkhouse. In June Coleridge would enter in his notebook:

Σαρα = Sara ~~Monkhouse~~

Sunday night . . . a dream—that W.W. and D.W. were going down to Wales to *give her away* . . . O no! no! no! . . . only let me die before I suspect it, broad awake! Yet the too, too evident, the undeniable joining in the conspiracy with M and Δ [Dorothy] to deceive me, and her *cruel neglect* and *contemptuous Silence* ever *Since!*

Everything seems to indicate that Asra did love him, but had the strength to extricate herself. This time her silence would be absolute; and, as such, ultimately, end the Wordsworth connection: where Asra was, he would never go.

There was, however, as yet in May 1810, at Allan Bank no question of a break. Coleridge was free to return whenever he chose. Instead he remained at Keswick, doing nothing but read as Dorothy, alas, could now say scornfully. Meanwhile on 12 May Willy entered the world. And when by July Catherine had walked a few steps, Dorothy and William, still in some doubt about going, set off as of old, but not as of old—to hitch rather than hike to Coleorton, where, after staying with the Beaumonts, William left her to join Asra in Wales. When he had gone Dorothy was, she wrote, 'in such low spirits I hardly knew what to do with myself'— but took the measures she would always take, and went for a walk 'to put aside my thoughts'. From Coleorton she made her way to the Clarksons at Bury St Edmunds, alone this time and by night on top of a coach, fighting the cold buttoned up in no guard's coat but 'in Mary's thin blue coat and shawl'. Here she herself now met and acquired a life-long friend in the foreign correspondent of *The Times*, Crabb Robinson, at thirty-five about to read for the Bar, who escorted her back and around London: 'Miss W., without her brother's genius and productive powers, shared all his tastes and feelings.' Put up by the Lambs, with whom she felt more at home 'than anywhere out of our own house', her own powers, however, proved too much for poor Mary, and no one should ever, Charles vowed, stay again.

Not till late October did she curtail a round of visits: Catherine was dangerously ill with whooping cough. Journeying north, Dorothy passed a chaise travelling south from Allan Bank. In this were seated Coleridge, 'Mar-plan' Montagu and his wife—in an already inflammable situation.

Montagu, two years earlier, had married as his third wife his housekeeper and hostess, Mrs Skepper. Elegant and clever enough to capture Montagu (now doing exceedingly well at the Bar) and to simulate Wordsworthian simplicity, the third Mrs Montagu talked too much and William disliked her; though he did not refuse Montagu's request that a son of his should go to Ambleside not Eton, and at week-ends inhale the truth at Allan Bank. He did, however, warn the less cautious Coleridge against being captured by Mrs Montagu, for such and nothing less was her aim—to bear him off to be cured by Montagu's example, with the assistance of their London doctor. Coleridge had fought, failed, and at Keswick sat facing himself; had lately written William a friendly letter, and taken a more important step—had found an Edinburgh doctor in whose hands he was about to place himself for cure as an opium addict.

The Montagus dissuaded him; the climate would be fatal, and their own doctor in London could not be bettered. But Montagu, apart from being the woolliest of idealists, was punctilious, industrious and teetotal. The thing could never work; and when the trio, *en route* from Keswick for London, called at Grasmere, William—perhaps while Coleridge vanished indoors with Mary—seized the chance to tell Montagu so, using, said Dorothy, 'many arguments . . . but in vain . . . After this William spoke out and told M the nature of C's habits', and Montagu then agreed with William's first suggestion, 'that it would be better for C to have lodgings near him. William intended giving C advice to the same effect; but he had no opportunity'. There was only time for a jesting word with Coleridge, who said that he 'felt very well in his head', meaning, presumably, not for the mad-house yet; to which William, in the same vein had replied that when an autopsy had been performed on Schiller 'his entrails were eaten up while his brain was sound'.

William later acknowledged that he had been entirely wrong to say anything to Montagu on 'so delicate a subject'. Though at the time, Dorothy wrote, he believed he was only preventing what was common talk at Penrith spreading further. But Montagu had seen the light himself before reaching London, and immediately wrote to tell William 'that he had repeated to C what William had said to him and that C had been very angry'. This, as Dorothy observed, was wholly gratuitous, since Montagu could have spoken for himself. She was reckoning without Mrs Montagu, who, joining in, led Coleridge to believe that William had not only denounced him—his closest friend—to Montagu; but had done so in front of his wife, a total stranger.

In Hudson's Hotel, Covent Garden, the air was rent with cries: 'No Hope of me! Absol. Nuisance! God's mercy it is a Dream . . . Wordsworth has *commissioned* me to tell you . . . whirled about without a centre as in a nightmair, no gravity . . . A compressing and strangling Anguish . . . O

Asra! Asra what have you done in deceiving him who for ten years did so love you . . . A Friend and a Lover . . . are not impossible . . . Yet what . . . circumstances ought to have led me to see long ago, the events of the last year . . . have now forced me to perceive—No one on earth has ever LOVED me'.

Not till the following May did the shrieks travel north. Neither Southey nor Mrs C. had received any letters. There was nothing unusual in this, and nothing to worry about when Mary Lamb could report him in good health and spirits, Charles adding: 'Coleridge has powdered his hair and looks like Bacchus . . . ever sleek and young. He is going to turn sober but his clock is not struck yet'. Meanwhile at Grasmere they had their own grounds for despair, with Catherine 'as near gone as possible'. The equinoctial gales had not begun as yet, but when they did smoke must come again, no cure for the coughers; and Allan Bank was abandoned for primitive Hackett, the cottage of a former old servant. The first morning they 'sate in hot sunshine on a crag . . . and William read part of . . . the Paradise Lost'. It seemed like a breath of the past. But that evening William left, and Dorothy, having seen him on his way, got lost in the night—the night that for long had been falling around her. When had it started to fall? When, carrying a candle, she had stumbled in the smoke over a chair? When would it end, would it ever end, this 'climbing over high walls that' she 'should have trembled at by day', stumbling on 'often above the knees in mud'? She was 'quite composed' until she came on a cottage. But then, she wrote, 'when I laid my hand upon the latch of that cottage door . . . and . . . entered I could not speak for weeping and sobbing'.

They were no sooner back at Grasmere than they fled again—this time from scarlet fever, to Windermere. Only now does Dorothy speak of Coleridge. 'Nothing can more clearly prove the hurry in which I last wrote than that I never mentioned [his] departure. The consulting [the doctor] is quite a farce . . . For my part . . . I dismiss him as much as possible from my thoughts'—she is bitter, but even here contradicting herself. And three weeks later is 'going to write to him'. She was wasting her time. But, by February, 'it would pity anyone's heart' she wrote, 'to look at Hartley, when he enquires, as if hopelessly, if there has been any news of his Father'.

By March there is news of a kind—from Mary Lamb again, all too plainly on the verge of confinement: 'she knows there is a coolness between William and C'. There was none on William's side. Dorothy could assure her. Meanwhile, with the Crumps now anxious to enter their own temple, they themselves have got the Parsonage House which Dorothy thinks can be made 'a very canny spot . . . much more like a home of ours. It will be a large cottage'. They have sworn, however, never again to live with workmen in, and 'at present it makes' her 'sick to look at it'. 'At present' is 12 May 1811, a year exactly since she last saw Coleridge, of whom there did now come news from Mrs C.: 'We find',

Dorothy wrote, 'that C is offended with William . . . He writes as one who had been cruelly injured—He says "if you knew in detail of my most unprovoked sufferings . . . and with what a thunder-clap that . . . came upon me . . . you would less wonder . . . that a frenzy of the heart should produce"' in some part '" a derangement of the brain"''. Dorothy 'burned with indignation . . . a pretty story . . . "Coleridge has been driven to madness by Wordsworth's cruel and unjust conduct towards him"'. William, for his part, immediately applied to Mrs C., asking her to enclose what he wrote to Coleridge, since the latter obviously would not open his letters. This Mrs C. declined to do, on the very natural grounds that he might in future cease to open hers. But 'Time', Dorothy thinks, 'will remove the cloud from his mind', as it does the cloudburst from her own. Although 'It has been misery enough, God knows, to me to see the truths which I now see . . . I only grieve at the waste and prostitution of his fine genius . . . and I do grieve whenever I think of him'.

Accommodating as are the Crumps, they have now been forced to move with workmen in, and 'pell mell rainy days'. They cannot gravel the paths until the river falls; meanwhile the children are constantly wet and dirty. Apart from this, the house has only three disadvantages: that it loses the sun as soon as it rises; its being too public—easily cured by planting shrubs—and that the field which surrounds it is waterlogged. This cannot be drained, it will have to be fenced off. Otherwise 'there is no comfort wanting'.

Today, surveying the Rectory—no longer exposed to the road but deep in shrubs, the sea of mud drained, and across the river a flourishing Garden Centre—it is hard to credit the site as that of so much misery. They had gone, it transpired by the autumn, from bad to worse smoke-wise. In other ways, too, things went from bad to worse. In January Coleridge came for six weeks to Keswick, collecting the boys from Ambleside and, to the latters' astonishment, driving through Grasmere without stopping. 'Hartley', wrote Mrs C., 'dared not hazard a remark'; she was left to explain 'the paradox, and H. turned white as lime when I told him that Mr W. had a little vexed his Father by something he had said to Montagu—which through mistake had been mis-represented'. It could not have been more wisely or more gently said. But only now did William and Dorothy themselves learn the extent of the mistake— Montagu's fatal words, retailed by Southey: 'Wordsworth has *commissioned* me to tell you that for years . . . you had been an absolute Nuisance in the Family' and 'that he has no hope of you'. Schiller's entrails, too, had by now been transmogrified—into words spoken not by Wordsworth to Coleridge, but addressed to Montagu who passed them on: Coleridge, 'a rotten drunkard' had 'rotted his entrails out by intemperance'. At which William exclaimed: 'He [Montagu] never said that!'

Coleridge now had a new grievance: his veracity was questioned. In short, Wordsworth had used Montagu with the deliberate intention of ending their friendship. William now, for the first time, thought in identical terms: Coleridge was glad of a pretext to break with him. He declined to go to Keswick, though Dorothy implored Mrs C. to get Coleridge to come to them. This he could hardly do. Instead he returned to London, whither in April William followed him.

With Mary sent ill to Wales, Dorothy and Asra, smoke-bound, anxiously followed negotiations. For to such a pass had things literally come. William wisely refused to subject himself to what, in private, must be a fruitless hysterical outburst. Lamb found William cold, but Crabb Robinson thought 'healthful coolness preferable to the heat of disease'. And only through Crabb was the situation saved—in so far as anything could be saved from what Coleridge called 'the hot water of that bedeviled cauldron Explanation with alienated Friendship', Above the tragic meaningless clamour Dorothy's voice travels, small, distinct, sending her message via William: 'When you see him . . . give my love to him. I suppose he will now receive it'. But her own note now is tragic: 'I am sure he does not know the depth of the affection I have had for him.'

So she wrote on 17 May 1812 in what Asra pronounced a 'hateful house' in a 'deadly situation'—deadly indeed on the night of 3 June, when lame Catherine raced Willy upstairs to sleep as a treat in her mother's bed, where Dorothy found her 'with her eyes fixed'. She died that same night. The shock was fearful; and Mary's agony worse. Had she been at home it *must* have been prevented. Dorothy's state was such that William took her to stay with Jane Marshall, now, with a family of eight, living in the district at Watermillock. When on 23 July he fetched her home Dorothy nearly met her own death, attacked by a fit of giddiness and only narrowly saved by William on the edge of a precipice. De Quincey, in London at the time of Catherine's death, now spent his nights flung down upon her grave. His grief must, it seemed, bind them for ever. Mary's condition made the children frightened to go near her, and in November William took her away; but all was undone when, returning through the churchyard, she, too, flung herself down on the small grave. Two weeks later Thomas—gentle, bookish, dove-eyed, William's hope and favourite—followed Catherine, dying of pneumonia after measles. He was six and a half. Dorothy was this time again with Jane Marshall, and brought back by William mortally stricken. The house was a living grave overlooking the graveyard; and within three months they had arranged to move.

Meanwhile Coleridge had written twice within the week; Catherine's death he had ignored, but Thomas was, of all the children, 'nearest to' his 'heart'. 'I so often', he wrote,

> have him before my eyes sitting on the little stool by my side, while I was writing . . . and how quiet and happy and affectionate the little fellow would be if he could but touch me, and now and then be looked at!—O dearest Friend! What comfort can I afford you? What comfort ought I not to afford, who have given you so much pain? . . . There is a sense of the word, Love, in which I never felt it but to you and one of your

Household—! I am distant from you some hundreds of miles, but glad I am that I am no longer distant in spirit . . . An aweful truth it seems to me . . . that one mere thought, one feeling of Suspicion or Jealousy or resentment can remove two human Beings farther from each other, than winds or seas can separate their Bodies. . . .

He would come at once but that his play was being put on. This was that same tragedy parts of which Dorothy had heard him recite at Racedown on the occasion of their first meeting. Rewritten it was now renamed *Remorse*. By Remorse, he explained to Southey, he meant 'The Anguish and Disquietude introduced into the Soul by Guilt'. He must wait till rehearsals were over, but then he will come after Christmas. Instead he went to the sea at Bexhill.

XXI

Forlorn! The very word is like a bell
To toll me back from thee to my sole self!

John Keats, *Ode to a Nightingale*

1813–1820

We are going to have a *Turkey*!!! carpet—in the dining-room, and a
Brussels in William's study. You stare, and the simplicity of the dear
Town End Cottage comes before your eyes, and you are tempted to say,
'are they changed, are they setting up for fine Folks?' . . . No, no, you
do not . . . but you want an explanation and I must give it to you.

The date is September 1813, the address Rydal Mount, and Dorothy's
explanation to Catherine Clarkson not just that the Turkey 'will last 4
Scotch'; 'Our Master was all for the Brussels and to him we yielded—a
humour took him to make his room smart'. A humour, in fact, conceived
within a month of their moving on May Day, when Dorothy, that evening,
had been the last to leave the Parsonage House casting a parting look
upon the graveyard. It was the end of four cruel months of waiting in
idleness, cruel since the four could have been two; or at least relieved by
plans and making curtains. As it was the obnoxious outgoing tenant, Mrs
North, had moved by March but left some wine in the cellar and, on these
grounds, refused to release them earlier or so much as let them see inside
the house.

The Brussels, in short, was not a carpet but an inspired gesture
designed to set 'the Females' in 'a buzz', to put heart into the broken and
debilitated Mary, with William himself in no better state. His humour a
humour to infect them with sale fever, to arrive home with an enormous
cornice and curtains, 'admirable', observed Dorothy, 'were we to leave
this house (which God forbid) and got another with 3 sitting rooms . . . I
think they will come to be cut up for sofa covers'. But the sales as he
guessed, and as Dorothy wrote, were just the thing for Mary; and he bore
them both off to one in a barn, at which they stayed to the very last, 'the
beds were sold by candle-light and all walked home in the bright
moonshine, I with a water decanter . . . and William and Mary with a
large looking-glass—oval with a gilt frame . . . very cheap—1£ 13s.' They
are now, as William intended, 'quite bewildered' by too much furniture:
'This comes of [?buying] pennyworths'.

From it also comes Dorothy's power to write as she now does, if—still in September—the carpets 'popped in . . . and with a smile and a tear' she 'set down the foolish thought'. But her description of the sale and William's cornice—'He would fain persuade us that his curtains—and with a stripe above ¼ broad—are handsomer than our own'—is not written to Catherine Clarkson but Sara at Stockton. Nor is her tone here only explained by the sale. The note is new—caught from Sara herself and Mary, as is shown by a letter from Mary this October:

> Dearest Sarah. William has mentioned our *agreeable* visitors. Think of having Mr Blaken[e]y glue'd to us from morning to night! I am glad you and D. are spared this punishment. Yet I could have liked that you should have seen what a mountain of vanity he is . . . W. bears him with patience—Nay I think he likes him for they never cease talking, and they agree in all things . . . We had H. Lowther and his Bride i.e. they dined here . . . and then when they went this Blossom arrived . . . Miss G. is terrible! Her Sofa is come, a most ugly thing, but I do not say so. I want you my most dear Sister painfully . . .

William has written in the same letter to Sara asking her where and when he can meet her, if possible at Hawes in Yorkshire, some forty miles distant, though he 'will come even as far as Stockton. But what I myself should like best would be to meet you at Hawes, and what I should like infinitely the worst would be that you should prolong your stay, and deprive us of your presence and company for I love you most tenderly . . . We look for Dorothy home on Wednesday by . . . Mr Blakeney's carriage, which I hope she will not miss'.

Many new notes are sounded here, and not only that which Dorothy has caught from Mary's example in suffering. William, loving greatly, suffered more than most fathers; and Dorothy, in her own incurable anguish, could not be the support that Sara had been. She herself has been at Kendal to order Thomas's tomb-stone from where she did break down in a letter to Sara, 'Dear Sara I am little fit for it—do what I can the thought of him rends my heart and hard work I have had . . . to bear up often and often'.

There were lesser things to rend her heart, such as De Quincey's total, seemingly inexplicable indifference both to Thomas's death and their dire affliction. When Catherine died Dorothy had written instantly to him, as 'My dear Friend', breaking the news—'I wish you had been here to follow your Darling to the grave'—while even Mary had been roused, wrote William, knowing how he 'would participate her distress'. His participation then had, it would seem, paradoxically been the cause of his now showing none—Catherine's death the cause, or so he implies in the *Opium Eater*, of his first in the full sense becoming one. But by 1811 (and as merely their tenant at Town-End) he had within months of moving in, 'polled the Ash tree', wrote Sara, 'and cut down the hedge all around the orchard—every Holly, Heckberry, Hazel . . .' The moss hut, too, had vanished from its place. And 'D. is so hurt and angry she can never speak to him more'. This grossly insensitive act she had, in fact, forgiven. And possibly living at Rydal she did not hear of the strangest beggar to call yet at Town-End, drawn there by some strange instinct in 1816: a Malay, who had 'stood in his turban and loose trousers of a dirty white relieved upon the dark paneling'; and been, as an Asian, given a lump of opium 'large enough to kill some half dozen dragoons' which he had bolted at one mouthful. At least she was spared knowing that his ghost would haunt her cottage to dominate in dreams 'the avenging terrors' that must lie in wait for the opium eater. Without it she knew enough, knew what by 1814 Mary had guessed—that De Quincey's diarrhoea was 'such a one as C.'s, no doubt'. Typically, but unlike her, Sara could take it. 'Quince', she wrote, 'doses himself with opium and drinks like a fish.' For Dorothy, passing the cottage by day 'always blinded or but with an eye open', the Malay, if personally unknown to her, cast a longer and more baleful shadow. 'Mr de Quincey', she wrote in 1817, with what has been taken as pure snobbery, 'is married; and I fear I may add he is ruined . . . At the uprouzing of the Bats and Owls' only did he emerge to repair to a farm, the Nab, 'and the consequence is that Peggy Simpson . . . presented him with a son ten weeks ago.' They are now married 'and with their infant son . . . spending their honeymoon in our cottage at Grasmere'.

But Sara had not the reasons to love De Quincey that Dorothy had. She had not been twice fooled, betrayed and dropped; but on the contrary been beloved, and withdrawn of her own volition. Younger, earthier, of a less delicate fibre, to Sara, delight though she did in William's children, their death could not be the blow this was to Dorothy—one that literally brought mutilation. 'Much of the knowledge gained from books' she now felt was slipping from her, and sorrows, she wrote, 'weaken the memory so much that I find reading far less use than it used to be to me . . . were it not that my feelings were as much alive as ever there would be a growing tendency for the mind to barrenness'. Gardening in 1813, three women in a row, banded together to stave off the memory of Thomas—always their 'best helper' in the garden—'Sara', Dorothy wrote, 'is mistress . . . of that concern. I am contented to work under her'.

Rydal Mount was not as today almost symbolically interred, one may feel, in its Victorian garden. 'The place is a paradise', Dorothy wrote, as if incredulous at waking there her first morning to sunlight and not to the smoke, the gloom, the pain of the Parsonage House. But, despite being so newly freed from this, it had been for Dorothy—and, in the sense she meant it, only for her—'a bitter pang when the parting hour came and we left Grasmere Vale'. If, however, her 'inner thoughts *will* go back to Grasmere'—and before her own final parting hour return to take up their habitation there—she loved Rydal with its views 'so various and beautiful' an invalid 'need never stir out of the garden'. She could not see Rydal

Water, but she could see Windermere, still watch the moon conspiring with Silver How; still herself retire to the kitchen to bake for such old friends as the Town-End Ashburners and others—friends she vastly preferred to those who now called in droves on the tenant of Lady Fleming of Rydal Hall. They had moved a mere two miles but had indeed left Grasmere Vale and for more than a new social milieu. That Southey was now Poet Laureate and William's the less prestigious appointment of Distributor of Stamps for Westmorland (not a glorified post office but equivalent to the local department of Inland Revenue) troubled her not at all. Scott—rich and generous—had declined the Laureateship in favour of Southey who, as William said, had 'a little world dependent upon his industry', the Aunt-Hill, his own five children and Coleridge's. William, in any case, could never have been in the running. The Distributorship, procured him by Lord Lonsdale, entailed considerable 'dancing about the country'; but, by employing a clerk-cum-gardener, would leave him free for poetry, help pay for the children's education and, Dorothy wrote, would now 'enable him to assist in sending Hartley to college'.

In this they were all over-optimistic. William's was not a gratuity, his earnings dependent on how many 'Pawnbrokers . . . Dealers in Thread, Lace, medicines . . . persons letting to hire Stage coaches' etc. required licences, stamps or stamped paper. Meanwhile the office also entailed visits to Lowther Castle where Dorothy, with an eye to the sale of poems, reported his meeting 'the Duchess of Richmond and *heaps* of fine folk'. There was nothing degrading in the old tradition of patronage, and nothing servile in William's attitude. Her old acquaintance, Wilberforce, by now himself a grandee, meeting him at Sir George Beaumont's found him 'very manly, sensible, full of knowledge, but independent almost to rudeness'.

All this had seemingly little immediate bearing on Dorothy's life. But if she, like Mary, was 'out' when the gentry called, change was in the wind—change which, as she looked forward to 'long evenings and winter quiet', she could scarcely have foreseen in the arrival of Basil, her perpetual joy at Racedown, now sadly ill in mind, and it proved body. Posted north, to be cured by the infallible Wordsworth rites, he had proceeded to Keswick and was sitting with Southey in his study, when, wrote Mrs C. to Poole, 'hearing a bustle upstairs . . . we ran up—think what must be our astonishment and grief—when . . . we saw this poor youth . . . with Southey hanging anxiously over him, just as a few months before we had seen poor George [her brother] bringing up streams of blood from the lungs—it was a most striking coincidence never to be forgotten!' This letter is vintage Mrs C., but for one thing only—she could not be her transparently honest self. 'The poor youth' had been supported to a cottage across the garden, that of an old friend of Southey's, a Miss Barker, where 'Miss B. and Miss W. take [it] by turns to watch his bedside'. Mrs C. has 'not been able to be of much use', has not, in fact, so much as entered the cottage where Dorothy remained for three long months. For the truth was a violent fall-out had, soon after Dorothy's coming, occurred between Miss B. and the laureate's ladies. Dorothy's role was difficult in the extreme, going as she must 'to the other house', where, she wrote, 'I have much ado to prevent quarrels with me also'.

This, on 24 March 1814, did not prevent her writing, not to Coleridge, but to his host at Bristol: 'I write at the request of Mrs Coleridge'. Mrs C. had only Tom Wedgwood's annuity (he had died while Coleridge was in Malta). Josiah had lately withdrawn his contribution, thus reducing Mrs C. to some sixty-five pounds a year and greatly increasing Southey's burden. Dorothy now took up her pen both about money and about Hartley's future education. For Hartley was seventeen and, though Dorothy did not now say so, 'in the weak points of his character resembles his Father very much—though he is not addicted to sensual indulgence— quite the contrary—and has not one expensive habit.' Had, it might be said, no single terrestrial one. 'His oddities', indeed, 'increase daily'. His father ought to come and place him in a new school. But precisely because he ought to, she fears he will not. 'And how is H. to be put through College?' 'These perplexities', she wrote to Catherine Clarkson, 'no doubt glance across his mind like dreams.'

That fact was that, as so often, she had divined not only Coleridge's state but in almost his very words that same spring, as opium held him in a thrall from which there seemed no escape: 'The worst was that in *exact proportion* to the *importance and urgency* of any Duty was it of fatal Necessity sure to be neglected.'

Dorothy's attitude was no mere fruit of the past. The Coleridge boys had a second home at Rydal. And Hartley, in 1815, was settled in, not by his father, but by William at Merton College, Oxford—after being tutored by Southey and with funds raised by him and William from Montagu, Poole, the Beaumonts and even Cottle. Matters were not improved in 1817, when Coleridge's old suspicion that 'somewhere or other there existed a radical difference' between his and Wordsworth's aims in poetry was explored in the *Biographia Literaria*. Coleridge, in fact, in this made mincemeat of Wordsworth's critics. But if William admitted to skimming through parts only, it is unlikely that Dorothy's own skimming took her further than the chapter headings: 'Rustic life (above all, low and rustic life) unfavourable to the formation of human diction.' 'The language of Milton as much as the language of real life, yea incomparably more so than that of a cottager.' 'The characteristic defects of Mr Wordsworth's poetry in their proportion to the beauties.'

In 1819 her voice would still ring with scorn—and incomprehension. It was at this time that Rydal Mount received from Mrs C. a note by coach so glorious was the news: Hartley had been elected a Fellow of Oriel! Poor Mrs C., so small had been her taste of the sweets of life, 'can hardly believe it possible'. And such is her pathetic intoxication that 'Miss W.' becomes 'my kind friend Dorothy', who says all 'that her good heart

dictated'. But with a blissful Mrs C., Derwent and Sara for Christmas—
and with Derwent to put through university somehow—Dorothy's heart
found other things to say to Catherine Clarkson: 'Would you believe it
possible, Coleridge expressed a wish that Sara [with slight curvature of
the spine] . . . could . . . be placed under the care of Mr Gillman!! the
cleverest medical man with whom he was ever acquainted!!' The
acquaintance was by now of three years' standing. But for Dorothy this
was still too short a time—to credit the impossible; that the courageous
battle, which could not be won alone, had ended at last.

Greta Hall, however, was, in 1814, no longer dearest C's 'desert home'.
Besides, '*now* above all other times' she 'should have wished to be at
Grasmere' for William is actually printing *The Excursion*. 'It has been
copied in my absence, and great alterations made', some of which only she
had seen when she returned home for a week. 'But the printing has since
been going on briskly and not one proof sheet has yet met my eyes.' How
has William not felt, as she felt, that her place at this time was at Rydal?
For, had he urged that it was, she would have been there. And, if for some
weeks she could not be, he could have ridden across to discuss alterations
with her. But now there is Mary to copy and in Sara an able critic. With
the deaths, moreover, of their two children William's marriage to Mary
has entered a new phase. No longer will his aversion to letter writing allow
him to write to Mary and Dorothy jointly. Mary will have letters of her
own—and letters quite unfit for Dorothy's eyes. Mary has not waited in
vain. Strengthening over the years William's love for her now is passionate
love.
   Meanwhile by the end of April Dorothy was back—in time, perhaps,
still to see some proof-sheets. But then the reviewers went to town, one
'beginning', as William wrote, 'with these elegant and decisive words:
"This will not do."' Yet Lamb in a letter called *The Excursion* 'a day in
heaven'; and Hazlitt—in three monthly instalments—achieved the
almost impossible feat of praising '*more* than' Dorothy 'should have
expected'. Fortunately she had not in August seen his final onslaught in
which (because William described Aggy—parsimonious Agnes of Town-
End) he wrote of 'the depraved and inveterate selfishness' reserved for
'those boasted mountain districts'; and, not content with being nearly
ducked at Keswick, 'had the audacity', Dorothy wrote outraged, 'to
complain that there are no courtezans to be found in the country'. It was
fortunate since in August she was alone. The Irish jaunting-car had once
more taken off for Scotland with, as its passengers, Mary, Johnny and
Sara.

Some member of the family must always remain at Rydal in charge of
what Sara called 'the plaguey stamps'. And such now for almost ten weeks
was Dorothy's role. Mary had never recovered her spirits or strength since

the children's deaths. But physically Sara, too, was far from strong. And within three days of their return, Dorothy—though with 'great difficulty in resolving to leave William and Mary so soon'—had volunteered to escort her to Tom's in Wales. There she did prepare two new volumes of William's, *Poems including Lyrical Ballads*, for Longman. But one alteration to these, at least, was sent, as he wrote to a friend, 'to Miss Hutchinson and my sister'—in that order. There, too, she once more toured the Wye —with Tom Hutchinson, only to be summoned home by William. Willy was ill and 'when I have any anxiety', William wrote, 'I always wish for you'. The least illness on the children's part now filled their parents with terror, and had coloured Dorothy's deep reluctance to accede to Annette's wish and go, at this season, to France for Caroline's wedding. Caroline's future husband, Jean Baptiste Martin Baudouin, was the brother of a young French officer who, a prisoner-of-war in England, perhaps known to Annette, had somewhat mysteriously come to Rydal. Delicacy may have dictated that Dorothy should attend the wedding and not William. Certainly it was she who, in 1814, shouldered all correspondence with Annette. But by now to William's aversion to letter writing had been added what seems to have been trachoma, severe enough at times to condemn them to sit without candles and to make him fear total blindness.

For Dorothy's sake the wedding was postponed till the following spring. But then Napoleon escaped from Elba. Royalist Annette, resuming her dangerous underground role, was with Caroline in grave peril, and their plight uppermost in Dorothy's mind. She nevertheless rejoiced at being spared a journey she had dreaded, the more so since she *was* needed at Rydal—once again to guard 'the plaguey stamps'.

Her three months' stint during this summer of 1815 was gruelling, ill and with all three children ill. She dared not tell William and Mary, and when the children recovered a damp day still put her in a panic. She could only, however, feel thankful that their parents were absent: 'I always suffer a thousand times more from my Brother's unconquerable agitation and fears when Willy [aged five] ails anything than from any other cause.' And doting though Dorothy literally herself did on the children, she could not approve of William's weakness. To Sara she had written the previous spring: 'It is impossible unless you have seen it to have any idea of the Father's folly over this child'. By 1817 she was still complaining, 'really, his Father fondles over him and talks to him just as if he were a year old'. Delicate as Willy and Dora both were, her attitude becomes the more surprising when one considers that Southey had, a year before she wrote this, lost his only son, the light of his eyes. 'Southey you know has uncommon self command', but would never again, she feared, be his old gay boyish self. Despite this it was largely her doing that Willy was, at nine, dispatched to school in London, where Charles Lamb could answer her own anxious questioning: Willy's 'genius I take it leans a little to the figurative . . . Not that I accuse William Minor of hereditary plagiary . . . Rather he seemeth . . . purposely to remain ignorant of what mighty poets have done . . . before him. For being asked if his father had ever been on Westminster Bridge, he answered that he did not know'. Here in a long inimitable letter Lamb had, perhaps, put his finger on the trouble-spot. For Johnny too, though Dorothy is sure 'not a Dunce in soul', 'is certainly the greatest dunce in England', and served his sentence at Sedbergh Grammar School; while Dora, being 'extremely wayward' (as her aunt had been!), went for cure to Miss Dowling's establishment.

To return to 1815. No sooner had William and Mary returned to relieve Dorothy at her post than there was Charles Lloyd's wife to be relieved— with eight children, Lloyd himself now totally deranged and unable to bear her out of his sight; or bear only Dorothy or Mary. 'To me he has never objected', Dorothy wrote; 'he liked me when he was well and the same liking has continued during his woeful depression'. Eventually William helped to take Lloyd to Birmingham doctors, while for some three weeks Dorothy took over the motherless household. But the very night before Lloyd left they had heard of the sudden death of his sister, Priscilla, Christopher's wife; and Dorothy when free might be wanted there. But Christopher wanted no one. Meanwhile there was their own pressing need—to obtain from Richard security for all their capital, for which, said Dorothy, they 'had not a single bit of paper to show'. Richard, in 1814, had actually married—his maid, begotten a son, and so tied up their money that should he himself die this would not be theirs until his infant son's coming-of-age. Thus it was that a fortnight before Dorothy's forty-fourth birthday she was once more alone with William climbing Kirkstone. It was 'frosty without snow' and she never in her youngest days remembered revelling more in an excursion.

When the following spring, however, Richard did die in London William was only then, with Montagu's help, able to extract a death-bed settlement; and was still for a further year, Dorothy lamented, 'kept from his old employments' by 'Richard's affairs—delays of lawyers—difficulties of getting debts settled—threatenings of a Chancery Suit', etc., 'everything', she mourned, 'to disturb him'.

But with the money out of Richard's clutches and properly invested, the wind had again for Dorothy changed. Henceforward she could emulate Sara, self-styled 'the real Jaunter'. But so too, when she was at Rydal, could William and Mary. In the intervals she continued to go where she could with William, in 1818 to the hustings—on the wrong side, that of the landed gentry against the rights of the people, or so thought Keats of Wordsworth, his poet hero. Keats's attitude is illuminating—and of more than his own youthful incomprehension as, dining at Bowness on Windermere in June 1818, he learnt from the waiter of Wordsworth's apostacy: 'Sad-sad-sad, but the family [the Lowthers] have been his friends always. What can we say?'

We can of course say that the Lowthers had been nothing of the kind; but that Catherine Clarkson would have agreed with him: Rydal, she confessed to Crabb Robinson, was at this time 'so Torified' as to be 'a little draw-back . . . even to me'. William's course, however, was perfectly logical; the Industrial Revolution was under way, and with it his old horror of the mob had, however irrationally, revived. He was back in Paris in 1792 and Dorothy this time was at his side. But for once she had, and knew it, gone too far. When another election came round, she would be and keep away, leaving William, as Sara said, 'to enjoy the sport'.

Keats had in London that January hastened to call on Wordsworth as one whose lines were always on his lips. He had been kept waiting an age —only to encounter the Distributor of Stamps for Westmorland, in stiff collar, knee-breeches, silk stockings and unseemly haste to dine with another Distributor. What he could not know was Wordsworth's state— or the reasons for this—in London, that he would not, as Sara said, 'stir without one of the Females', detested his silk stockings quite as much as Keats did and was, in a flap, being hauled into these by Mary. Keats knew only, and lamented, that Dorothy's brother had 'left a bad impression wherever he visited in town by his egotism, vanity and bigotry'. Things were not improved by now finding 'Winandermere' likewise 'disfigured' by 'the miasma of London', while 'Lord Wordsworth, instead of being in retirement, has himself and his house full in the thick of fashionable visitors quite convenient to be pointed at all the summer long'. This, however, failed to deter him from calling on Wordsworth next morning: 'He was not at home nor . . . any . . . of his family'. Keats 'much disappointed' wrote a note 'and stuck it up over what I knew must be Miss Wordsworth's Portrait'.

That Keats posted his note where he did was surely no accident. Familiar as he was with *Tintern Abbey*, by far the most interesting object to him in the room must have been the now vanished portrait. Scanning this and in it catching a glimpse, perhaps, of 'the shooting lights' of those 'wild eyes', he may have remembered the lines 'Oh! yet a little while / May I behold in thee what I was once'. And had Dorothy entered the room beheld this for himself, and seen the paradox—that if the Mount could hold a being so unpretentious, spontaneous, accessible, vital he must, in the matter of Wordsworth, think again.

As it was he had simply come too late—for Town-End. Had he encountered the poet who, sitting at breakfast, 'ate not a morsel, nor put on his stockings but sate with his shirtneck unbuttoned, and his waistcoat open while he did it', Keats—himself bohemian, sardonic, intellectually stringent—must have found in William a kindred spirit. And in Dorothy's cottage covered with scarlet beans found his niche no less than Coleridge did. Had he, in fact, called at Rydal a mere eighteen months later he must still have found something to surprise him: 'Doro [Dora] and the [Lloyd] girls hurrying the father with his shaving to accompany them . . . to skate—He partly attending to John and Derwent who are at work with Greek—Dorothy and I with our desks before us *attempting* to write in a hurry . . . all this . . . going on in two rooms . . . constant opening and shutting of doors—messages and arrangements, *to from* and *by* all the parties, that', or so thought Sara, 'a more *agreeable* scene of confusion you could not imagine'.

But with a disillusioned Keats as our progenitor, and William as the polestar of Dorothy's life some further elucidation must seem called for. For it cannot be denied that Wordsworth was in London, as Keats depicts him, his own worst enemy; and at his worst in 1817. During that same London visit he had his portrait painted, and Sara's letter to Dora is revealing: 'It does not strike the London people as being such a good likeness because here your father is not in his thoughtful way . . .' He was not indeed; but smarting under the reception of *The Excursion, The White Doe* and *Miscellaneous Poems.* It was hardly an auspicious moment for friends to arrange a first meeting with Coleridge since the estrange- ment: 'For the first time in my life', Crabb Robinson wrote, 'I was not pleased with Wordsworth'. But who had harboured the Coleridge boys at weekends; who stood by Mrs C., in two years the recipient of one letter from their father; who raised the money to send Hartley to Merton? 'I smiled', William had written in 1815, 'at your notion of Coleridge reviewing The Ex[cursion]. I much doubt whether he has read three pages of' it. In other words Coleridge at Allan Bank—or such is the implication—had taken no faint interest in William's work, work under- taken sick at heart. When Coleridge did, in fact, read the poem in the spring of 1816 it was to write deploring its truisms to Lady Beaumont who showed the letter to Wordsworth. Whereupon the latter's sole reaction was to write to Coleridge in a humble troubled vein: 'Pray point out to me the most striking instances where I have failed . . . And believe me my dear Coleridge in spite of your silence Most affectionately yours . . .'

But for Wordsworth, having where he had failed publicly expounded in the *Biographia Literaria* (published seven months before their meeting), the publication was tantamount to treason; and this, despite Coleridge's having written there of 'the unexampled opposition Mr Wordsworth's writings have been doomed since [1798] to encounter'. 'Unexampled opposition' over twenty years, however, is unlikely to leave one open, suave, relaxed. But doomed he had been from the first to encounter this— and as a boy at the hands of those he despised. His course from Penrith must for genius have been a headstrong one—and had led not only to *Guilt and Sorrow*, the final title of 'Salisbury Plain', but to open warfare with Grub Street. Diffident, obdurate, he developed a carapace from behind which he pontificated.

But beneath the carapace lay something very different—a man whose need was love untinged with awe. And the devotion of a Sara Hutchinson, breezy, astringent, sturdily independent, cannot like Dorothy's be explained away. Even a bigot, it seems, may know what is sauce for the gander, and Sara's sauce was her speciality. When a young admirer, Edward Quillinan, paid his first visit and, out of shyness, arrived late, to encounter an angry patriarchal poet gyrating his chair, it was Sara who, entering the study, 'saw at once' as Quillinan wrote, 'that there was some awkwardness between us . . . civily accosted me, rallied the poet for twirling his chair . . . appropriated it to her own use' and, having laughed him into a good humour, 'sent him out to show me the garden and terrace'.

Dorothy could not have written, like Sara, that William, beset by guests and trying to compose, 'was agreeable only by fits'. And it was with Sara, not Dorothy, that on the Clarksons going too far for abolitionists even and having 'the Sable Queen' of Tahiti to stay, William wasted an afternoon concocting a skit on Ben Jonson that does not appear in the *Poetical Works*—'Queen and Negress, chaste and fair'. 'Oh! how they laughed!' Dorothy wrote, 'I heard them into my Room upstairs'.

She was not jealous of Sara, but her own method of making William relax had been replaced. The tension with which he lived remained. But Dorothy's cure—the untrammelled eye—lay too close to the cause when, as the locals said, 'it was potry as did it'. Meanwhile she shared him with not one but two women; to these would shortly be added a third in Dora, William's adored and adoring but in no way blinkered daughter. Dora, too, as Hartley Coleridge wrote, 'drew him out to gambol with her in the childishness that always hung upon her womanhood'.

Such were the women William loved, by whom he was beloved—but also, in the current phase, mobbed up. By temperament over-anxious and for years with all to shoulder, Dorothy needed this ambience no less than William. Already it might seem she had made her exit, the perfect electrometer been swallowed up in the perfect dogsbody. But ultimately she had gained, not lost. The Grasmere Journals could never have emerged from Rydal Mount, the pulse and throb of such poetry was silent for ever; but with this too had gone the haunting fears, proved phantoms in the shared light of a common day. To Mary and Sara Dorothy owed a balance she had lacked, a confidence that would now let her come forward not as the poet's sister but in her own right, a role new to her—'I, Dorothy Wordsworth'.

I am alone waiting in the square for my companions and, seated on the steps of a house, I take my pencil . . . I will describe this Square— houses yellow, grey, white, and *there is a green one*! Yet the effect is not gaudy. Half Grecian church, with gothic spirit . . . Bells continually tinkling. *There* goes a woman to her prayers, in a long black coat and bright blue stockings. *Here* comes a nicely dressed old woman leaning on her staff. . . .

The year is 1820 and she is perched—why not?—on the steps of a house in a small Belgian town. One notes that she is alone in the square awaiting her fellow-travellers. Or it may be 'Here I sit alone in the *voiture* . . . W.,M., and' the host of the inn 'talking endlessly'. But any moment serves her—to seize the moment, the group assembled to see them off: 'There stands the *fille de chambre*', her own pretty Rosalie, 'there the waiter with his napkin, and porters and other helpers with their gold ear-rings and leather or fur caps by the half dozen. They expect nothing from us, for they have got their pay, but *there* they stand'—and still, one feels, stand, as 'fresh to the feelings of being in a foreign land', the travellers, like Dorothy's prose, 'drove briskly forward, watchful and gay'.

The result is a masterpiece, inexplicably neglected perhaps because it is not the Grasmere Journals, because the voice is not the voice of the rain falling in Grasmere, but one that takes us along at a rattling pace. Or perhaps because what has tended to be extracted from this is Dorothy on William's Pedestrian Tour, to the detriment of her own *Tour*. For the two things are, to my mind, quite distinct. The first is a pilgrimage—but with the shrine behind her and placed there by her own act of recollection. Approaching the Alps, 'this land so dear to the imagination . . . I remembered the shapeless wishes of my youth, wishes without hope', she now wrote, '—my brother's wanderings thirty years ago and the tales brought to me . . . at Forncett; and often repeated as we paced together on the gravel walk . . . by moon and starlight'.

She did remember these; would on sighting the Alps give a scream which, as Mary said, made them all think that something had happened. And something had; but not, I think, as much as has been suggested. She did—as Crabb Robinson, who joined them at Lucerne, noted—wish to see exactly what William had seen. But her avidity did not end here. Cities tumble from her pen, avalanches sound like 'the rattling of innumerable chariots'—this simile is not for nothing. Her *Tour of the Continent* is no mere scenic tour, it is predominantly a human one.

Nor does she as in imagination at Forncett climb with William, but, as in real life one does, with a Miss Horrocks. Miss Horrocks is the sister-in-law of Mary's cousin, Tom Monkhouse, who is on his honeymoon (Dorothy's third). William is walking with Mary on the other side of the river. This, like Miss Horrocks, however is incidental. If her stake in William is smaller, it is secured to her—secure enough for her to share Mary's relief when, beset by night in the carriage with fleas, and by William beset with fleas, he removes at last to the empty Monkhouse carriage. 'Never were people more glad to get rid of their worst enemy than we were to part with him', Dorothy wrote. '. . . We shook our garments and sat down in quiet.' And when 'the small tormentors' began again they whiled away the time watching the flashes of lightning over the Jura. She has caught the note from Mary, but the point is she has caught it; that William will certainly read what she says about him, and will be hard put to turn this into poetry. Nor will it serve him much better to read of 'this salle where I now sit', where, with all the rest of the party in bed, she continues to sit on alone, 'the story of Cupid and Psyche now before my eyes as large as life . . . The paper is in panels with large mirrors between in gilt frames . . .' And then, by staying up, she sees what others have missed, the diligence come in and unload—'a lap-dog walking about the top . . . viewing the gulph below'—and depart again with a monkey as its outside passenger. Their own postilion from Bruges wore a white nightcap, and had a full-blown rose stuck in his mouth. Even confined as she is in Cologne to a window, being 'ill in her usual way', as Mary wrote, Dorothy may own to feeling weak, but this will not lessen the impact of her powers of observation—vital, microscopic, insatiable. She is watching the ferry,

> a square platform, not unlike a section cut out of a thronged market place . . . When the boat draws up to the mooring-place a bell hung aloft is rung . . . carts with their horses wheel away—rustic yet not without parade of stateliness—the foreheads of the meanest being adorned with scarlet fringes and the trappings with brass nails . . . Peasants male and female, sheep and calves . . . Two young ladies trip forward, their dark hair *'basketted'* round the . . . head, green bags on their arms . . . next a lady with her black hair stretched upward . . . and a skull cap at the top like a small dish . . . A girl crosses the platform with a handsome brazen ewer . . . Soldiers—a dozen at least—are coming in. There is a sunburnt daughter of toil! Her olive skin whitens her head-dress; and *she* is decked in lively colours. . . .

How much she sees from a window, how much more she learns as she walks. For—so populous are Dorothy's Alps—that one might almost forget that she crossed these twice on foot, occasionally riding an ass, and in great heat. As with the beggars at Grasmere, she questioned all and sundry, since, Mary wrote, 'she never hesitates—going in to the kitchens, talks to everybody there—and in the villages, on the roads . . . makes friends . . . gains information . . . jabbers [French and] German everywhere. She astonishes us all.'

XXII

Farewell, impassioned Dorothy

'I RESOLVED TO keep a journal . . . because I will not quarrel with myself, and because I shall give Wm Pleasure by it when he comes home again.' So Dorothy had written in 1800. Twenty years later both goals, it might seem, were behind her. It is, however, easy to forget how deep-laid were the sources of stress in her—to forget as she loved and sorrowed and slaved the fight she would always have in order not to quarrel with herself; with a temperament that could still in 1820 make her, as Mary wrote, 'ill in her usual way'. That Mary could say this comes as a shock, since from her own letters one would assume that she had long ceased to be so. She had strengthened, had matured, but to simplify the pattern is to underrate the toll and the achievement. 'As high as we have mounted in delight / In our dejection do we sink as low'—without this state, in Dorothy perennial and acute, and her remedy, things 'all for themselves', we might never have heard of a poet, Wordsworth, or heard, across two centuries, redbreasts singing in a garden.

But nor, in the former case, might we in 1828 have tracked her to Whitwick near Coleorton, where she arrived to housekeep for Johnny, now the Rev. John, in this his first curacy. 'We shall not, alas!', wrote William, 'see her again for half a year.' The half year at Whitwick still held good when, in December, Lord Lonsdale offered John a parish near Whitehaven. Dorothy's reaction might seem surprising: had John 'continued here another winter I should have done so also', she announced unequivocally. This cannot be explained as in Whitwick with John a reincarnation of Town-End alone with William, even if his 'lowly parsonage' was indeed lowly and as such ideally suited to her taste—a roomy thatched cottage with a quaintly tumbling look and thatch over the latticed bay-window. Poor John was, as Hartley said, 'a laborious ass'. And if Dorothy found it 'a good country for walkers', with from one hill—twenty-one miles distant!—'a most extensive prospect', this was hardly a substitute for Helvellyn and its views on one's doorstep.

But Dorothy gave her own revealing explanation: 'In the first place I am more useful here than I could be anywhere else, and, in the second, am very comfortable.' She does not, as would be characteristic, link comfort with usefulness, but specifically distinguishes her reasons. And the second might astonish one from her lips. But to muse, taking stock, by the fire at Whitwick was—she had not, perhaps, realized until she got there—what she had long needed.

Mary, it was true, now called Rydal 'Idle Mount'. The newspapers would have announced to Robert Jones the names of some of their visitors, Dorothy wrote in 1825, 'Mr Canning, Mr Scott etc. etc.'; Jones, had he come, 'would have had no *quiet* enjoyment' and was 'not made for *bustling* pleasures'. She had herself increasingly sought escape from these—on the moors outside Halifax, in Wales, on the Malvern Hills, in Herefordshire, Scotland, the Isle of Man. And the year she and William had planned to climb Snowdon she had, instead, stayed away nine months—to avoid the added bustle of an election. She could not miss out London and so miss seeing the Lambs. For though Charles had at last got released from the India House, this he had partly wanted for Mary's sake, who, with age, withstood her attacks less well. Henry Crabb Robinson, 'Aunt's lover' as Dora *would* call him, had written to tell her of the last of these, and was sorry that Charles had taken a house at Enfield: 'The solitude is much too great for him.' And Charles, it had long sadly seemed, was unsuited to retirement, or to the undiluted strain of Mary.

But the person it made her saddest, always 'strangely sad' to part with was Catherine Clarkson at Playford, near Bury St Edmunds. After leaving there she had written 'I was with you all the day—in your own bed-room first; then by the parlour fire . . . the thought of you is now so much with me that I hardly seem to dwell upon what will no doubt enliven my journey'. Her note *is* elegiac. 'A haunting comes upon' her that Catherine Clarkson may be ill again. But she is, one cannot help feeling, haunted by more than fears for one who is for her 'My dearest Friend'. Haunted by fear of losing the being to whom, in her letters, her voice carries no echo of Mary or Sara; who stands, still stands for Eusemere where, for years after the Clarksons left there in 1804, she would return to wander through the rooms and rejoice at finding these unchanged; rooms where so many memories of the brief, most precious era of her own life still lived on. But she must wrench herself from Playford to delay at Cambridge, where Christopher's four motherless boys 'wished me so much to stay, and talked so feelingly of their loneliness . . . I could not find it in my heart to leave them'.

The Master's Lodge at Trinity was too lonely and grand for her own taste. But if it remains the hardest place to picture Dorothy issuing forth to tea with Derwent Coleridge at St John's, it was also the place where William first tasted fame. For acclaim had come at last, had, in 1820, met them almost like a further wave when, stepping off the boat after the continental tour, they had stayed for the first time in the Lodge; stayed to see Christopher in his capacity, too, of Vice-Chancellor conferring his first degrees in the Senate House. It was the undergraduates, however, who had anointed William. For Keats—then dying in Rome and, it was said, hastened to his end by the spite of reviewers—had been only the vanguard of a generation that shared none of the prejudice of its elders.

But rejoice though Dorothy must in William's hard-won triumph, this meant either an overflowing Rydal, William surrounded by visitors, or, fame combining with fortune, William increasingly away. Had already in 1823 meant one six months' separation while he and Mary travelled in Belgium and Holland, and then hung on in Harrogate while Dora drank the waters. For herself, Dorothy could remember, this had meant meeting the coach and that, in spite of her 'heroical wishes' for their delaying as long as Dora needed, she *was* disappointed at not seeing them on top of it—'at first grievously disappointed'. Though she 'soon got the better of that', she could tell Quillinan. But 'Oh!', she had written to him, 'that I could have kept you longer! I was very sad and melancholy all the morning after you left me, wandering about the garden'. For it had then been just over a year since Jemima Quillinan had died, had first been deranged after the birth of Rotha . . . That had once, it came back to her, been Coleridge's name for herself, and was now, it seemed, the name he called Dora by . . . But of what had she been thinking? Oh yes, that poor Jemima, who had then died horribly of burns, with 'Q' away—since these it had seemed were healing—and leaving Dorothy in sole charge. She had been glad that Mary was 'spared the last awful scene', but not glad of the reason. 'Never', she had written with truth to Jane, 'Never in my whole life did I pass so wretched a day' as when she learnt that Mary had left at midnight, William somewhere near Bampton having been thrown from his horse, hitting his head against a wall. Never, as she sat now hearing the fluttering of the fire, would she forget her terror and suspense. For 'had the wall been an inch nearer his death must have been certain'; and William's the grave she had stood by the following week.

As it was she had settled up all Q.'s affairs on his very naturally quitting the district. She had missed him, missed the dashing dragoon, missed his Irish charm as he stationed his mettlesome steed under her window and interrupted her as she tried to settle to copying that endless *Tour* which no one would want to read. And now there was Dora in love with Q., as anyone who saw her provocative postscripts to Dorothy's own letters, or to William's, to him might have guessed. Hartley Coleridge suspected it for the reasons that William did not, suspected that Dora 'would be a healthier matron than she is a virgin, but strong indeed', he wrote, 'must be the love that would induce her to leave her father, whom she almost adores, and who quite doats upon her'. And with Q. living in London, and all of them in Cambridge, Dorothy at the eleventh hour had been obliged to dash off a note cancelling Dora's visit: 'She was home-sick—the Father sick to have her at home, and so they settled it.' And perhaps there would be nothing more to settle. Q. had never proposed, preferred his cigars it seemed to a wife, had no house, no job and no prospects. William would never consent to so feckless—and Roman Catholic—a husband for a daughter so delicate. The doctors had said, definitely said that it was not consumption when she had been so desperately ill, a mere four months after the death of Isabel, at fourteen Southey's youngest, most beautiful daughter. But gay and enchanting as Dora contrived to be, and always wanting 'Aunt' to go with her when she could sally forth with the Southey girls, she remained as her mother said 'a complete *air* gauge'. Had it been Sara Coleridge one might have understood it, frail as she was and hard as she had slaved to help put Derwent through university—first, at twenty, with her translation from the Jesuit Latin of Dobrizhoffer's *Account of the Abipones*, then tackling mediaeval French. How so fragile and flower-like a creature 'Dobrizhoffered it all out' defeated Charles Lamb 'to conjecture'.

At least Mrs C. had something to be proud of. For Hartley's affair had nearly killed her—even if Sara H. was right, and Oriel had seized the first excuse to get rid of him. William, after all, had, at Hartley's age, got tight drinking Milton's health in Milton's rooms. And if the Dean had found Hartley drunk in the gutter, Oriel had itself, perhaps, been the cause— been of all places the last for Hartley; with dons like Keble and Newman, combined with the rule that Fellows must not consort with under-graduates. Mrs C.'s advice had seemed silly enough at the time: 'One thing I have warned him against, that of flying about in the open air and uttering his poetic fancies aloud', for 'this he constantly does . . . and when we are sitting . . . with the Curtains drawn, between the whistling of the wind, we hear him whizzing by, and sometimes his Uncle calls out to him "Whither so fast Endymion?" alluding to his visits to [old] Lady Diana Fleming . . . about whom H. cannot bear to be teized.' Mrs C. had done her best, on the old score—appearances. But Hartley would never conform —as conform he must, looking as he did or Dorothy found him, 'the oddest creature you ever saw—not taller than Mr De Quincey—with a beard as black as a raven. He is exactly like a Portuguese Jew'. Whatever the truth it had been a cruel thing for Mrs C.; and Hartley's guilt was pitiful, as was his father's. For Coleridge had taken the whole blame; and, on the grounds of his neglect, moved heaven and earth to get Hartley taken back.

Dorothy herself had known nothing of any of this until, on their return from the Continent, they had gone to see Coleridge in Highgate. And such had been his anguish that her heart had at last softened. But William had thought as Southey had: 'The scheme of sending him to be under his mother's eye is preposterous'; and so it had proved. For Hartley could not face his mother's eye, even 'steady' as he for some years was teaching with Mr Dawes in his old school. And cut off from Keswick, from home, from all those he loved, could only and did fall back on Rydal: 'many a Run', as Dorothy could still in those days report, 'has he had up and down the Terrace', while 'composing a pretty sonnet', 'such a Run as he used to take at six years old'. But then had come longer flights. Dorothy no longer worried as she had done, beloved as he was, not only in every inn, but in every cottage throughout the vale. 'His Friends through me'—the 'Friends' being chiefly the Wordsworths—helped meet the debts that now came home to roost, from the least respectable sources, on poor Mrs C. Flight from loneliness, failure, guilt—in such a guise did the ghost of Coleridge flit now over the hills and through Dorothy's mind.

But Coleridge himself had actually, the summer before she left, been rolling along in a carriage beside the Rhine with William and Dora. The two men had got along famously, Dora said. Outwardly how little had changed, if one half shut one's eyes—with Coleridge still encased in pastoral black and William still in his old attire, striped pantaloons, fustian gaiters and 'strange thick-hoofed shoes'; and taking off on the spur of the moment, as in the Alfoxden days, even Mary had not known when or where. . . . Tomorrow Willy was coming to say goodbye to her, Willy always her 'first charge and care' after his nearly dying at eleven of dropsy and asthma, when William, distraught, had brought him home for good. Since then he had had little schooling, and his future was a problem. But now he was going to Bremen to learn German . . . Meanwhile she had planned one nice long walk—with the result, or so it was then supposed, that Dorothy now became Willy's 'first charge and care'.

For Willy arrived only to nurse her in an agony she 'should never have believed possible'. 'What a shock it was to our poor hearts,' wrote William. 'Were she to depart the Phasis of my moon would be robbed to a degree that I have not the courage to think of.' 'The old women at my bedside', Dorothy herself wrote, 'talked to each other as if quite sure I must die.' Not for three months was she fit to move, and, breaking her journey at Halifax, was again in July violently ill; and back at Rydal forced 'to enact the invalid'—of all roles the hardest for her to sustain.

The first of her many letters now is moving in more ways than one. In it she makes no mention of her illness, but is full of the visit of 'the Bridal Pair so engrossingly interesting to themselves'. These were Sara Coleridge, after a seven-year wait newly married to her cousin Henry. Dorothy watched them off: 'Dear little Sara who seats herself with such dawdling efforts in the pony chaise with her helpful Husband to pack her up in her wrappings.' No one has ever tucked the rugs so tenderly round Dorothy's knees as she climbed, all fragility, into a chaise. And if Dora, 'all independence on her pony', is about to ride with the couple to Coniston, happily she will have a male companion, 'for to be solitary . . . with a Honey-moon pair is not quite the most satisfactory thing in the world'. For the winter she must keep to her bed, only in April 1830 to emerge and write, 'surely it is no punishment to be confined to this beautiful spot'. By the summer she could leave it—in a chaise; by the following one, August 1831, spend ten days on Belle Isle, Windermere, 'compared with Rydal Mount dull, and to the feelings confining. But what I like least in an island . . . is the being separated from men, cattle, cottages, and the goings-on of rural life'.

Three months after writing this, felled by a fresh attack, she was cruelly confined to a smaller island—and William by June had abandoned hope.

Coleridge 'and my beloved Sister', he wrote, 'are the two beings to whom my intellect is most indebted, and they are now proceeding, as it were *pari passu*, along the path of sickness . . . towards the grave'.

Writing to the Lambs the following spring, he described reading Lamb's *Love me, love my dog* 'to my poor Sister this morning, while I was rubbing her legs'. This, said Dorothy, 'was my good brother's office twice in the day—if but once how he groaned and lamented'. And she is at times able to quit her bed if not her room. But perhaps it was her cheerfulness—that, as Sara said, 'her patience never forsakes her'—which led William to burst out to the Lambs 'in tenderness of heart I do not honestly believe [she was] ever exceeded by any of God's Creatures. Her loving-kindness has no bounds. God bless her for ever and ever!' 'Surely', wrote Dora, 'such love as he bears her is of no common nature'. While Dorothy herself wrote of the night when 'my poor brother went to lie down on his bed, thinking he could not bear to see me die'. And it must have been the renewed sense of her central place in his life that, more than anything else, sustained her.

At times she rallied sufficiently to sit on a chair in the garden. The cost of her courage, however, might pass unrealized had she not, when well enough, kept a diary: she must go and lie down; she had wished to rest on the sofa and hear William read from the poem on his own life; but instead 'had a melancholy pleasure in the sound of his voice—with now and then a word' giving 'the key to what was employing their thoughts'. Other entries, bare of comment, tell us all too much: 'The Fiddlers went their rounds. Found me awake.' But her fortitude comes through most fully in the poems she lay composing when too ill to write or read or sew:

> I felt a power unfelt before
> Controlling weakness, languor, pain;
> It bore me to the terrace walk;
> I trod the hills again.

In December 1834 a robin flew in to live with her, 'its soft warbling', Mary wrote, 'is most delicious and soothing to her feelings'. She was happy—perhaps in comparing her lot with others. For though Coleridge had died as the Grand Old Man of Highgate, the autopsy etablished his sufferings as all too real. The heart was hugely enlarged and in his right lung an enormous cyst—a condition, said Dr Gillman, 'which must have had its commencement nearly forty years before his death'.

Asra had five times made her way to Highgate, and Coleridge had left her a ring and his Chapman's *Homer*. To Dorothy by now Lamb's death meant more: 'His sister survives', she would write, 'a solitary twig patiently enduring the storm of life. In losing her brother she lost all . . .' She had always seen herself in Mary Lamb; the resemblance when she wrote this would be complete.

Meanwhile there was poor Southey with his wife in a madhouse. Whereas she herself was mending. If proof of this was needed William, after a year when he could not so much as read, was writing again; and confident enough to go, taking Mary with him, to London about a job for Willy. They returned to Dora in a decline, Asra with what seemed lumbago, and Dorothy once more daily expected to die. 'Father', wrote Dora, 'keeps up his spirits most patiently, though at times I see his heart is almost breaking.' It was Asra, however, who died—of rheumatic fever. For Dorothy a worse fate was in store: twenty more years of a life that was not merely posthumous but which made her the reverse of her former self—a violent, greedy, tyrannical, spoilt child. Were it not that such is the character change wrought in those who suffer from brain damage caused by arterial sclerosis, this might have seemed—as it has been taken to be—a natural revolt on the part of Dorothy's psyche. Only William could calm her in her worst moods; and about two things she was always lucid—no detail of their life alone at Town-End was forgotten by her, and she could always complete a line of poetry.

But if Hartley, who no longer saw her, heard her and wished that he had not, her own mental suffering was intense: 'My dearest Dora', she wrote in 1838,

> They say I must write a letter—and what shall it be? news—news—
> I must seek for news—My own thoughts are a wilderness 'not pierceable
> by power of any star'*—News then is my resting place—News! news!
> Poor Peggy Benson lies in Grasmere Churchyard beside her once
> beautiful Mother. Fanny Haigh is gone to a better world. My friend
> Mrs Rawson has ended her ninety and two years pilgrimage—and *I*
> have fought and fretted and striven and am here beside the fire. The
> Doves behind me at the small window—the laburnum with its naked
> seedpods shivers before my window and the pine-trees rock from their
> base . . .

In 1841 Dora married Quillinan. William, repeating Dorothy's performance, could not, at the last, face the wedding. Six years later Dora died at Rydal—of consumption too long unrecognized. William, a heart-broken old man, seemed to find his sole enjoyment in pandering to Dorothy's every whim. This poor Mary thought bad for both; but, she wrote, 'her death would be to him a sad calamity'. William's death, however, came first. And with it for a day the complete return of Dorothy's faculties. 'Miss Wordsworth', wrote Quillinan, who was in the house, 'is as much herself as ever she was in her life.' She was quiet, considerate, concerned for William, but did not receive the final news with the violent outburst of grief Mary had dreaded. Instead 'O death where is thy sting, where grave thy victory?' she had murmured, being pushed in her chair past William's door. Soon she would join him—and five years

---

* Dorothy is remembering Spenser's *Faerie Queene* (1.i.7), recalling the Forest of Error, in which Una and the Red Cross Knight 'wander to and fro in wayes unknowne'.

later did so, on 25 January 1855. De Quincey had taken his leave of her earlier:

'Farewell, Miss Wordsworth! farewell, impassioned Dorothy. I have not seen you for many a day—shall too probably never see you again, but . . . from two hearts, at least, that knew and loved you in your fervid prime, it may sometimes cheer the gloom of your depression to be assured of never-failing remembrance, full of love and respectful pity.'

Select Bibliography

(The place of publication is London unless otherwise indicated.)

Wordsworth, Dorothy	*Journals* second edition ed. Mary Moorman (Oxford, 1971) *Journals* ed. E. de Selincourt (2 vols, 1941) *George and Sara Green, a Narrative* ed. E. de Selincourt (Oxford, 1936) *The Letters of William and Dorothy Wordsworth* ed. E. de Selincourt. Vol I revised Chester L. Shaver, Vol II revised Mary Moorman, Vol III revised Mary Moorman and Alan G. Hill (Oxford, 1967–1970)
Wordsworth, William	*The Complete Poetical Works* (1930) *The Prelude, 1798–99* ed. Stephen Parrish (1977) *The Prelude* (1805 text) ed. E. de Selincourt, corrected by S. Gill (Oxford, 1970)
Wordsworth, Mary	*Letters* ed. Mary E. Burton (Oxford, 1958)
Wordsworth, Dora	*Letters* ed. Howard P. Vincent (Chicago, 1944) *Her Book* (1924)
Hutchinson, Sara	*Letters* ed. K. Coburn (Toronto, 1954)
Coleridge, S.T.	*The Poetical Works* ed. Ernest Hartley Coleridge (1912) *Letters* ed. E. L. Griggs (4 vols, Oxford 1956–9) *The Unpublished Letters* ed. E. L. Griggs (1932) *Letters* Selected by Kathleen Raine (1950) *The Notebooks* ed. K. Coburn (3 vols, 1957–73) *Biographia Literaria* ed. J. Shawcross (1907)
Coleridge, Sara	*Minnow among Tritons: Letters of Mrs S. Coleridge to Thomas Poole* ed. S. Potter (1934)
Coleridge, Hartley	*Letters* ed. G. E. and E. L. Griggs (1936)
Coleridge, Edith	*Memoir and Letters of Sara Coleridge* (2 vols, 1873)

Select Bibliography

Cottle, Joseph — *Early Recollections of S. T. Coleridge* (1837)

De Quincey, Thomas — *Reminiscences of the English Lake Poets* (Everyman's Library, 1911)
Confessions of an Opium Eater (World's Classics, 1902)

Hazlitt, William — *Complete Works* ed. P. P. Howe (1930–34)

Keats, John — *Letters* ed. M. Buxton Forman (Oxford, 1947)

Lamb, Charles — *The Letters of Charles Lamb: to which were added those of his Sister, Mary Lamb* ed. E. V. Lucas (3 vols, 1935)

Robinson, Henry Crabb — *On Books and Their Writers* ed. E. J. Morley (3 vols, 1938)
Correspondence with the Wordsworth Circle ed. E. J. Morley (2 vols, Oxford 1927)

Sandford, Mrs Henry — *Thomas Poole and his Friends* (2 vols, 1888)

Southey, C.C. — *Life and Correspondence of Robert Southey* (6 vols, 1849–50)

Bateson, F.N.W. — *Wordsworth: A Reinterpretation* (1954)

Byatt, A.S. — *Wordsworth and Coleridge in their time* (1970)

Chambers, E.K. — *Coleridge: A Biographical Study* (1938)

Coburn, K. — *The Self-conscious Imagination* (Riddell Memorial Lectures, Newcastle-on-Tyne 1970)

Davies, Hugh Sykes — *Thomas De Quincey* (British Council, 1964)

Gill, Stephen — *The Salisbury Plain Poems* (New York, 1975)

Griggs, E.L. — *Coleridge Fille* (Oxford, 1940)
Thomas Clarkson, the Friend of Slaves (1936)

Hanson, Lawrence — *Life of S. T. Coleridge: Early Years* (1938)

Hayter, Alethea — *A Voyage in Vain: Coleridge's Journey to Malta in 1804* (1973)

House, Humfrey — *Coleridge* (Clark Lectures 1951–2)

Lawrence, Berta — *Coleridge and Wordsworth in Somerset* (1970)

Lefebure, Molly — *Samuel Taylor Coleridge: A Bondage of Opium* (1974)

Legouis, Emile — *The Early Life of William Wordsworth* (1921)
William Wordsworth and Annette Vallon (1922)

Lowes, J.L. — *The Road to Xanadu* (1927)

Lucas, E.V. — *The Life of Charles Lamb* (1921)

Margoliouth, H.M. — *Wordsworth and Coleridge* (Oxford, 1953)

237

Moorman, Mary

William Wordsworth: A Biography (2 vols, Oxford 1957–65)
William and Dorothy Wordsworth (Royal Society of Literature, 1970)

Pinney, Lady Hester and Evans, Bergen

Racedown and the Wordsworths (R.E.S. Jan. 1932)

Rawnsley, H.D.

Reminiscences of Wordsworth among the Peasantry of Westmorland (1968)

Raysor, T.M.

Coleridge and Asra (Chapel Hill N.C., 1929)

Read, Herbert

Wordsworth (Clark Lectures 1930)

Sackville West, Edward

A Flame in Sunlight ed. J. E. Jordan (1974)

Selincourt, E. de

Dorothy Wordsworth (1933)

Whalley, George

Coleridge and Sara Hutchinson and the Asra ·Poems (1955)

Index

239